Our Turn!

The ultimate start-up guide for female entrepreneurs

by

Alpesh B. Patel & Nikki Royston
with Nishika Patel

Hh Harriman House Publishing

HARRIMAN HOUSE LTD

43 Chapel Street
Petersfield
Hampshire
GU32 3DY
GREAT BRITAIN

Tel: +44 (0)1730 233870
Fax: +44 (0)1730 233880
Email: enquiries@harriman-house.com
Website: www.harriman-house.com

First published in Great Britain in 2005
Copyright Harriman House Ltd

The right of Alpesh B. Patel, Nikki Royston and Nishika Patel to be identified as the Authors
has been asserted in
accordance with the Copyright, Design and Patents Act 1988.

ISBN 1-897-59747-9

British Library Cataloguing in Publication Data
A CIP catalogue record for this book can be obtained from the British Library.

Printed and bound by Cambridge University Press.

Contents

About the authors

Alpesh B. Patel

Alpesh is the founding director of Agile Partners Asset Management, one of the best performing hedge funds in the world in 2004. In 2005 he was made International Dealmaker for the UK Government's Global Entrepreneur Programme within UK Trade and Investment. In that role he is responsible for searching intellectual property in India of outstanding value and making it investment ready with a UK angle.

His business interests include founding director of InvestingBetter.com, a non-executive Chairman of Aranca, a director and shareholder in WorldSpreads Plc and director and shareholder of Pinnacle Capital.

Alpesh is a founding board member of TiE-UK and has been Visiting Fellow in Business & Industry, Corpus Christi College, Oxford University. He is involved with several Oxford Business School Committees.

Alpesh has written a weekly column in the *Financial Times* and is a regular markets and business commentator on CNBC Asia, CNN and the BBC. He also co-hosted a weekly show for 3 years on Bloomberg TV.

Alpesh is on the UK-India Roundtable, established by the UK and Indian Prime Ministers to examine how to expand all facets of bilateral relations. He is also on the board of the Indo-British Partnership and a Trustee of Chatham House.

Alpesh is the author of 10 investment and business books translated into 6 languages. He has a degree in Philosophy, Politics, Economics from Oxford University and in Law from King's College, London and is a non-practicing barrister.

alpesh.patel@tradermind.com

Nikki Royston

Nikki Royston is a freelance writer, based in Vancouver. After becoming disheartened by the male-dominated workplace, she took the decision to begin working for herself. Nikki has edited women-focussed websites, including the 'Mothers Who Think' site, and www.the-bag-lady.co.uk, a global directory of women in business.

She has three children, two of whom were born in the first three years of setting up her own business/working for herself, proving that business and domestic life can work together.

Nishika Patel

Nishika Patel has a Masters Degree in Journalism and has experience in international journalism. She has formerly interned at Bloomberg in London and is currently a full-time journalist.

Foreword

The buzzwords of recent years have been trumpeting the apparent advent of 'human capital'; we have always known that good people contribute to the best results, but the battle for that talent has become fiercer as individuals have become less willing to hang around for an employer who is giving them neither the reward, recognition nor opportunity that they can find elsewhere. Over the last 30 years, opportunities for women to excel in the world of business have increased significantly; there is now a concerted effort on the part of Government, the private sector and individual organisations to ensure that the available talent pool is maximised by including women on a full and equal basis.

This activity stretches beyond the world of employment – 27% of the self employed population is female[1] and women started 30% of businesses in 2004[2]. Currently, just 15% of businesses are majority owned by women[3], contributing some £130 billion to the UK's economy[4]. As Jacqui Smith pointed out, if women started businesses at the same rate as men, we would have an additional 150,000 new businesses each year[5], which is vital for our enterprise culture.

We in the banking sector recognise the great opportunity this is. At HBOS we are ahead of the game in having created a Women in Business unit that works specifically to understand and address any issues that pertain particularly to women; whether they be around access to finance, attitudes to debt and risk, networking styles, non-traditional working patterns or unfamiliar sectors. Naturally, we are sensitive about over-segregating women, hence our activity is focused not around 'special' products or superficial offers, but on ensuring that our mainstream offering is appropriate, appealing and accessible to all our customers, including women, as they develop their businesses. We are working on creating a culture that is genuinely inclusive and which automatically recognises the benefits that natural diversity can bring.

Within the HBOS group, Corporate Banking's vision is to 'Look at things differently'; something at which, due to their different experiences, approaches and attitudes, women excel. It seems to me only common sense that we should be focusing on, fostering and encouraging our female talent, both colleagues and customers alike, to help them reach their potential.

You'll also find a lot of common sense within these pages, along with some first rate advice and opinions from those who have carved professional success from particular challenges and who are not afraid to discuss where and how they believe their gender has played a part on that journey.

Madeleine Albright once said "There is a place in Hell for women who don't help other women".

I hope you'll find plenty of help here.

Dennis Stevenson

Chairman, HBOS

August 2005

---

[1] A Strategic Framework for Women's Enterprise, Small Business Service, 2003.

[2] As quoted within the Scotsman Saturday November 4th 2004.

[3] Small Business Service, 2003; Carter, Mason and Tagg, 2004.

[4] Rt Hon Jacqui Smith, Minister for Women and Equality speaking at 2nd Prowess conference, Nov 2004

[5] Industry minister, Jacqui Smith, 2004

Preface

We are often asked 'Why not Men in Business?' and our answer is always the same: 'if you feel there is a market need, go ahead and set it up.' But we believe there isn't the same need; history has dictated that the traditional business models and styles were instigated and developed by men. They thus tend to involve men naturally and generally suit men pretty comfortably. Without doubt, there are fundamentals in business that cross any gender divide (the right finance, a great idea, big sales, strong management) but the approach that women take and the styles they exhibit in dealing with these issues can often be subtly but crucially different from that of their male contemporaries. The result is that traditional models and styles don't always sit quite so comfortably with them and they look for different avenues and ways to run their businesses or their careers. It is vital that business providers and employers take cognisance of this fact and ensure that what they offer is appealing to all their customers – and banking is no different.

Bank of Scotland Corporate's award-winning Women in Business team is committed to helping support and encourage those women who are starting or growing a business and continues to lead the way with its groundbreaking programme and materials. 'Our Turn!' is a valuable addition to the range of information, services and advice that the team accesses or provides for customers and colleagues and I am sure you will find it instructive, interesting and a really good read. I am delighted to be the sponsor of the Women in Business team within the HBOS Group, and to watch their activity embody our 'Look at things differently' Corporate vision and to see the numbers of female businesses grow and flourish as a result.

Brian Johnston

Head of Corporate

Bank of Scotland

Part of the HBOS Group

Introduction

"When it comes to entrepreneurship and job creation, ours is an increasingly woman's world."

President George W Bush

Why a book for women in business?

After all we don't expect to see a book about men in business do we? Yet there are many websites devoted to 'women in business' the world over. Is it needed? Are we being patronising? Are we setting back the cause by compartmentalising women in business?

We feel there is a genuine role and value of such a book. These include:

1. Dealing with issues which are simply not covered in other business books because they relate specifically to women based on detailed research which shows women approach business issues differently.

2. Never look a gift horse in the mouth. If someone is giving you a helping hand because of your specific characteristics – take it.

Why this book is different

The number of women entering business has been growing for years. Yet there are surprisingly few entrepreneurial, business books directly for them.

This book is grounded on research but mixed with businesswomen interviews in the style of the best-selling US business books (which have surprisingly not tackled this area head on) which combine 'studies with stories' to make the book widely appealing and accessible.

It's funny but it's true…

As well as serious differences between the sexes there are the humourous anecdotal, non-serious ones too. We want this book to be entertaining as well as informative. For that reason, let me start by quoting from the BBC on differences between the sexes – happy reading!

THE DIFFERENCES BETWEEN WOMEN AND MEN

MEN

Women understand colour. They seem to know what to wear all the time. Men just think red is nice, pink is nice, so why not have them together?

Jeremy Vine

Men have no opinions about curtains.

Stuart Maconie

Women have the If you need to be told I am not going to tell you gene.

David Bergin, Switzerland

Men like to have all their stuff (DVDs, CDs, etc) on show to impress their mates. Women like to hide things in cupboards.

Mark Nelson, UK

Ask a woman in the street how to get somewhere and she will direct via shops. Ask a man and it will be via pubs.

Fred, UK

Men appreciate the importance of a 42 inch plasma screen. Women do not.

Jonathan, UK

Women can use sex to get what they want. Men cannot, as sex is what they want.

Eoin Dempsey, Ireland

Men speak in sentences. Women speak in paragraphs.

Steve Munoz, US

For men, 2am is time for sleep. For women, 2am is time for a discussion about where our relationship is going.

Luke, UK

WOMEN

Women have the Oh dear, the toilet paper is on its last sheet; must replace it immediately gene. This is entirely absent in men who have the Oh s..t! Can you pass me a toilet roll, love? gene!

Jenni Murray

On being told that someone has bought a new car women usually ask what colour it is - men ask what sort is it.

Anna Ford

Women know instinctively what is dangerous or not recommended for babies in their care. Men, generally speaking, do not.

Sian Lindsey, Netherlands

Women have a built in calendar gene - we remember birthdays, anniversaries and appointments effortlessly.

Linsday, UK

Women put things on the bottom stair to take up next time she has to go upstairs. Men just step over them until told to pick them up.

Karen Kelsey, UK

A multi-tasking gene is clearly only owned by women - men can never prepare dinner so that everything is ready at the same time.

Kelly , UK

Women pick up on subtleties and then think about them. Men need things explained IN CAPITAL LETTERS before the message gets through.

Morag, Edinburgh

At weddings, women cry then get drunk. Men get drunk, then cry.

Debby, UK

When faced with flat-pack furniture, men never read the manual. Yet they spend hours reading manuals for cars or bikes they will never own.

Linda, UK

Men can store useless information. Like the top speed of a car they are never going to drive, let alone own.

Rob, UK

Only women can understand other women.

Jon Lipscombe

Woman have the diary gene. (And no, they do not make your bums look big).

Ben Appleby, UK

If you told a woman that you had just returned from a trip to the surface of the Moon, she would show her interest by asking who you had gone with.

Howard, UK

When men want something they ask for it. When women want something they make a point distantly related to the subject and wait for a response.

David Lawson, England

Men need a round of applause for emptying the dishwasher. Women think E on the petrol gauge means enough.

Peter Richmond, Canada

Men have a gene which makes them blissfully unaware of impending emotional outbursts, but which sometimes backfires resulting in the registering of physical pain.

Gary, UK

Men refuse to pay more than £5.00 for a hair cut as it is not that important.

Mark Tomlinson

Men know that common house spiders are far less dangerous than scorpions.

John S, UK

Women enjoy planning a wedding.

Tom Howes, UK

Men can balance an infinite amount of rubbish in the bin, without noticing it is full.

Yvonne Eccles, England

Women know when all you want is a glass of wine, nodding sympathy and a good whinge. Men offer a solution.

Wendy, UK

Women are missing the parking a car in between two straight white lines in an empty car park gene.

Jane, UK

Men do not even bother to look for something, then ask where it is and hope that it was the woman who put it away.

Kate, Isle of Man

Women have an ability to make men think they are in charge.

Sheila, UK

Men use I or me when they should use we or us. Women use we or us when they should use I or me.

Clair, England

Women have the we must name our car gene.

Louise, UK

Men have the capacity to sleep through most sounds, whether it is a baby crying, dog barking, or doorbell ringing.

Val Soanes

Women drive on the stretch of road they can see. Men move through the landscape by car.

Anne Taylor, UK

Men have an anorak gene, which triggers a lecture on thermo dynamics when asked a simple question requiring a yes or no answer.

Deborah, UK

Women eat curry if they like it. Men eat curry to prove they can.

Paul Angel, UK

Women could never invent weapons that kill, only ones that make you feel really bad and guilty until you surrender.

Dan, UK

Men can watch an entire film without having to ask who is that, what does he do?

Alistair, UK

Girls cannot climb trees. Furthermore, they cannot be in my gang.

Dominic Green, UK

A man can choose and buy a pair of shoes in 90 seconds over the internet.

Paul, UK

Women pee together. Men do not acknowledge, let alone speak to each other when peeing.

Angus, London

Men can drive without having to look at themselves in the mirror.

Christian Paterson, France

Women make lists upon lists of things for men to do when they know very well we will never do them.

Brian Mac, US

Men CAN get a bus through there!

Bob Ellis, UK

Men can write their names clearly in the snow.

Riccardo, UK

Men manage to sit in public places with their legs wide open without noticing how startlingly unattractive it is and how they get in the way.

Jane Penrose, UK

Women are the only ones with the noticing gene - we notice when something is dirty/nearly empty/out of place and then we bring into play the doing something about it now gene!

Sarah Wilson, UK

Women know what to do when someone starts to cry. Men tend to shuffle out of the room mumbling something about doing the grouting.

Lucy, UK

Men will do something and not think about the risks involved then be sorry after. Women will think about the risks involved before hand.

Diane McKay, England

Men have the ability to make a la, la, la, not listening face.

Laura Humphreys, England

Men have the shed gene, where being locked up in a small wooden structure in quiet contemplation with a collection of garden equipment counts as stimulating entertainment.

Lorraine, UK

Men have a gene which enables them to answer any question, no matter how complex or important, with Mmm.

Rachel, UK

Women do not get turned on at the thought of two men together.

Donna, South Africa

Men can watch six different channels at the same time and know the name of none of the programmes they claim to be following.

Niamh Brown, Singapore

Women can smell old trainers at 100ft, men have to hold them to their nose.

Sally, UK

Men start a sentence and...

Cliff Grover, UK

Men enjoy publicising their faults on BBC websites; women enjoy publicising men's faults on BBC websites.

Paul, UK

Men are paid more for doing the same job. :-)

Nigel Harris, UK

Women keep carrier bags hidden away in a cupboard. They even keep carrier bags within carrier bags!

Matt, UK

Men look at going down the gym as a physical activity, to women it is a social event.

Robert, UK

Women think that a good place to keep the TV controller is on top of the TV.

Christopher, UK

Women can get by with 10 or 20 CDs. Men need 200 plus.

Damien Bove, Leeds

Women recall every outfit they have worn for the past two decades. Men cannot remember what they were wearing yesterday without looking on the floor next to the bed.

Tom, London, UK

....women finish it for them

Jane Grover, UK

Men have the empathy with computers gene. This means they are more likely to be found fiddling about with one rather than doing something useful.

Sarah Savill, UK

Women have the take things personally gene.

Emma, UK

Women parallel process, men parallel park.

Petal, UK

A woman would look at a sexy man and not be noticed. Men just stare.

Isabelle West, UK

Men have a gene that enables them to maintain a vice like grip on the remote control while reclining on the sofa studying the insides of their eyelids.

Jane, UK

Women know that washing machines have programmes for every kind of fabric, colour and quantity and use them appropriately. Men will put a month's supply of laundry through the 40 degree cycle (safest guess), regardless of any other detail.

Janine MacLean, UK

If a man knows an acquaintance has given birth to a baby, he will remember the sex and name - if you are lucky. If a woman is told about a birth, she will remember names (first and middle), weight, time, how long the labour took and whether medical intervention was required.

Marcia, UK

Source: BBC

Facts and figures

Perhaps the most telling piece of information about women and business are the facts and figures.

1. Women in management

Women comprise 30% of managers in England, 29% in Scotland and 33% in Wales.

Women and Equality Unit published May 2003

Managerial occupations remain strongly gender-segregated. While women make up 73% of managers in health and social services, they only make up 6% in production.

Women and Equality Unit published May 2003

Women's representation also varies by sector. While 40% of managers in the public sector are female, in the private sector it is just 28%.

Women and Equality Unit published May 2003

Data from the National Management Salary Survey in 2001 revealed that the average female manager earned £34,789, while the average male manager earned £40,289. Women managers therefore earned around 86% of the average annual managerial salary of men.

Women and Equality Unit published May 2003

2. Women in the boardroom

In all UK listed companies

Less than 1% of chairmen are women.

Women and Equality Unit published May 2003

4% of executive director posts (including Chief Executive Officer) are held by women.

Women and Equality Unit published May 2003

6% of non-executive director posts (employed largely to offer strategic, specific and objective advice at board meetings) are held by women.

Women and Equality Unit published May 2003

Overall, 4% of directorships are held by women.

Women and Equality Unit published May 2003

In FTSE 100 companies

Just over one in ten non executive posts and one in 40 executive posts are held by women.

Women and Equality Unit published May 2003

Only one company had a female Chief Executive Officer, in 2002.

Women and Equality Unit published May 2003

Only 7.2% of directorships are held by women and 39 firms have no female directors.

Women and Equality Unit published May 2003

16 of the top 20 FTSE companies had women directors, but only eight of the bottom 20 firms.

Women and Equality Unit published May 2003

Only one company had a female Chief Executive Officer, in 2002.

Only 7.2% of directorships are held by women and 39 firms have no female directors.

Women and Equality Unit published May 2003

3. Women in politics

Parliament

The 2001 General Election returned 118 women MPs to the House of Commons, a decrease of two from the previous election. Women represent 18% of all MPs.

Women and Equality Unit published May 2003

24% of British members of the European Parliament are female.

Women and Equality Unit published May 2003

33% of Cabinet Ministers are women.

Women and Equality Unit published May 2003

4. Women in public services

7% of Chief Constables and 9% of Assistant Chief Constables are women.

Women and Equality Unit published May 2003

Women in judiciary

6% of High Court Judges are women - six out of a total of 107.

Women and Equality Unit published May 2003

21% of District Judges (Magistrates' Courts) are women - 22 out of a total of 105.

Women and Equality Unit published May 2003

Women in public appointments

34% of all the boards of non-departmental public bodies, nationalised industries, public corporations and health bodies are held by women.

Women and Equality Unit published May 2003

Sources

1. 'Women and Men in Britain : Management', EOC, 2002.

2. Review of the role and effectiveness of non-executive directors, Derek Higgs, January 2003.

3. The 2002 Female FTSE report: Women Directors Moving Forward, Dr Val Singh and Professor Susan Vinnicombe, Cranfield School of Management, November 2002.

4. Key indicators of women's position in Britain, Dench et al, WEU, November 2002.

5. Room at the Top? A Study of Women Chief Executives in Local Government in England and Wales, Pam Fox and Mike Broussin. Bristol Business School, undated.

6. The Lord Chancellor's Department, January 2003.

7. Public Bodies 2002.

8. Department of Health, February 2002.

5. International comparison

Norway - women formed 7.5% of the directors of the largest private sector companies.

USA - women make up 12.4% of the Fortune 500 company boards. There are 6 female CEOs in Fortune 500.

Australia - women hold 5.35% of seats on top 500 companies, 5 women chair top 500 boards, 2 are deputy chairmen.

Sweden - 7.3% of board directors are women in top 297 companies.

Spain - In December 2002 only 24% of top 300 companies had women directors. None of Spain's ten largest companies has a women director.

Canada - In 2001, women held 9.8 percent of all board seats among the FP500 companies. Nearly one-half (243) of the FP500 companies have at least one woman board director.

Women and Equality Unit published May 2003

"Progress is slow, but an increasing number of women are being appointed to boards. In 2002, 48% of women directors in the FTSE 100 were appointed in the last three years, whilst only 37% of the men were appointed during this time scale. One significant problem is that the pool from which directors and CEOs are drawn from is very small. During 2001 women who were currently on boards received an average of three invitations to become a non-executive director. This provides confirmation that invitations are going out to this select band of 'proven' women."

Women and Equality Unit published May 2003

Sources

1. The 2002 Female FTSE report: Women Directors Moving Forward, Dr Val Singh and Professor Susan Vinnicombe, Cranfield School of Management, November 2002.

2. Review of the role and effectiveness of non-executive directors, Derek Higgs, January 2003.

3. Women Directors on Top UK Boards, Singh, Vinnicombe and Johnson, Cranfield School of Management.

4. Data supplied courtesy of Val Singh, Cranfield School of Management.

6. Start-ups

"There is no such thing as a stereotypical entrepreneur. People in the process of setting up or who are actually running a business are very diverse - men and women, young and old, from different ethnic, social and educational backgrounds."

Department of Trade and Industry: Women's Enterprise

"Women comprise 26% of the 3.2 million self employed in the UK which equates approximately 824,659."

Business Startup 2003 (www.bstartup.com)

"The most frequently cited reason for women (as with men) starting their own business is the search for independence and control over one's destiny."

Business Startup 2003 (www.bstartup.com)

7. Equality

"Compared with their female counterparts, men are nearly twice as likely to believe they will have an opportunity to start up a business in the next six months. They are also nearly twice as likely to think they have the skills to start a business. And men are more optimistic about their future finances than women."

Department of Trade and Industry: Women's Enterprise

"Research shows that 24% of men are actively engaged in entrepreneurial activity compared with 11% of women. This is reinforced by the UK 2002 GEM (Global Entrepreneurship Monitor) study which found that men in the UK are over 200% more likely than women to start a business. This gulf between men and women business owners remains constant whether or not they are involved in bringing up children."

Department of Trade and Industry: Women's Enterprise

The figures show that:

"Women constitute 27% of the total numbers of self-employed people in the UK."

Labour Force Survey

"About 12% to 14% of businesses are wholly owned by women, compared with 44% by men."

SBS Household Survey & Federation of Small Businesses

"Women are outnumbered by their male counterparts with three times as many men than women starting their own business."

Business Startup 2003 (www.bstartup.com)

"66% of women business owners (compared to 56% of men business owners) tend to reflect on decisions, weighing options and outcomes before moving to action. In addition, women are more likely to gather information from business advisors and associates."

Business Startup 2003 (www.bstartup.com)

"18% of women compared to 10% of men are more likely to turn to business support organisations than men."

Business Startup 2003 (www.bstartup.com)

"Women entrepreneurs describe their businesses in family terms and see their business relationships as a network whilst male entrepreneurs think in hierarchical terms, following clear rules and procedures."

Business Startup 2003 (www.bstartup.com)

"90% of men and women believe that it is now easier for women to start their own business than in recent years, due to cultural change and increased opportunities for women."

Business Startup 2003 (www.bstartup.com)

"A significant proportion of men feel that women have a key advantage when starting a business, due to being 'better with people' (21%) and having a better image (23%)."

Business Startup 2003 (www.bstartup.com)

"The number of women entrepreneurs is now increasing significantly and are often more adventurous than men when starting their own business. Whilst most men stay firmly within their comfort zone, some 45% of women choose to start up in a line of work completely different to what they have done before."

Business Startup 2003 (www.bstartup.com)

"9% of small businesses are wholly owned by women compared to 44% wholly owned by men."

Business Startup 2003 (www.bstartup.com)

"Female business ownership is a relatively new phenomenon. 15% of new firms are owned by women, dropping to 12% for firms aged between 4-5 years and decreasing steadily by age of business."

Business Startup 2003 (www.bstartup.com)

"Women entrepreneurs are likely to be younger than their male counterparts."

'Lifting the Barriers To Growth' Federation of UK Small Business (www.fsb.org.uk)

"Women owned businesses are disproportionately over-represented in the 22-34 age band and to a lesser extent the 35-44 aged band. Relatively few women business owners come into the age band of 55 plus."

'Restricted Access: Women Owned Business' Prowess (www.prowess.org.uk)

"Women owned businesses are under represented in such sectors as manufacturing, construction, transport and agriculture."

'Restricted Access: Women Owned Business' Prowess (www.prowess.org.uk)

"Women business owners are less likely to use IT, internet and online services to communicate and cite an inability to understand new technology as an issue."

'Restricted Access: Women Owned Business' Prowess (www.prowess.org.uk)

"Women are more likely to use informal sources of finance, such as personal savings to start and sustain their business in favour of obtaining bank loans and overdrafts."

'Restricted Access: Women Owned Business' Prowess (www.prowess.org.uk)

Men bow

Perhaps it is ironic but when one in six of the world's population are embarking on a business venture or the pursuit of wealth, they pray to a woman. Men, business leaders including some of the richest most successful businessmen in the world, pray to a woman. These are Hindus, followers of the world's oldest faith and they number nearly one billion. In this 'pluralistic monotheistic' faith (i.e. they believe in one God manifested as many gods) the deity representing wealth is the goddess Lakshmi (from where the word 'luck' comes). Indeed the world's third richest person is named after this goddess.

Lakshmi is depicted as a beautiful woman of golden complexion, sitting or standing on a full-bloomed lotus and holding a lotus bud, which stands for beauty, purity and fertility. Her hands represent the four ends of human life: *dharma* or righteousness, *kama* or desires, *artha* or wealth, and *moksha* or liberation from the cycle of birth and death.

Cascades of gold coins are seen flowing from her hands, suggesting that those who worship her gain wealth. She always wears gold embroidered red clothes. Red symbolises activity and the golden lining indicates prosperity.

Let no one doubt that successful businessmen bow to a woman – albeit a goddess.

Alpesh B. Patel

London 2005

alpesh.patel@tradermind.com

1 That men are from Mars and women from Venus

"Life on the planet is born of woman."

Adrienne Rich

> - That women are different.
> - How women's approach to business differs.
> - What women do well.
> - What women do poorly.
> - What women can learn from men and men learn from women (not a chance of that happening!)

Before we get into the advantages of being a woman in business and how to exploit them – and the disadvantages and how to overcome them – let's get a feel for how women, and the issues surrounding women are viewed. Are women seen as unsatisfied, incapable, not credible, likely to fail due to children over business success? Are things really changing? Are the changes superficial? How are some business women winning?

Who are the most influential women in the eyes of the public? Who is the most influential woman in business? The role models certainly exist, but when men and women talk in the relative anonymity of web postings there is a mixed picture of hope and frustration too.

Carly Fiorina, then boss of Hewlett-Packard and Compaq	–	48.99%
Cherie Booth, top QC and member of Matrix Chambers	–	19.53%
Marjorie Scardino, chief executive of Pearson	–	9.52%
Meg Whitman, chief executive of eBay	–	8.23%
Nicola Horlick, chief executive of SG Asset Management	–	6.94%
Martha Lane Fox, managing director of Lastminute.com	–	6.78%

1239 Votes Cast
Results are indicative and may not reflect public opinion

Source: BBC

Public opinion

Members of the public and their views on the issue of women in business appear below in italics. Our views are expressed above each one.

Get over equality

Should we stop trying to straight jack women into becoming like men? Should not the emphasis be on different overall abilities? Or is it a form of discrimination in itself to highlight differences? What would be most advantageous to a woman in business – to pretend there are no differences between men and women or to highlight the differences?

Our research suggests emphasising the differences on these occasions – where the audience you are appealing to appears to agree to differences and it plays to your advantage. This may not necessarily be gender-related.

"I would say that the only obstacle that women are facing is their obsession in trying to become 'equals' to the male gender. We are not equal, we never will be (biologically speaking and taking evolution into consideration). So why can't we all just let it go and move on? As a woman, I aim to do the best I can in my professional life, rather than try to live up to a long-term myth."

Rana Jawad, Belgium

"Competition for talented employees is stiffer now than ever. The kind of manager that would favour an inferior male over a more talented female will be running a below average operation which will die a natural death in due course. There may be free rides in the law and politics but in business the only question is whether you are capable of making a real contribution, regardless of gender."

Brian, UK

"The thing that is the most aggravating to observe in today's society, is that the feminist fight of the early 20th century tried to push women into the male dominated world, but not the other way around. It is time for women's professions to be equally valued as those of men. As soon as the rules of business are changed from being male oriented, women will be part of it."

Thorey, Iceland

"Why do men always get suspicious when a woman is doing her work well? Without making too much noise, without taking the credits, without making useless interim reports about other interim reports, a woman does not stand a chance. And then there are the men who can easily judge if a woman is suitable for her job: she must be tough and definitely not emotional – no better look for a male candidate again."

Cecile, The Netherlands

"I have a part-time job that I thoroughly enjoy and am respected and appreciated for, get to spend time with my son for half the working week, spend time with my friends and mum during the day. Who isn't fulfilling their potential? I've never been happier. My husband leaves for work before 8am and returns after 6pm. He can be on call and has to deal with problems all day! Yes, he is vastly better paid than me, but he often says he would swap places. Why is that considered as 'doing better'? Keep your high flying career – I'm doing just fine!"

Catherine, UK

"Although a few women have made it to CEO here in the US, the prevailing numbers are still men. I think there will be glass ceilings for women for several more decades. There is a general attitude that women are not suppose to be tough."

Brenda, USA

"I agree that women do have to push harder. But most of the women bosses I have been around tend to be more difficult and prickly to work for; they seem to get more power crazy than men."

Mick Lloyd, UK

"Since starting work 14 years ago, most of my bosses have been female and I can honestly say that having a female boss is far better than having a male one."

Jason, Manchester, England

"Women have never had it so good. The problem is that they are never satisfied, and whatever men do it will never be enough for them!"

Ray, UK

Pretty woman – bad professional?

How are you supposed to dress and retain credibility as a woman? Women in the legal profession in the UK are not even meant to show their hair under their legal wigs. That is the androgynous extreme. After all, the judge, who is invariably male, may lose focus.

Equally, dress too well and will you be considered lightweight, flaky or shallow? Will emphasis on your appearance detract from your abilities and highlight (or remind the male decision-makers) that you are a woman? Or are we being paranoid?

"I am a Canadian woman working in Paris. The difference I notice here is that it is very difficult for a woman to obtain a high position unless she is extremely tough and not very attractive. In my industry – technology – you rarely see an attractive woman at a high level position. For a young woman, like myself, who is very ambitious and wants to succeed, I find that being somewhat attractive immediately impedes my chances of success."

Mary, France

"I am a British Woman working as a Computer Engineer in Northern California. I got tired of constantly having to work to excess to prove myself in IT departments in the UK, so I moved to the USA. It was like a breath of fresh air! Here, they are not allowed to ask you about your family life in interviews and the men seem to work just as hard in raising their children. There are still not very many women working in IT, but they get paid the same and have the same opportunities."

Imogen Shepherd, USA

"I would happily stay at home and be a house-husband so my wife could further her career. Unfortunately, she studied archaeology and so has no career. People looking for equality should try the academic environment. Even in my field (physics and engineering) people are judged on intelligence and ability, not gender."

NB, UK

"I think the biggest obstacle to women's careers is people's attitudes. Society expects women to take the responsibility of looking after the family, while men earn the bread. Imagine if it was the norm that men stayed at home to take care of the children and do the housework. The topic of debate nowadays would be 'men and their careers'."

Chermaine, Germany

"I am sure a lot of women don't want to be leaders. But if a woman wants something she'll go and get it."

Elena, Russia

"I will know that women have succeeded in business when I hear a man express genuine concern about how he is going to balance his family and career."

Wendy, UK

"I'm 30 and entered the business world with no opinion on whether a man or a woman was more suited to a particular role. I worked for several years in an American corporation and the senior management roles there were equally split male/female – it was a non-issue. Where I now work is very different however – a large steel firm, senior management is all male and in their late fifties, women are viewed as administrators and secretaries only and often referred to as 'girls'."

Nick, UK

"I work as a software engineer as does my husband. I believe he has a point when he says it's easier for women to get jobs as software engineers because companies want to increase the number of women they employ. However once we have the job it's a different story. I've had men saying to my face that they don't believe that women are capable of being good software engineers. I decided to

prove them all wrong and worked really hard but I still had to watch men with less experience/qualifications being promoted over me.

I then changed jobs and was faced with having to prove myself all over again to an extent that a man just wouldn't have to. I'm faced with the expectation that I just won't be as good as the men on the team. Now I'm so disheartened with it all I'm planning to change career, to something more woman friendly."

Anon, UK

"A few of the posters here have suggested we should define success. Patience, folks; we're only going to have to wait a few more years to find out. If both parents worked and their kids shove them into an old folks home because they owe their parents nothing, will the mums who stayed home with their kids and who, along with their spouses, are kindly, lovingly treated in their old age because of the strong bonds that exist, be the successful ones? It will be interesting to watch. I stayed home with my children and, even though I am far from old yet, I am cared for with loving kindness now and have no expectation of being put on an ice floe to perish any time in the future."

M, Canada

"The only people who succeed in business are the shareholders and the fat cats who sit at the top of the ladder."

John, Scotland

"I'm not sure that it's a matter of choice anymore – I think that for a brief, glorious, moment, it was, and the choice was made. That choice is now firmly embedded in house prices, the workplace, the complete lack of a culture outside work (OK, except for those with very young babies). For most women now, there is little option but to work."

Steve, UK

"The most successful person in Britain today is the authoress, J.K. Rowling. Not only has she made pots of money in a very short time she has bought pleasure to millions around the world, and like Enid Blyton, will be remembered for a long time."

Anthony, England

"I work in manufacturing and the women I really admire are the ones brave enough to take on traditional male blue collar jobs. We see a number of female lorry drivers and I'm talking seriously big lorries and I cannot tell you the admiration I have for them."

Malc, UK

"Whilst women of around 30-45 years of age are of that generation where they felt they had to "have it all" and success is measured by career progression, I think women just starting out in professional life of my generation will make quality of life choices. We have realised the goal in life is happiness which is

gained by finding your true potential and achieving it, not 'getting to the top at all costs'."

Deborah, UK

"I think more than a few women are having an easier time of it moving up in the corporate world. But, in spite of this there are women who cannot break out of the secretary/admin role and move up the corporate ladder. 'Once an admin, always an admin' still rings very true out in the business world. I think it's who you know, not what you know that helps."

Margaret, USA

What price women in business?

So you've heard about the superwomen; ten kids, four jobs, happy husband and CEO of her own company…or something similarly impossible.

But hang on, can you have it all? How do you get into business with the time that takes, spend time on your marriage, raise kids, if, as the presumption continues that the man can certainly not stay at home as house-husband? After all, he can't breast-feed.

What about the kids? The women will bare guilt if she is away and not fulfilling the usual role won't she?

"I used to live next to a couple who are both lawyers. They work from dawn to dusk and more. They are homogonously [sic] rich and their kids are raised by a series of babysitters. I happened to be the teacher of these children and they were distracted, lonely little kids. You can't both have full-time management careers and well-balanced kids."

Benny, UK ex-pat

"Modern business demands a wide range of skills. Many of them are the 'softer skills', which women excel at. If people really want to make it (whatever that may mean), men or women they can. However there is a price to be paid and maybe fewer women are prepared to pay it. My wife is a successful senior manager and we have two small children. However, it is very hard for both of us to juggle work and family. The options are there for everyone and it is up to them to make their choices."

Chrisp, UK

"Several of my friends got good jobs after leaving uni, then got married, then got pregnant. They all took full maternity leave with full benefits and then quit their job as soon as they were legally required to go back to work. Such blinkered action gives massive amounts of ammunition to the 'boys only' club."

Col, UK ex-pat

"I get pretty tired of this modern trend of women versus men in the boardroom. There have always been women at the top, but it wasn't until the 70s that so much amalgamation started and the huge corporations formed. I can't imagine why any woman with intelligence would want to be in those positions. After working for 48 years in high pressure environments, I believe the best job in the world is being at home with your kids. I had five wonderful years with mine and would never have worked if I didn't have to. I would never put money first and abandon my children, as modern women do."

Patricia, Australia

"When we see women being lead out of the office in handcuffs, like the execs at Adelphia, then we will know they have made it."

Don, USA

"I think there is some truth that mothers are less likely to be promoted due to the amount of time they have to spend dealing with their children. Personally, I don't think the business community can change that – it's home life that must change. Men should be given a few months off after a child is born, just like women get."

Monica, Chicago, USA

"Choice is the key. As a man, it seems that I do not have the choice of staying at home to raise the children, see them at sports day, read bed-time stories, or help them through difficult times. I see them in the morning as I iron my shirt before going to work and at weekends – it is not enough. Women have total choice, there's an end to it – and good luck to them. They have a good deal. The debate should now focus on men for a change."

James Millar, England

"If a woman thinks that being female is automatic justification for a boardroom position, perhaps it's time they considered the millions of men who also don't get the top jobs either. At least women have the choice to revert to a more traditional family role – what choice does the average man have?"

Paul, UK

Success...such excess

Raising great kids, having a clean home, being a house-wife...nope that is not the stuff of success. Or at least that is one debate women seem to be having. Some will argue the multi-tasking exhausting work of being a mum is a mark of success. Others will quietly feel they have not achieved unless there is a title in a job that they can point to...something in the hands of others bestowed upon them.

We all want to feel successful and important, having made a difference. A good parent is not doing it for many women. Will being in business fill the hole?

"Surely it depends on how you define success. None of the women I know have risen to the dizzy heights of the boardroom, but I would not call the majority of them failures, since most of them lead varied and fulfilling lives. Maybe more so, as they don't have to spend their time point scoring at endless tedious meetings!"

Pads, UK

"I agree with the comments of Pads, UK. It's really time we moved on from judging people's worth by the job they do or how much they earn doing it."

Jane, Wales, UK

"The main issue isn't high flying executives. Most women earn low wages doing essential but often under valued jobs. Many also have to cram in caring for their kids, as do some men. We need better pay and status for low paid women. And we need more support for all working parents, especially better and cheaper childcare. By the way, I'm a man with no kids, so some of us can see beyond our own wallets!"

Ben Drake, York, UK

"When I left university a couple of years ago I lost count of the number of times I was asked about my plans for a family by male interviewers. I work very hard and am determined to achieve everything I want out of my career, but I feel that if children were such an issue for employers when I was 22, I feel their assumptions on this issue will become more detrimental as I approach my late 20s."

Helen, UK

"My role models are the vast majority of female entrepreneurs in Asia. It's time to acknowledge their business skills, without getting into this male-female debate. Most of the so-called successful executives are there not because of their merits – it's a mafia-like closed system up there."

Tridiv Borah, Germany/India

"It's interesting to note that it's the men in this column saying women don't have a problem. My experience has shown that it is very hard for an intelligent and self-confident woman to climb the ladder in the same way a man does. I work in the technology field and the discomfort that men feel with my knowledge and skills is quite obvious. Just the fact that it is still women who must choose between career and children says that we have not reached parity."

Lesley, USA

"Lesley, I too work in technology. It always irritates me when women complain they don't have a chance in these industries and that men are holding them back. In my experience women are not interested in computers or technology. Here in Britain there has been a considerable drive to get more women into software and engineering but it doesn't seem to be working. The interest just isn't there."

D Williams, UK

"If you think it's biased in business and technology, you should look at transport. A 50:50 employment policy is impossible to achieve in our industry. I want to end up as a boardroom member and will go head to head with anyone, black or white, male or female to achieve that goal. We've had female prime ministers, CEOs, astronauts, fighter pilots, doctors and professors. There is no longer any excuse. If a woman wants the same job as I do, she'll have to compete against me for it. If she's good enough she can have it."

Alex, UK

"I have worked in the IT industry for six years. I manage a team and earn more than most men in the department so I think the opportunities are there. The problem is that a lot of women think they can't do it, so they don't try."

Sarah Flynn, UK

"There are fewer women at the top because they still take the lead role in bringing up children. Hopefully this is because they choose to and not because they feel they must. I suspect househusbands are just as rare as businesswomen."

Katy, UK

"Women are not holding the higher positions due to personal choice. We fought for choice – and that's what we've got. We can't expect there to be anywhere near as many women in the top positions, when the majority are making the decision not to rise to the very top."

Nicola Lagan, England

"My team leader is a woman of whom I have the greatest respect – she doesn't whine or moan about her sex, and she knows her job. She is a great example of what can be achieved by hard work and the ability to affect her career by her actions and communication skills. Less whining, more action please!"

Nick S, UK

"Men and women are different and excel in different fields. But if a woman decides to give all her time to her career she must forget about a traditional family. In Albania there are no differences in the wages, so a man and a woman can have the same wage for the same work. It may be because we come from a communist experience in which there was almost a full parity between the two genders. However, even though we are a poor country, this is a good example for the wealthier nations to take."

Dori, Albania

"I would suggest that it is not women who are less likely to succeed, but mothers. If a male employee took days off without giving notice, because his child was sick, and then rushed home at finishing time to pick the kids up from a childminder, then he would be less likely to be promoted too. The people who succeed are the ones who put in the extra work, and often mothers are unable to do this. This is due to their choices."

Fay, UK

"Women go on and on about needing to be equal to men at work. You don't to the same extent however see men leaving a firm for six months to have babies, with all the damage it does to a firm's intrinsic productivity base. A fair salary for a fair performance, I say."

Rich, UK

"Only a few weeks ago we were told equal pay for women is still very much a myth in the UK, despite all the legislation. There are few incentives for us women to rise to the top. If I was a senior executive and still only earning 80% of my male counterpart's salary, I'd wonder why I bothered."

Kaye, Liverpool, UK

Expectations and rights

We live in a society where we know we are granted rights by legislation. Our expectations differ. But does that mean when we don't get what we want we blame others? After all, one hundred years ago, you never expected to be a woman in business.

Today you believe it is your right to have the opportunity. If it doesn't happen then is it too easy to blame others? Or is it really others people's fault for failing to live up to the ideals encapsulated in equal opportunity laws?

"I'm black and don't use my race as an excuse for not succeeding so it's time women stopped using their gender as one. My mother worked and raised kids, facing sexism from my family who expected her to stay at home, never mind the workplace. She wasn't whining or writing chick-lit about it, she was putting the hours in to get on. She didn't have these fashionable excuses ('Oh the men close ranks') and didn't allow us to use them either. If hard-done-by women worked as hard as they complained, every company would have a female boss."

Flynn, England

"The obstacles for working women are not just in industry; you try taking a child for vaccinations, checkups or to the dentist outside working hours. You have to take time out of work. There is very little childcare for before/after school and if a child is ill, there is nothing a working mother can do other than take time off work. The government wants us to return to work, but will not help to set up an infrastructure that allows it."

Carol, England

"Women are not failing, they have choices which will affect their careers. When I had my first child I understood that my career would be affected. We all have choices; I could have coped by employing a full time live in nanny like Mrs Blair, but it wouldn't have suited me. As for the industry being male dominated – that is more due to the choices made by women and not by men excluding us. How many mothers are prepared to forgo seeing their children grow up, miss sports day and other school activities? I believe I made the right decision that my family is more important to me than a career."

Caron, England

"Of course women succeed. Marie Curie in medicine, Mother Theresa in charity, Florence Nightingale in nursing, Cecil Frances Alexander in hymn writing, Elizabeth Fry in prison reform etc. All useful activities. I could give a list of men who have recently lost millions of pounds of other people's money of whom several are now in prison. And yet these men are deemed to have succeeded in business."

Anthony, England

"I can't employ women in senior positions in my company unless they apply for a job that I have available. I can't promote women if they don't already work for me. The facts are that less than 10% of job applicants at my company are women."

John, England

"The most influential woman in British industry must be Patricia Hewitt; however that doesn't necessarily make her the best role model. Business people don't tend to be well-known outside their own environment so it is unsurprising that so few business women are house-hold names: how many FTSE-100 CEOs of either sex could most of us name?"

Susan, UK

"Can we please stop this "Women are so hard done by" nonsense? Men and women are different and excel at different things – face it! It's like a woman saying 'When it comes to growing moustaches we have been dealt a bad card – men have it so easy'!"

Craig, England

25

2 Starting out

- Why do you want to get into business: the right reasons, the female reasons.
- The biggest obstacles and getting around them.
- Using the gender advantage.

According to no less a source than the United Nations: "Men traditionally have had better opportunities for self-employment as women face more constraints than men in developing their businesses. These constraints include things such as: less access to credit and larger markets; mobility constraints; more workload in the family and household; lack of networks needed to facilitate business development; and lack of know-how concerning ICT, corporate and public sector procurement."

More locally, a three-year study by the Paisley Enterprise Research Centre, looking at the barriers women face in entering business and the ways in which they can be helped to overcome them identified up to 270,000 women in Scotland aged from 16 to 64 as 'would-be entrepreneurs' at some time in their lives. But, currently, only 34,000 are actively interested in starting out on their own.

Consequently the Scottish Executive identified, "…an expanded mentoring programme for businesswomen, with networking events to enable them to come together and find out about the support services available; an enlarged funding programme for women going into business, together with an information campaign to ensure they are aware of the financial support available; and marketing and PR campaigns targeting potential women entrepreneurs."

One thing is clear. You have nothing to fear except fear itself and that is not macho bluster. That is well researched analysis – the way a woman would analyse things – not gung ho!

So as it is the point of the book, let's first highlight the problem, then more importantly, look for solutions for 'women in business' or women wanting to get into business. We clearly want to exploit every resource at our disposal, whether or not we're the 'put upon' minority/majority. But we want to target those resources at the potholes on the road to success.

Why?

If you're like most entrepreneurs, then most of the reasons why entrepreneurs go into business will apply to you. With many women the emphasis can be more intense on some of the main reasons. These are just some of the reasons we found as key drivers from our surveys. The important point here is that you are not alone, even if entrepreneurship can feel lonely at times:

"Having looked after the kids for a number of years, I want to do something fulfilling in a different way."

"I always wanted to be my own boss."

"I reckon I can do things better."

"I have a great idea."

"I never had the opportunity until now having got married, busy with other things."

What is clear is that entrepreneurship is a calling, a passion. It might be fuelled by a life change or removal of pre-existing obstacles, but when the call comes, women feel they have to answer it. Unfortunately the bigger problem we have identified is often the lack of confidence to do so. From our surveys some of these reasons seem societally pre-programmed, others are due to genuine obstacles faced by all budding entrepreneurs regardless of gender.

However, our aim here is to remove those obstacles which are more perceived than real, by again highlighting that you are not alone:

"I don't know where to start."

"I'd like to, but it's not me."

"My husband wouldn't let me."

"I have a good salary, I'm afraid of giving that up for what I know I would enjoy more."

In this book you will see answers to obstacles which are simply not as great as you might have thought.

What?

Maybe it is to do with testosterone, or because of conditioning, but of the three major types of business ambitions, our anecdotal surveys find women go for the smaller type:

1. Accelerated large-scale expanding business growth with international scope.
2. Micro-lifestyle business intended for income replacement.
3. Slow consolidated non-urgent business growth.

Why do more women than men seem to be in 3 than in 1? Some typical responses:

"Didn't think about it."

"I wouldn't have the time or resources."

"It's not what I'd want, I'd be happier with smaller."

"I'm not that type of person."

"I've still got kids and a husband to look after."

"I don't have the people or the money to hire them."

"I don't think the business has that kind of potential."

"There would not be enough customers."

Still feeling alone?

Firstly, in case you think it is not for you, let's see how perceptions of obstacles can be lowered when we show you just some of the headlines around the world relating to women in business – for god's sake if they're all doing it, and some must be doing it well, then why not you?

Times Are Changing For Woman Entrepreneurs

"As a woman entrepreneur, and the current President of the Women Entrepreneurs of Canada, (WEC), I have had the opportunity to take a close look at the issues..."

WebProNews, KY – 29 Mar 2005

QC lauds women entrepreneurs

"...lauded some 6,000 women entrepreneurs for leading the fight against poverty through their participation in the Task Force Sikap Buhay (TFSB) livelihood..."

Philippine Star, Philippines − 18 Mar 2005

Women targeted as new entrepreneurs

"...an information campaign to ensure they are aware of the financial support available; and marketing and PR campaigns targeting potential women entrepreneurs..."

Scotsman, UK − 8 Mar 2005

More Than 30 Million Women Worldwide Are Entrepreneurs; Mentoring ...

"...This suggests that women entrepreneurs may take a more conservative approach to business formation, perhaps because of their higher involvement in necessity..."

mysan.de (Pressemitteilung), Germany − 8 Mar 2005

WOMEN ENTREPRENEURS IN RURAL INDUSTRIES

"Under the REGP, women entrepreneurs are entitled to a higher rate of margin money assistance as compared with general category entrepreneurs..."

Press Information Bureau (press release), India − 17 Mar 2005

ICCI urges IDB to facilitate women entrepreneurs

"...Bank (IDB), other Islamic banks and financial institutions to allocate a special window for providing services for the projects of women entrepreneurs in the..."

Pakistan Times, Pakistan − 7 Mar 2005

Award for women entrepreneurs from Inner Wheel

"Inner Wheel Club celebrated Women's Day by presenting 'Women Entrepreneur Award' to Vasundhara Ravi of Visible Difference Beauty Clinic..."

News Today, India − 10 Mar 2005

Small Business SBA recognizes entrepreneurs' contributions

"...And the SBA's Nevada District office honors entrepreneurs locally for their accomplishments in various segments such as women-owned and minority-owned firms..."

In Business Las Vegas, NV − 19 hours ago

'Make Mine a $Million Business' Program Aims to Propel Chicago ...

"Two powerhouses for women entrepreneurs have teamed with a financial services leader committed to the growth of women-owned enterprises to launch the Make Mine..."

Business Wire (press release), CA – 21 Mar 2005

A 2004 report from the British Chambers of Commerce provides local evidence of the growth:

"In 2001, the UK was ranked 26th out of a possible 29 countries, in terms of balance between male and female entrepreneurship. By 2002 this situation had improved and the gap had narrowed slightly with the UK ranked 23rd out of a possible 37 countries. In 2003, the UK ranked 7th of 14 countries comprised of participating G7 and EU countries, but the gap between male and female entrepreneurship was still wider than in Canada, the US, Germany, the Netherlands, Belgium and Italy. Part of a global pattern of reduced entrepreneurial activity across the world, total entrepreneurial activity (TEA) for women in the UK fell from 4.3% to 2.3% between 2001 and 2002. Female TEA in the UK regained some momentum in 2003, increasing to 3.8%, compared with an 8.9% rate for male entrepreneurship."

Capabilities

Do you feel you don't have the skills? We could say 'maybe you don't' or 'everyone, including good entrepreneurs think that way'. Guess what we found?

- Women in full-time employment are the most likely of all female groups to see good opportunities (48.9% of all respondents) and to think that they have the skills to set up a business (36% of all respondents).

- Women in part-time employment have the second highest fear of failure rate (37%) and do not see entrepreneurship as a good career choice in comparison with women in all other employment categories.

- Disabled women are the most likely to see entrepreneurship as a good career choice, but are unlikely to know an entrepreneur and unlikely to think that they have the skills to set up a business. They have the highest fear of failure rate of all employment categories.

- Male homemakers are more positive about their capabilities than female homemakers, hardly any fear failure at all, and 41.2% of them know entrepreneurs. However, only 43% of them see entrepreneurship as a

31

good career choice. In contrast, female homemakers do see entrepreneurship as a good career choice – 61.8% of them responded positively to this as a question, and a much higher proportion of women see entrepreneurship as a high status activity compared with men (74.7% compared with 43.8%).

- Both male and female students are similarly unlikely to know an entrepreneur or to see good opportunities. Male students are substantially more likely to think that they have the skills to set up a business, (44.0% compared with 28.6% in the female population) but are more likely than women to fear failure (31.1 % compared with 24.8%).

- Retired women are more likely to see entrepreneurship as a good career choice than men. However, they are much less likely to think that they have the skills to set up a business than any other grouping except the unemployed women in our sample (responses were 25% and 23.5% respectively).

- Unemployed women and men are more unlikely than any other group to know an entrepreneur and unemployed women are the least likely of any group to see good opportunities.

TEA: Total entrepreneurial activity by country and year

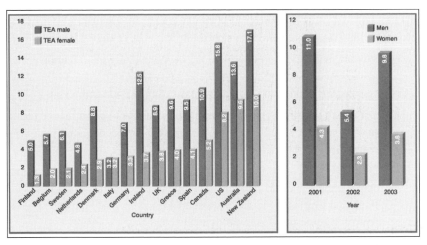

Source: British Chambers of Commerce

TEA: Total entrepreneurial activity by UK region

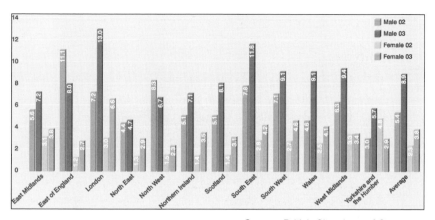

Source: British Chambers of Commerce

The impact of qualifications

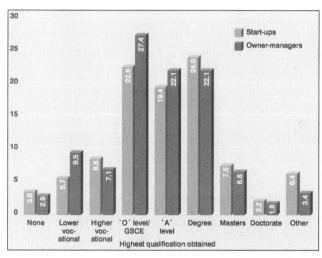

Source: British Chambers of Commerce

Finance as a barrier – real or perceived?

Both male and female businesses require on average around £20,000 in start-up money, according to GEM data. Female entrepreneurs will, on average, put in £10,106 of their own money at this stage, while men will put in £13,500 on average. This leaves an initial start-up funding gap for male-owned businesses of £6,500, and a gap of £9,894 for female-owned businesses.

Where does the money come from?

- 27% of women compared with 17% of men will obtain this money from their close family.

- 36% of women compared with 21 % of men will obtain this finance from government sources.

- The majority of start-up finance comes from banking sources (43% for women and 46% for men) but there is no statistically significant difference between male and female usage of bank finance.

- Female business angels will invest a median amount of £20,000 into start-up businesses compared with £17,142 by male business angels.

A number of points can be highlighted from the data on female financing presented this far:

- Women invest less personal resources in their businesses than men.

- Women are more likely to obtain finance from friends and family and government sources.

According to the British Chambers of Commerce, women are less likely to apply for external finance, but when they do, are more likely to succeed with gaining funding sources except individual investors (informal investors) and non-bank unsecured loans.

It is interesting to look at the reasons why women fail to gain finance in order to derive some guidance for future actions. GEM UK asked a set of questions about why a respondent had been rejected for external finance. This was done to establish two things:

1. To look at any link between failure to gain specific types of finance and failure to gain an alternative.

2. To look at failure, both by type of finance and by the reasons for failure (for example to establish the probability that if an entrepreneur had a weakness in the business proposition in one area, then they would also have weaknesses in other areas).

The results were striking. First, if a woman does not get access to one source of finance (for example, a bank loan), then she is highly unlikely to gain access to any other sort of finance.

Second, the reasons why women fail to gain access to any particular funding source are only weakly correlated to the type of financing as a general rule. A notable exception is a significant positive correlation between failure to gain finance from an individual investor and having a weak management team.

Third, there are exceptionally strong correlations between the different reasons for failure to access finance.

In other words, according to the report: "irrespective of the type of finance a woman tries to access, there is strong evidence to suggest that if a female has a weak management team, she will also have costs that are too high; be unwilling to share ownership; fear debt; have a proposition that is too small and restricted for investment; have an inadequate business plan; have a business whose nature is not suitable for investment; and not be investor ready."

Okay, let's put that to one side for the moment. In this book we're going to help you get to investor ready and ensure you know what it takes to get investment.

But it helps not to be white!

Levels of total entrepreneurial activity are high amongst ethnic minorities generally, but black Caribbean women are the most entrepreneurial. In GEM 2003, TEA amongst this group was 11.3%, higher than male TEA for the UK population as a whole.

Analysis on attitudes from GEM UK 2002 brought out the following points:

- Fear of failure is highest amongst the white population at 34.5% and lowest amongst Caribbean people at 30.6%.

- Overall, African people are the most likely to see good business opportunities.

- There is a strong positive correlation between knowing an entrepreneur, seeing good opportunities, and skills to start a business amongst Asians and Africans. This would suggest that these communities work well to generate a culture of entrepreneurship and share information and knowledge about setting up a business.

Well, one can completely understand the immigration policies of Western governments then! Of course part of the reason Asians are entrepreneurial, speaking from personal experience, is lack of choice. Take co-author Alpesh Patel. Two hundred job applications – all rejections. Hmm. Probably a bad candidate. Or you may want to read the author biography again.

Women leave the boardroom to start a business

A record number of women are escaping the male-dominated work place and branching out on their own, according to new research published in August 2004. A report from the Chartered Institute of Personnel and Development found organisations driving talent away and suggests that many capable women are choosing to build a business of their own.

Male-dominated rules normally associated with 'being at the top' can limit women entering the boardroom and help them make the decision to go it alone. One interviewee from the report said, "I see the trappings of higher status, more money or a bigger car as geared towards a male perspective of success".

The high-potential women who left corporate life to set up on their organisations stated that the political and 'clubby' atmosphere of the boardroom frustrated their efforts.

The study, named 'A bird's eye view', looks at three types of career woman and the factors which decide whether or not they enter the boardroom or choose to set up their own business:

Corporate high flyers – those who have stayed within the corporate life and have achieved senior roles. These women fall into two categories: those who are dedicated to making a difference in their organisation and those who are dissatisfied with what top jobs offer.

Soloists and pioneers – those who have struck out alone, either working on their own, or setting up businesses on their own terms. These women tend to work at least as long hours and as hard as in a corporate life, but feel that the way they manage their work-life balance brings them greater satisfaction than if they'd stayed and pursued a board level career.

Submarines – talented women who have chosen not to work towards traditional career advancement, but have put their energy into other areas. These women put other priorities ahead of work, as work is not engaging or rewarding enough to compete with other elements in their lives.

The problems and prejudices that women still encounter in the workplace

Co-founder of lastminute.com Martha Lane Fox is well aware of the kind of barriers professional women still face in offices and board rooms across the UK.

"I think the climate for women is hideous," says Ms Lane Fox. "In all the meetings I go to, I never meet women. It is so depressing."

Research from Cranfield University has found that about 93% of FTSE 100 firms have no women visible at director level. One theory says that women are having to prove themselves above normal standards set for men.

Pay gap

Fewer women at senior management levels partly explains why the pay gap in the UK between men and women is about 18%, based on an average hourly wage. Inevitably, women also choose to spend time out of the job market raising families and do not accumulate as much work experience as men.

Nevertheless, campaigners still feel the gap is not closing quickly enough:

"We don't want our daughters' generation continuing to debate how we tackle the pay gap," says Julie Mellor, chair of the Equal Opportunities Commission (EOC).

For part-timers (in 1998, 44% of all employed women worked part-time) it is even worse. They earn 41% less on an hourly basis than full-timers. By contrast, in the Netherlands, the same pay gap between part-time and full-time is only 7%.

Prejudice

Research shows that part of the reason for the pay gap is that work done by women has historically been undervalued. Many professions that attract women are often graded at a lower point in the pay structure than male-dominated occupations, even if there is no real difference in skill levels.

This is a particularly British problem, with nurses in Australia earning above the national average wage, while British nurses earn less.

Okay, this we know and lord knows we're not into self-pity. Don't worry, we're about to get back onto what women in business can do.

Where have all the women gone?

One of the biggest obstacles to employing more women in areas where they are not well-represented, such as senior management positions, is a lack of qualified candidates.

Patricia Hewitt and Harriet Harman – both government campaigners for women – have opted for a softly, softly approach, choosing to initiate change through influence.

With equal pay, for example, the government wants to encourage – rather than force – companies to ensure their staff are paid equally by carrying out voluntary 'pay audits'.

"There is little that can be done to give you a quick fix," says John Forth, a senior research officer at National Institute of Economic and Social Research. "Legislation for pay audits is not going to get passed very easily, even though that route would provide the most noticeable short-term solution."

The real test will come as more educated women enter the workforce. Only time will tell whether the weight of new generations and fresh attitudes will slowly do away with the old duffers.

Do you fit the mould?

The GEM 2004 Report on Women and Entrepreneurship provides an in-depth global look at women's entrepreneurship.

Key findings in 2004

In 2004, GEM estimated that about 73m people were involved in starting a new business in the 34 countries that participated in the study. Of those, about 30m were women. The average level of female total entrepreneurial activity (TEA) rate across the 34 GEM countries varied from 39.1% in Peru to 1.2% in Japan.

In every country of the study, men are more active in entrepreneurship than women. The largest gap occurs in middle income nations where men are 75% more likely than women to be active entrepreneurs, compared to 33% in high-income countries and 41% in low-income countries.

Overall, opportunity is the dominant motivation for women's entrepreneurship, similar to men. Nonetheless, many more women than men are involved in entrepreneurship because of the lack of alternative job opportunities.

In low and middle-income countries, the peak years to become involved in entrepreneurial activities for women are ages 25-34. In high-income countries, on the other hand, the peak years for women are ages 35-44.

In low income countries, the majority of active entrepreneurial women (54%) have not completed a secondary degree. In high-income countries, on the other end, women with post secondary education are the most likely (34%) to start a new business.

As in the case of men, and regardless of per capita income, the largest majority of women involved in starting a new business hold other jobs.

Regardless of per capita income, a strong positive and significant correlation exists between knowing other entrepreneurs and a woman's involvement with starting a new business.

"Our results suggest that employed women who know other entrepreneurs are the most likely to start a new business," said Babson Professor Maria Minniti, one of the authors of the report. "These women tend to be older and better educated in high-income countries than in low and middle-income countries. We also found that a woman's perceptions of environmental opportunities as well as confidence in her own capabilities are a powerful predictor of her entrepreneurial behaviour."

The GEM report shows that across all countries, a strong positive and significant correlation exists between opportunity recognition and a woman's likelihood of starting a new business. Women who perceived the existence of business opportunities were more likely to make the decision to start a new business.

Additionally, across all countries, a strong positive and significant correlation exists between a woman's belief of having the knowledge, skills and experience required to start a new business and her likelihood of starting one. Conversely, a strong negative and significant correlation exists between fear of failure and a woman's likelihood of starting a new business.

Other findings

Subjective assessments about the availability of opportunities, the ability to exploit them and the possibility of failing in doing so are all crucial factors in a woman's decision to start a new business.

In the US for example, the majority of businesses started by women employed less start-up capital as compared to men ($33,201 vs $65,010 respectively), used known technology and targeted existing markets. This suggests that women entrepreneurs may take a more conservative approach to business formation, perhaps because of their higher involvement in necessity driven entrepreneurship.

Women tend to have slower early growth trajectories. The vast majority of women involved in starting a new business expect to create five or fewer additional jobs within a five-year period. In low and middle-income countries, only 1% of women's new businesses qualify as having high employment potential. The percentage increases to only 1.6 in high-income countries.

Clearly, if you are writing a business plan, one key thing to do is revisit it and ask why you have made the decisions you have. Being in business is about getting out of your comfort zone. Have you simply made choices because they are comfortable and are they comfortable because of your gender?

Again from GEM:

Policy implications

"In order to be effective, policies with respect to entrepreneurship need to be tailored to a country's specific context," said Prof. Minniti. "This is particularly important for women since they tend to be much more sensitive than men to conditions in their local environment. Nonetheless, across all countries, it is clear that support policies by themselves are not sufficient to increase women's involvement in entrepreneurship. Women are particularly sensitive to their social environment. Mentoring and network support, especially at the local level, are at least as crucial in boosting women's attitudes with respect to business leadership and new venture creation as financial support."

Policy implications for high-income countries

"High-income countries need to sustain innovation rates and encourage the involvement of women in entrepreneurship, especially when faced with an aging labour force. Areas of importance for policy makers should include promoting entrepreneurial education at the college and post-graduate level and encouraging more women to pursue technical degrees and to commercialise their ideas. Coordinating policy to encourage equal benefits for women in the workforce, whether in traditional or entrepreneurial business roles, is vital."

The lesson for UK entrepreneurs is get out and learn. Don't just take it for granted and 'muck in'. Where there is policy identified and you've not benefited from having that gap filled, fill it within yourself, by yourself – including, for instance, your fear of Excel spreadsheets.

Policy implications for middle-income countries

"More than in other groups, women in middle-income countries shy away from starting their own businesses. Areas of importance for policy makers should include to instill fundamental aspects of the entrepreneurial mindset and to increase the attractiveness of entrepreneurship as an income producing activity for women even when they have access to jobs in manufacturing or in the public sector."

Policy implications for low-income countries

"Much female entrepreneurship in low-income countries is motivated by necessity, thus starting a new business represents an effective and flexible way for women to emancipate themselves and provide for their families. Areas of importance for policy makers should include literacy and financial assistance."

TEA: Total entrepreneurial activity by gender and country

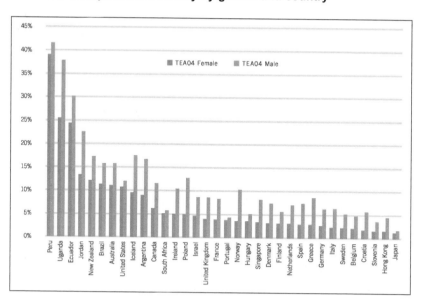

Source: GEM

Solutions

So, you need a helping hand. Any good entrepreneur faces obstacles. They also know how to leverage every single iota of resource. Below we list the key obstacles and some resources for you to tap into to remove obstacles (or at least make the obstacle less daunting) and we offer some quick bullet-point solutions.

Networking

We have a chapter on the subject (chapter 4) including a list of websites.

Finance, angel investors and business plan know-how

Again, we devote a whole chapter to this (chapter 5). Of course, the usual forms of funding are savings, credit cards, angels, friends or family and bank loans.

Government level solutions

Whilst lessons can be learnt from other countries, such changes can take time, so we should see what we can do anyway. Looking at programmes in other countries we can see that this book must address skills development, networking, getting credit and rights. These come up time and time again as the most likely obstacles to you succeeding as a woman in business.

Canada has a range of programmes aimed at creating conditions to support women entrepreneurs in starting and expanding businesses. For example, the 'Step in and step out' programme:

- offers services such as counselling, training and planning to those owning small and medium-sized businesses;
- supports women entrepreneurs if they feel discriminated when refused credit from the banks; and
- gives legal support in access to loans and banking services.

'The Economic Development for Canadian Aboriginal Women Initiative (EDCAW)' program has been established to provide support to aboriginal women with economic and business development. Activities undertaken are:

- networking;
- training;
- advocacy; and
- pilot projects to improve access to capital and business resources.

Opportunities for women – not a local problem

The table over the page shows far fewer women are in self-employment than men. You might not think this a major problem. You might think this is far removed from winning a supplier contract. But the issue is of such grave concern that there is a United Nations division dealing with this issue. As the United

Nations Development Fund for Women put it:

"Women, and especially poor women, are the least able to benefit from globalization and the most likely to suffer from the rapid changes societies undergo during macroeconomic restructuring. There is a growing awareness of the important link between women's poverty at the micro level and macroeconomic policy-making. It is increasingly clear that the ways in which governments allocate resources and make decisions about fiscal and monetary policy have gender implications due to men's and women's different roles in social reproduction and as formal or informal sector workers, producers, consumers, tax payers and citizens."

	United Kingdom						High income	
	1980	*1990*	*1995*	*2000*			*1980*	*2000*
Labour Force								
Females (% of total labour force)	39	42	43	44			38	43
Employment								
Distribution of labour force by employment status								
Wage and Salaried								
Male (% of males employed)	89	80	82	85				
Female (% of females employed)	96	91	92	93				
Self-employed								
Male (% of males employed)	11	18	18	15				
Female (% of females employed)	4	7	7	7				
Contributing Family Workers								
Male (% of males employed)		0.4	0.3	0.2				
Female (% of females employed)		1.1	0.8	0.6				
Women in administrative & managerial positions (% of total workers in this occupational group)			33					
Female Wages (% of male wages)								
Agriculture	77	92		94				
Non-agriculture	70	76		80				
Manufacturing	69	68		68				
Unemployment rates								
Male (% of males labour force)	8.3	7.0	10.1	6.1			5.5	5.4
Female (% of female labour force)	4.8	6.5	6.8	4.8			7.0	6.7

Nevertheless...

Government statistics show that more women than ever before are starting their own business. Their reasons and contributing factors for this are extensive, but it's revolutionising the face of business and changing the traditional stereotype of the grey-haired middle-aged, male entrepreneur.

Here are some statistics and facts on the changing role of women in business:

How many?

A quarter of the UK's 3.2 million self-employed workers are now women.

Labour Force Survey 2003

30 per cent of business owners are women.

Labour Force Survey 2003

Female entrepreneurs now account for 6.8 per cent of the UK's working population, double the figure than in 1979.

Labour Force Survey 2003

The difference between male and female owned start-ups narrowed by 40 per cent in 2002.

Global Entrepreneurship Monitor 2003

Four in every 100 women aged 18 to are active entrepreneurs.

Global Entrepreneur Monitor 2003

Almost five per cent of the female population expects to start a business in the next three years.

Global Entrepreneur Monitor 2003

More than one in five women believe there are good opportunities available for them to start a business.

Global Entrepreneur Monitor 2003

A third of the female population would start a business if it wasn't for the fear of failure.

Global Entrepreneur Monitor 2003

43 per cent of enquiries to Shell Livewire, the international scheme to help young entrepreneurs, are from women.

Shell Livewire 2003

38 per cent of startup business owners contacting The Prince's Trust in 2002 were women.

The Prince's Trust

Who?

Women aged between 35 and 44 are more entrepreneurial, as are women with graduate qualifications and those from higher income groupings.

Labour Force Survey 2003

Where?

The highest number of female start-ups are based in London, where 8.4 per cent of the female workforce are self-employed.

Labour Force Survey 2003

Female entrepreneurs are least active in the North East.

Labour Force Survey 2003

Why?

54 per cent of women start a business so they can choose what hours they work, compared with only 35 per cent of men.

Figures extracted from On the move: Women & Men Business Owners in the United Kingdom, IBM, February 2002

Types of business

25 per cent of male entrepreneurs are engaged in the construction industry, compared with just 5 per cent of females.

The Small Business Service

There is little difference in the percentage of men and women attracted to industries such as manufacturing and transport, retail and distribution, but female entrepreneurs are more likely than men to work in sideline businesses.

The Small Business Service

Where improvements can be made

Men are still twice as likely to start a business as women.

Global Entrepreneur Monitor 2003

The UK has a comparatively low level of female entrepreneurship with the rest of the world in all categories.

Global Entrepreneur Monitor 2003

Entrepreneurial activity is highest among employed males aged 35-44.

Global Entrepreneur Monitor 2003

What the experts say

"There are still too few women starting out and growing a business. We need to eliminate the barriers that remain, be it access to finance or to childcare or because of some other form of discrimination. If women started new businesses at the same rate as men, we would have more than 100,000 extra new businesses each year."

Patricia Hewitt, former secretary for state for Trade and Industry

"It is good to see the gap between male and female entrepreneurship is narrowing."

Will Hutton, CEO The Work Foundation

Ending on a positive note: It's a woman's world

The role of the entrepreneur has traditionally been a male one and statistically more men than women still choose to start their own business. However, a growing number of women are deciding to go it alone and the gender gap is narrowing every year.

Starting a business is now a viable career option for women and while barriers to entrepreneurship undoubtedly still exist, four in every 100 women are active business owners.

Business opportunities now exist for women of virtually any financial, social and domestic circumstance. The internet and mobile technology are particularly responsible for opening up entrepreneurship to people that might previously have been unable to make the necessary commitment to the traditional 9-to-5 business.

It's now possible to start a business with little more than a good idea, a computer and a mobile phone. While it requires as much dedication and hard work as it ever did, in many circumstances there's far more flexibility in when and how to work and communicate.

As more women enter the fray, attitudes are thankfully changing too. Businesses and financial institutions are embracing the trend and are actively seeking to work with a gender they previously spent little time, money or attention targeting – as women now make up 30% of all business owners, they'd be foolish not to.

Pleasingly, of the all the female entrepreneurs we spoke to in our profiles section, only one complained that she'd experienced discrimination or not been taken seriously for being a woman.

The Government also appears to have recognised the value of female entrepreneurs. In June last year, chancellor Gordon Brown said: "UK start-ups would rise by 50% if the start-up rate amongst women matched that of men."

Perhaps motivated by the need to boost the economy as much as by its moral conscience, the Government launched a scheme in September 2004 to encourage more female start-ups in a bid to eventually match start-up rates in the US, where 100,000 extra businesses are created by women each year than in the UK.

So, while there's still progress to be made to ensure women gain the same level of opportunities in business as men, the traditional obstacles of social and domestic responsibilities, lack of access to finance and plain old-fashioned prejudice are diminishing.

3 Finance for growth

"Visions are worth fighting for. Why spend your life making someone else's movie."

Orson Welles

- Why women don't consider certain types of finance.
- Getting money – how much do you need – a simple, accurate, convincing answer.
- What investors want – from the horse's mouth.
- How do you know what to offer investors.
- A non-experts introduction to balance sheets, cash-flows and profit and loss accounts: really it isn't scary – honest.
- We bet after this you can produce a profit and loss, balance sheet and cash-flow for your business in an hour – that includes 'depreciation and amortisation!'
- Business plans the painless way.

Studies show women are less likely to borrow for their businesses than men. Whether it is lack of financial suppliers catering to them, or a 'Venus' mindset – either way it can and does hamper them.

Two obstacles we want to remove in this chapter are how to do the financials and how to prepare the business plan. Without these you aren't going to get within a million miles of finance anyway, so you need to learn. The other thing many entrepreneurs do not know is who to speak to. Again, we help remove this obstacle for women entrepreneurs.

If we shine light into the darkness, more women entrepreneurs will join us. Now, we're going to run through things in a way a mortal, not an actuary, would understand!

Sources of finance

How do you know who to approach? Many people waste a lot of time pitching to the wrong people. The outstanding www.innovateur.co.uk summarises sources thus:

Sources of finance – 'Business Stage' and 'Finance Required' matrix

LMBO						VC/MB/B
Established			VC/B	VC/AIM/B	VC/MB/B	VC/MB/B /SE
MBO/MBI			PR/BA/B/ VC	PR/VC/B	PR/VC/ MB/B	VC/MB/B
Expansion		PR/BA	BA/B/VCT/ OF/VC	VC/AIM/B	VC/MB/B /AIM	VC/MB/B
Growth		PR/BA	BA/VCT/OF /VC	BA/VC/ VCT/AIM	VC/MB/B /AIM	
Early Stage	PR	PR/BA	BA	BA/VC/ VCT		
Seed	PR	PR/BA	BA			
Seeking £	- 10K	10k - 100k	100k - 2m	2m - 5m	5m - 50m	50m - 250m

PR   Personal Resources, Friends & Family

BA   Business Angels (private individuals with funds & business experience)

VCT   Venture Capital Trusts - funds that behave much like Business Angels

VC   Venture Capital companies

B   High Street Banks

OF   Ofex - a less regulated market that enables small issues - not liquid

AIM   AIM & Techmark - A less regulated stock market that is liquid

MB   Merchant Banks - Providing commercial debt / equity with a risk premium

SE   London Stock Exchange (parent of AIM & TechMark)

Business angels

These individuals invest in early stage companies. Ideally you want an individual who will also add value through input, experience, contacts. As a mentor they are there to provide support.

Venture Capital Report:
www.vcr1978.com

VCR are very experienced in this area. Their directory details VC sources and requirements and they advise on how best to package presentations.

Oxford Investment Opportunity Network:
www.oion.co.uk/companies/companies.html

National Business Angel Network:
www.bestmatch.co.uk/home/

A national network with a central register of opportunities.

Xenos:

www.xenos.co.uk

Pi Capital:

www.picapital.co.uk

A group of successful angels who invest individually or as a group.

Beer & Partners:

www.beerandpartners.com

Proclaims itself as the largest and most successful source of business angel capital in the UK.

The following charts give further information about business angels.

Profession of business angel

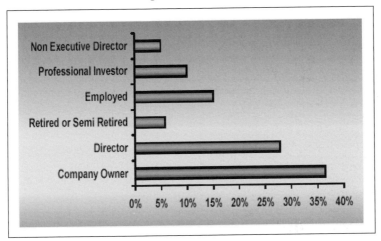

Source: InvestorPulse 2003 Business Angel Survey

Length of time as business angel

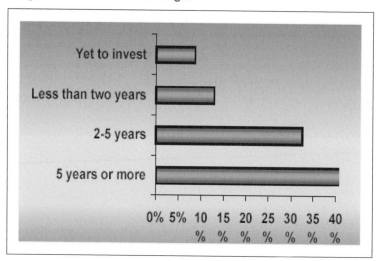

Source: InvestorPulse 2003 Business Angel Survey

Top five reasons for private company investing

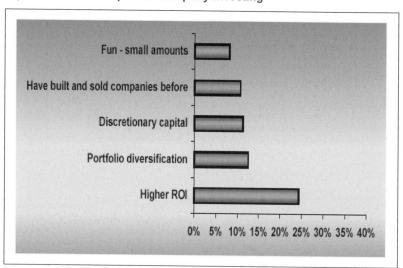

Source: InvestorPulse 2003 Business Angel Survey

Preferred stage of business

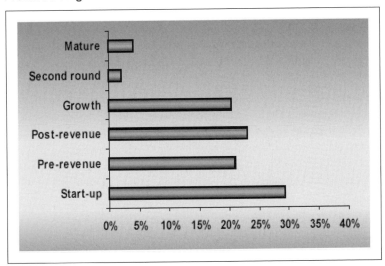

Source: InvestorPulse 2003 Business Angel Survey

Preferred source of investment opportunities

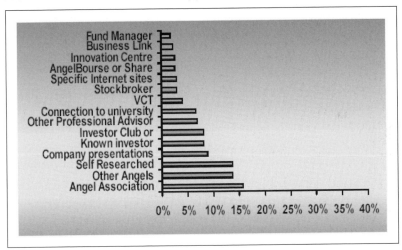

Source: InvestorPulse 2003 Business Angel Survey

So, what can you typically expect when contacting an angel network? This is one area of which many entrepreneurs, especially women, are unaware, so let's shed some light. We will use Beer and Partners as an example of one of the many professional units in this sphere. Another website I recommend you visit is C2Ventures (www.c2ventures.com). What follows is what Beer have to say.

What happens first?

"We would like to see a business plan. We are not looking for a work of art, but enough information to give us a preliminary feel for the type of business, whether it is likely to be suitable for investors, and the background of the people involved."

"If, on reading the plan, we do not think we can help, we will tell you right away; we will also try to explain why. This might be because we do not have enough investors keen on the sector, or in your area (we do not deal with overseas businesses for example), or we think that you are being unrealistic in your valuation of your business. In this case we will either return the plan to you at your request, or securely destroy it."

"We will quiz potential clients on the investment proposal and will seek answers to the key aspects of the proposal that our investors are looking for, i.e.

- Can the management team demonstrate that it has the ability to turn investment into profit? Is there anything in their track record that supports this?

- What is the 'discriminator' in your business? What makes your company different from its competitors and therefore more likely to succeed? Perhaps patent protections, proprietary information or other factors that will give comfort to investors that you are 'special'.

- What is the potential exit route, when and where is it? Remember investors are not looking for lifestyle businesses, they want to see growth, perhaps followed by a trade sale, float, sale back to the management or whatever.

- How much is really needed, when and why? Can funding be phased? What is the new money to be spent on – investors will not put money into a company merely to repay shareholder/bank debt, or to fund a lifestyle.

- What is the deal? How much equity are you prepared to sell? How did you arrive at the figure? Is there a skills gap in the team that a suitable investor can help fill?

- Are there any time or other constraints (apart from 'as soon as possible' – everyone seems to come to us too late!) or other factors that we need to be aware of?"

What are the fees?

"We do charge a non-refundable retainer fee to reflect some of the preparation work that we need to do. Our retainer fee must be paid before we start. This fee will also cover our out of pocket expenses incurred, for example in marketing you and your business to our investors, travelling etc.

This fee is a minimum of £1,000, where there is that (mythical!) perfect business plan, but is more usually in the £1,500 to £5,000 range. Most of the firm's income is of course geared towards success, for which our fees are 5% on the first £500,000 of funding, 4% on the next £500,000 and so on down to 2%, with a minimum success fee of £5,000. In addition, we will take an option or warrants in respect of shares in our clients, written on completion of the investment, at a strike price equivalent to the price at which shares are 'sold' to the investor and exercised normally when the investor exits. Usually this option is for 4% of the enlarged share capital."

Many business people do not know what warrants and options mean. Okay, let's clear up the jargon so we don't get scared off.

Enlarged share capital

When you set up your company it would be with a certain number of shares. It can be almost any figure, but let us say it was 80,000 shares. When your company gets money for equity, it means it issues and sells some of its shares to an investor for cash into the company. It sells these shares by issuing new ones and so you have more shares post an investment than you did before hand. The enlarged share capital refers to all the shares including new ones for new capital.

Why is this important? Because 10% of a company beforehand is maybe 8,000 shares and afterwards 10% maybe 10,000 shares. An investor needs to know how many shares he has.

Warrants and options

Again, don't be scared! Say you have an enlarged (i.e. post-investment) share capital of 100,000 shares and agreed that the company is worth £500,000 with your investor. Then each share is worth £5.

If you issue 1,000 warrants with a strike of £5 and expiry at some future date, that means the holder of the warrants (the investor or the middle-man) has the right, but not the obligation, to buy 1,000 shares for £5 each. Now say at some future date the company is worth £5m, then each share is worth £50. Clearly he will exercise his options, buy at £5 and sell on at £50.

Dilution

Let's say you set up your company with 80,000 shares and you own all of them. Now let's say the company issues 20,000 more, in exchange for £20,000. There are now 100,000 shares and instead of owning 100% of the company you own only 80% – that is dilution. No bad thing necessarily if you have a smaller stake of a bigger cake. But, you don't want to go from 100% to 1% if the 1% is not 100 times bigger do you?

So what do investors want then?

As Beer puts it: "At the risk of stating the obvious, investors will want to make a profit out of their investment. This means that, at a minimum, they will want to see the value of their investment double over, say, three years. They will want to see an exit route – no-one wants to be locked into an unquoted investment for ever, so there needs to be a clear exit strategy. This can be through a trade sale (who are the target buyers?) or a sale back to the management if cash flow permits. They will want a seat on the board; possibly they will want to fill a part-time role in the business. Indeed, they are likely to have a range of skills and contacts that will be extremely useful to our clients. Investors invest in people first, businesses second, so they need to be able to buy in to the proposal and to trust the team."

Quick guide to valuation

One of the things business women have difficulty with is what to offer the investor for their cash. That turns on how to value your business.

Okay, we're going to provide a very quick and dirty guide to valuations. The idea is with this knowledge you're less put off than a guide requiring a PhD in rocket science.

- Values are what you argue. Usually they are based on earnings multiples. So if your company made pre-tax profit of £100,000 and is valued on a price-earnings multiple of 5 then it would be worth £500,000.

- However, most young companies have hardly any earnings today, so you will not want to use a multiple of today's earnings but use future earnings. For instance, if you project in year three your earnings will be £1m, then you will want to use that. But of course that is speculative and has to be discounted to today's value. So you may say it is 5 x £800,000.

- Why '5'? It is a typical multiple for private companies.

- If your investor wants to double his money in three years, then he needs to have such number of shares in your company today, that in three years would mean they are worth double if he sold those shares based on the total value of your company. (You may hear the word 'internal rate of return' thrown in here – it basically means what annual return would have been (as an interest rate e.g. 30%, if given the initial investment, and given the exit in however many years).)

Let me explain. Your company in 3 years has net pre-tax profit of £1m. If you agree it is then worth £5m at that point, and an investor is willing to put in £100,000 today, how much of your company does he need to own for that to be worth £200,000 in 3 years? He needs to own 4%, because 4% of £5m is £200,000. So you need to work out what is 4% of your company (post-investment in today's enlarged share capital, say 100,000 shares i.e. 4,000 shares sold for £100,000 or £25 each, valuing the total company today at £2.5m).

Will the investor accept a valuation of £2.5m today? That depends on how likely they think it is you will be worth £5m in year three.

Valuation and the British Venture Capital Association

There can be few institutions more, perceived at least, male dominated than the British Venture Capital Association. And there can be few greater needs than for an entrepreneur to understand valuation of their business. So let's do women entrepreneurs a service and see what the BVCA says about valuation.

Earnings Multiple

32. This methodology involves the application of an earnings multiple to the earnings of the business being valued in order to derive a value for the business.

33. This methodology is likely to be appropriate for an Investment in an established business with an identifiable stream of continuing earnings that can be considered to be maintainable.

34. This methodology may be applicable to companies with negative earnings, if the losses are considered to be temporary and one can identify a level of "normalised" maintainable earnings.

This may involve the use of averaging of earnings figures for a number of periods, using a forecast level of earnings or applying a "sustainable" profit margin to current or forecast revenues.

35. In using the Earnings Multiple methodology to estimate the Fair Value of an Investment.

The Valuer should:

i. apply a multiple that is appropriate and reasonable (given the risk profile and earnings growth prospects of the underlying company) to the maintainable earnings of the company;

ii. adjust the amount derived in i above for surplus assets or excess liabilities and other relevant factors to derive an Enterprise Value for the company;

Guidance on the interpretation of underlined terms is given below.

"appropriate multiple"

36. A number of earnings multiples are commonly used, including price/earnings ("P/E"), enterprise value/earnings before interest and tax ("EV/EBIT") and depreciation and amortisation ("EV/EBITDA"). The particular multiple used should be appropriate for the business being valued.

37. In general, because of the key role of financial structuring in private equity, multiples should be used to derive an Enterprise Value for the underlying business. Therefore, where a P/E multiple is used, it should generally be applied to a taxed EBIT figure (after deducting finance costs relating to working capital or to assets acquired or leased using asset finance) rather than to actual after-tax profits, since the latter figure will generally have been significantly reduced by finance costs.

38. By definition, earnings multiples have as their numerator a value and as their denominator an earnings figure. The denominator can be the earnings figure for any specified period of time and multiples are often defined as "historical", "current" or "forecast" to indicate the earnings used. It is important that the multiple used correlates to the period and concept of earnings of the company being valued. "reasonable multiple"

39. The Valuer would usually derive a multiple by reference to market-based multiples, reflected in the market valuations of quoted companies or the price at which companies have changed ownership. This market-based approach presumes that the comparator companies are correctly valued by the market. Whilst there is an argument that the market capitalisation of a quoted company reflects not the value of the company but merely the price at which "small parcels" of shares are exchanged, the presumption in these Guidelines is that the share price does correctly reflect the value of the company as a whole.

41. In using P/E multiples, the Valuer should note that the P/E ratios of comparator companies will be affected by the level of financial gearing and applicable tax rate of those companies.

42. In using EV/EBITDA multiples, the Valuer should note that such multiples, by definition, remove the impact on value of depreciation of fixed assets and amortisation of goodwill and other intangibles. If such multiples are used without sufficient care, the Valuer may fail to recognise that business decisions to spend heavily on fixed assets or to grow by acquisition rather than organically do have real costs associated with them which should be reflected in the value attributed to the business in question.

43. It is important that the earnings multiple of each comparator is adjusted for points of difference between the comparator and the company being valued.

These points of difference should be considered and assessed by reference to the two key variables underpinning the earnings multiple – risk and earnings growth prospects. In assessing the risk profile of the company being valued, the Valuer should recognise that risk arises from a range of aspects, including the nature of the company's operations, the markets in which it operates and its competitive position in those markets, the quality of its management and employees and, importantly in the case of private equity, its capital structure and the ability of the Fund holding the Investment to effect change in the company.

For example, the value of the company may be reduced if it:

- *is smaller and less diverse than the comparator(s) and, therefore, less able generally to withstand adverse economic conditions;*
- *is reliant on a small number of key employees;*
- *is dependent on one product or one customer;*
- *has high gearing; or*
- *for any other reason has poor quality earnings.*

44. Recent transactions involving the sale of similar companies are sometimes used as a frame of reference in seeking to derive a reasonable multiple. It is sometimes argued, since such transactions involve the transfer of whole companies whereas quoted multiples relate to the price for "small parcels" of shares, that they provide a more relevant source of multiples. However, their appropriateness in this respect is often undermined by the following:

- *the lack of forward-looking financial data and other information to allow points of difference to be identified and adjusted for;*
- *the generally lower reliability and transparency of reported earnings figures of private companies; and*
- *the lack of reliable pricing information for the transaction itself.*

45. It is a matter of judgment for the Valuer as to whether, in deriving a reasonable multiple, he refers to a single comparator company or a number of companies or the earnings multiple of a quoted stock market sector or sub-sector. It may be acceptable, in particular circumstances, for the Valuer to conclude that the use of quoted sector or sub-sector multiples or an average of multiples from a "basket" of comparator companies may be used without adjusting for points of difference between the comparator(s) and the company being valued.

Valuation and Gate 2 Growth

Again, to help you understand these concepts on which all entrepreneurs, let alone women entrepreneurs, are weak, we include some examples:

Example 1 (P&L):

Sample Company Ltd. Income Statement (in '000€)	31.12.2000
+ Sales	11 136
= Total Revenue	11 136
- Cost of materials	135
- Personnel expenses	6 365
- Other costs	909
= EBITD	3 727
EBITD % of Total Revenue	*33%*
- Depreciation	2 014
= EBIT	1 713
EBIT % of Total Revenue	*15%*
+ Financial income	9
- Interest expenses	39
= PBT	1 683
- Taxes	321
= PAT	1 362
PAT % of Total Revenue	*12%*

Abbreviations used:

EBITD - Earnings Before Interest, Tax and Depreciation;

EBIT - Earnings Before Interest and Tax;

PBT - Profit Before Tax; synonyms: **EBT** - Earnings Before Tax;

PAT - Profit After Tax; synonyms: **Net Profit, Net Earnings**

Sample Company Ltd.
Income Statement

+ Sales
= **Total Revenue**
- Cost of Sales
= **Gross Margin**
- Operating expences
= **EBITD**
- Depreciation
= **EBIT** (Operating result)
+ Financial income
- Interest expenses
= **Profit Before Tax**
- Taxes
= **Net Profit**

Source: Gate 2 Growth (www.gate2growth.com)

So the intermediary has your plan and financials – now what?

Again as Beer puts it:

"Our job is to ensure that our clients' proposals are presented in the right way to as many suitable investors as possible, and we employ a variety of channels to achieve that end.

Our most effective means of bringing you in front of our investors has always been through personal contact. Our Associates know the more active investors, and deal with them on a wide variety of matters. So they will telephone these investors as soon as they see a proposal that is likely to interest them. Our investors appreciate this, since they are looking for deals. It is this knowledge of our more active investors that is the real strength of the firm.

Often we will also prepare a 2/3 page synopsis – approved and warranted by our client – which we circulate to targeted investors. All our Associates have on-screen details of our entire investor base, so they can target investors by sector, geography, or capital available. This may be to 10 investors or 100, depending on the nature of the investment proposal.

Finally we will prepare a 'coat trailer' for our regular Stop Press. This is up to 200 words, will not name our clients, but invite interested investors to seek further information from the Beer & Partners Associate responsible. Our client will approve the entry in advance, and will warrant information given. Circulation of the Stop Press is over 1,900 and growing, and will include all our private investors, the VC Institutions, and a large number of our other contacts (which we call 'gatekeepers'), such as stockbrokers, private banks, accountants, solicitors – indeed anyone we know who we believe has access to investors. Given the range of circulation, we cannot realistically control who will read the entry and you need to be careful not to disclose too much confidential or sensitive information, but provide enough to make our investors want to know more. The American phrase is the 'elevator pitch'.

Occasionally we send out an abridged version of the Stop Press entry to all our investors to make sure that they have not forgotten about our clients!

We also pass brief details to one or two of the more active business angel networks, and to some of the websites that are dedicated to our market.

If an investor wants to meet our client, he will need the up to date Business Plan in advance of the meeting, and we encourage our clients to send this, so that they have the chance to establish direct contact as soon as possible. Whilst our investors have signed a general confidentiality agreement with the firm, it is wise to reinforce this direct, particularly where there is market sensitive information in the plan. Our investors often have fingers in pies that we do not necessarily know about and we would always recommend caution in giving away too much sensitive information at too early a stage. At some point however, remember you will have to bare your soul. We will usually attend the first meeting with each investor, to ensure that the thing runs as smoothly as possible.

Remember that our investors are highly experienced, are likely to fully understand your market (that is one reason why they want to invest in it in the first place), and are very careful what they do with their money. We do not know many rich fools! We cannot emphasise too strongly the need to be open and honest with our investors, to answer all questions as fully as possible, and to respond to any requests for further information promptly. Our market is all about trust, and if investors have the feeling that our clients are being less than open, they will simply walk away, and quite rightly too. The investor is assessing our client and his or her ability to carry through the plan; the chemistry has to be right."

Due diligence next – when can I get the cash and get on with it?

"We have a role in the due diligence stage. Although due diligence will usually be relatively informal, we do need to make sure that our clients are providing additional information promptly and accurately.

We will also advise our client on any formal or informal offers that the investor might make, to ensure that all the key issues have been agreed, or at least discussed.

When the time comes to appoint solicitors, we can recommend suitable firms if our client does not have one of his own – after all the private equity markets are somewhat specialised and a solicitor with relevant experience is essential.

After this, we are on hand should problems arise – it is in our own interests after all that they do not! Whilst most of our investors are well known to us, some are not. Our clients should therefore undertake their own due diligence on investors. They are going to have to work with them, we do not. We will advise as needed."

Here are answers to some of the questions Beer are most often asked:

How long does it take?

"This is impossible to answer. So much depends on how well our client is organised, whether the investor will need extensive due diligence, and indeed how much interest we are able to generate early on. Research by the University of Southampton suggests an average timescale of 16/17 weeks. That is an accurate reply to the question, but not a useful one! We have concluded restructuring finance arrangements in a week, more usually it will take many months. So we always ask that clients plan the fund-raising exercise well ahead (as any banker will tell you, if the answer has to be quick, it has to be no!). For our part we work as quickly as our clients – and the investors – allow us; that has been one of the keys to our success so far.

We will do our best to keep you up to date with progress, though bear in mind that investors are generally busy, see many proposals, get side-tracked by other things and do not like to be hassled by us or by our clients. Everyone does need to have patience when dealing in the Business Angel markets."

What will it cost?

"Apart from our fees, you should plan for legal costs (get an estimate once Heads of Agreement are reasonably final), and accountant's costs, perhaps for EIS clearance or personal tax advice and due diligence costs. Bear in mind that you may have to pay facility fees if there is to be bank lending involved. Some investors will want their own legal fees to be borne by our client, but we would resist that (unless of course this cost is merely added to the amount invested without changing the 'deal')."

What can we promise?

"Nothing, except that we will do everything we can to market your proposal to our investor base. Although we do not agree to help a client unless we can add value, we can never guarantee success – we do not have power of the cheque book. Ultimately the decision whether or not to invest, or to accept an investment is out of our hands. It all depends on how well you can present yourself and the investment proposal, face to face, with an investor. Our job, in a nutshell, is to persuade as many potential investors to meet you as we can."

Filling in the financials

Do you look forward to filling in your tax returns? No, funny that, neither does anyone else except tax inspectors and accountants. Assuming you are in neither category, you will probably procrastinate about doing your company financials for your business plan, but if you are passionate about your business and want to be a woman in business you'll have to get on with it.

But, being a resourceful woman in business and reading this book, you will also try to make life as easy as possible. So scrap that three year degree course in accountancy, we're going to give you the run down.

By far the best and easiest software is downloadable free from:

www.innovateur.co.uk

The great thing is it does not need you to understand and calculate depreciations, amortisations and so forth. You can put in the figures you can handle e.g. costs of telephones and it will work out how, for the purposes of accounts, they should be handled and produce the balance sheet, profit and loss and cash flow for you.

By the way, the answer to the question 'how much cash will I need?' is found when you go through the cash-flow – it is the lowest negative point – because that is how much cash you will be short of – simple eh?

Starting out

The first point to start out with the spreadsheets is shown below. You would only fill in the white boxes, so don't worry about the others.

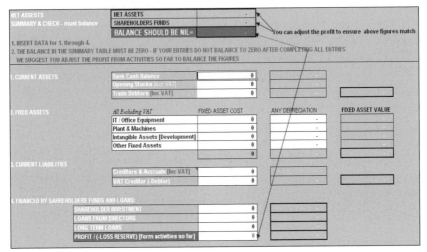

Source: Innovateur (www.innovateur.co.uk)

Okay, some simple points:

- Your business at the start could only have been shareholder investment (how much you put in to the company, directors loans (how much you lent the company) and long-term loans) and profits/losses from activities so far.

- The software will then make sure loans go towards net assets and profits/losses and shareholder investments go under shareholder funds. Why do net assets and shareholder funds need to match? Because where else would you have got your net assets from if not shareholder funds and vice versa.

Sales, cost of sales and distribution

Okay, you have sorted out your starting position. Next is your sales costs. See the image below.

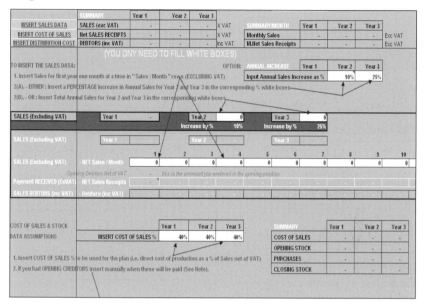

Source: Innovateur (www.innovateur.co.uk)

Don't worry if it is not very clear. Essentially it is simply this:

- You put in your calculations for your sales each month (this will be based on certain assumptions which form your notes to accounts).
- Then you just put in a percentage cost of sales (again assumptions in notes).
- And you estimate annual sales increases.
- The clever software from that can start working out your profit and loss and cash-flows.

Operating expenses come next – nearly finished

Source: Innovateur (www.innovateur.co.uk)

Here you just fill in your operating expenses like salaries. The software will then calculate the impact on your cash-flow and profit and loss.

Finally... the finance/loans and fixed assets bit

People often simply do not know how finance is put into a balance sheet, accounted for in cash-flows, how fixed assets costs are 'depreciated' or expenses over time on your profit and loss account show up on your balance sheet and impact the cash-flow.

Again, the software does it for you.

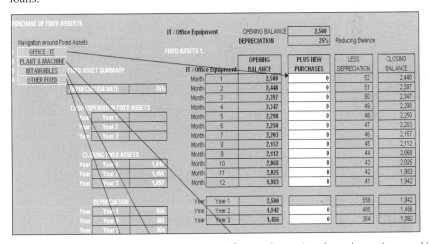

Source: Innovateur (www.innovateur.co.uk)

You first simply enter the equity (or cash from investors) you will receive and any loans.

Source: Innovateur (www.innovateur.co.uk)

Next enter the fixed assets you plan to buy. Now fixed assets are the cleverest way to understand how the holy trinity in accountancy interacts: the p/l; cash flow; and balance sheet.

If you buy an asset, it will show up on your balance sheet (because that depicts your assets and liabilities). The cash-flow is impacted by the cash going out. The profit and loss is hit by the expenses – but it is not expensed in one go, the expense is spread out over 3-5 years – depreciated – as that's the life of the machine going into earning profits.

Thankfully, the software does all of this for you, including changing one of the trinity as you alter your inputs.

Example balance sheet

Fixed Assets

IT / Office Equipment
Plant & Machines
Intangible Assets [Development]
Other Fixed Assets

Current Assets

Cash
Trade Debtors
Stock

Current Liabilities

Trade Creditors & Accruals
VAT Creditor (Debtor)
Other Creditors

Net Current Assets

Total Assets less Current Liabilities

Long-term Creditors

Long Term Loans
Loans from Directors
Other Creditors due after 1 year

NET ASSETS

SHAREHOLDERS FUNDS

Share Capital & Premium
Profit & Loss Account

Sample balance sheet

Sample Company Ltd. Balance sheet (in '000€)	31.12.2000
ASSETS	
Cash	30
Receivables	20
Inventory	50
Total Current Assets	**100**
Current Assets % of Total Assets	*24%*
Land & Buildings	110
Machinery & Equipment	200
Total Fixed Assets	**310**
Total Assets	**410**
LIABILITIES & EQUITY	
Creditors	25
Short-term Debt	25
Current Liabilities	**50**
Long Term Debt	**250**
Total Liabilities	**300**
Liabilities in % ot Total Assets	*73%*
Share Capital	100
Reserves	5
Retained Earnings	5
Total Equity	**110**
Total Liabilities and Equity	**410**

Current Assets - assets available at short notice, include cash, current accounts, receivables, raw materials, work-in-process, goods-in-stock;

Fixed Assets - consist of land and building, movable equipment, construction-in-progress, intangible assets, financial investments;

Current Liabilities - liabilities with term up to 1 year, consist of: notes-, accounts-, salaries-, taxes-, and dividend-payables; accrued expenses; short-term debt;

Long-term debt - debt/payables with term over 1 year, e.g. bank loans, mortgages etc.

Retained earnings - accumulated profit/loss from current + previous periods

Source: Gate 2 Growth (www.gate2growth.com)

Example cash flow forecast

CASH INFLOWS
Cash from Sales
VAT (or GST USA) from Sales
Loans from Directors
Long-term Loans
Share Capital Investment

CASH INFLOW IN PERIOD

CASH OUTFLOWS

Financing & Investment
IT & Office Equipment
Plant & Machines
Intangible Assets (Development)
Other Fixed Assets
Purchases for Stock
Bank Interest Paid/(Received)
Loan Interest Paid
Loan Capital Repayments
Director Loan Repayments

Administrative Expenses
Offices and Rates
Salaries & Employer NI
Utilities
Telephones
Insurance
Stationery & Post Office Equipment Rental
Website Costs
Accountancy Costs
Legal & Professional Fees
Travel & Subsistence
Motor Expenses
Sundry Expenses
Bank Charges
Other Services
Marketing Costs
Research Costs

Provision for Bad Debts

Sales & Distribution Costs
VAT (or GST USA)
VAT in Purchases & Expense Payment
VAT to Customs & Excise - Payment (Refund)

CASH OUTFLOWS IN PERIOD

NET CASH FLOWS

OPENING CASH

CASH BALANCE

Example profit & loss account

Sales
Cost of Sales
Gross Profit
Administrative Expenses
Offices and Rates
Salaries & Employer NI
Utilities
Telephones
Insurance
Stationery & Post Office Equipment Rental
Website Costs
Accountancy Costs
Legal & Professional Fees
Travel & Subsistence
Motor Expenses
Sundry Expenses
Bank Charges
Other Services
Marketing Costs
Research Costs
Provision for Bad Debt
Sales & Distribution Costs
Depreciation
Operating Profit (EBIT)
Interest Payable
Overdraft Interest (Interest Received)
Loan Interest Payable
Profit Before Corporation Tax
Corporation Tax
Net Profit/(Loss)
Dividends Payable
Profit to Reserves

Cumulated cash flows

Source: Gate 2 Growth (www.gate2growth.com)

What not to say in your business plan or to investors

1. **There is no competition.**

    Yeah, right, because you're just that good! No it means your mind is closed and you're desperate to see things the way you want to.

2. **The existing competition is lazy or stupid.**

    Again, well you're not getting my money. Firstly, they are not lazy or stupid. Secondly, if they were, that is not a competitive advantage for you. Trust us.

3. **Founders have invested £x of their time.**

    Forget trying this old one, where you value your time and say that is how much cash equivalent you've put in. Please don't treat the angel like a muppet.

4. **The channel partners will sell the product.**

    Speaking as an author, it's like saying to a publisher, 'the book will sell, if Amazon promote it heavily'. Grow up.

5. **We will take 1% market share of the $10 trillion dollar global market.**

   1% never sounds a lot. But 1% of the Chinese population is 10m for instance. Can you sell 10m? Similarly, just work out the raw numbers first, before pulling percentages from the sky.

6. **Where did the dosh go?**

   So many founders want to raise cash because it is a validation of their life. They don't itemise where the cash will go. Spell it out.

Sample business plan

Below is a sample business plan courtesy of www.innovateur.co.uk

XYZ COMPANY LIMITED
BUSINESS PLAN

Strictly Private & Confidential

XYZ Company Limited
The Old Manor House
Somewhere Down South
Avalon AV1 234B
Tel: 01234 567 890 Fax: 01234 567 891
E-mail: xyz@xyzcoltd.com

Executive summary

The executive summary is the most important part of the business plan. Many people will only read this. The summary in itself will not secure an investor, however, it can lose them.

Quality – the quality of the summary must therefore be outstanding and you should pay particular attention to it. Obtain critical feedback from others on your drafts.

Stand-alone – it is also used as a stand-alone document when introducing the project to others so it must be able to capture interest and entice the reader to take the next step and request more information – and secure a meeting.

Style – cogent and terse. It should be direct and organised as a series of bulleted paragraphs, each deals with one key area. No waffle.

Length – ideally one page, and certainly not more than two pages.

Content – it needs to:

- Introduce the project in terms of what area it is concerned with, what it is trying to do, and list the key individuals and advisors involved

- Describe the stage the project reached particularly in terms of the 'readiness for market' of its products, or product concepts, and outline any intellectual property, such as patents, that may support the products

- Highlight the main market characteristics, including size and growth, and specify the market opportunity that you are addressing

- State the central competitive advantages of your products and/or processes, how distinct they are from the competition and in what way, and how these are important to customers

- Summarise the objectives of the company in the short and long term, and quantify these with specific numbers. Outline the key strategies you will use to achieve them

- Include any "evidence of success" - this may be trade reviews, analyst comments, sales or partnership agreements, working prototypes, market testing, etc. which help to make the project more tangible to the reader and raises confidence in the project

- Highlight any other key issues that should be noted

Example Text:

- XYZ Company Limited is an Expert Design Consultancy focusing on Packaging Design Solutions for "Fast Moving Consumer Goods" (FMCG) in the Personal Care industry.

- It was founded in 2001 by Augustus James, a Director of the UK's leading Consumer Design Agency, Good Designs plc, who directed packaging design projects totalling over $100 million for Nike, Gillette, Channel and other global brands. Also on the executive board are Jill Mann, a Director of the Advertising Agency, Nero & Antonia, and by Julius Marcus, a Production Manager at the UK's largest packaging company, Boxes-R-Us.

Table of contents

Important Information: This document does not constitute a public offer or prospectus or invitation to the public. Only those who fall under the FSA definition of "High Net Worth Individuals", or "Sophisticated Investors" should review the plan. It will not be circulated to more than 50 such individuals. Investments in unquoted securities are highly speculative, carrying high risk as well as the potential for high rewards. There is no ready market for the realisation of that investment, or its valuation, or the risks to which an investment is exposed. The figures stated are purely illustrative and do not constitute a forecast. Before investing in a project readers are strongly advised to verify all material facts and information for themselves and seek advice from a person authorised under the Financial Services Act.

Introduction to the business and its management

Introduce the business and what it does / will do.

Describe concisely how the project came about and progressed to the present situation.

Explain who is involved, what are there positions, what relevant experience and qualifications do they have. Include a one-paragraph biography on each (full CV in the Appendix).

State what stage the business is at now. Highlight briefly the most salient features of the company's products and services – their competitive advantage.

Explain any "evidence of success" you may have – from customer orders, market testing, working prototypes, expressions of interest, industry recognition, etc. Outline any other factors that have increased the likelihood of success.

Do you have any Non-Executive Directors or Mentors who add value to the Board, and will give potential investors more confidence through their expertise, be they sector experts or generally experienced business people? List them with a brief biography highlighting achievements and relevant experience.

Outline any skill gaps you still need to fill, and how you intend to do so. If you do not recognise the skills gaps the investors will do and may feel your plans are unrealistic.

List your business advisors, if necessary with a brief description highlighting relevance.

Do you have any major alliances with other organisations, if so how do they add value / contribute to the business in outline terms. What is the basic nature of the relationship?

What is your organisational structure? (Include an organisation chart if appropriate – see example below).

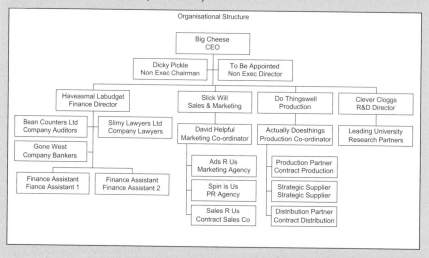

Outline where you want to go from here - what you want to achieve. What are the company's main aims and objectives? Quantify these. What are the next key stages and milestones?

Products and services

- Describe your products / services in clear and simple terms

- What consumer need is being satisfied by these products that is not being satisfied at present?

- Explain any performance advantages / value advantages over rival products

- List any other unique features

- Intellectual property – are any patents or trademarks involved or required?

- Price and pricing strategy – what price will you products sell at and what is the pricing strategy behind this decision. How does this compare with rivals?

- State the costs of production and distribution, and so the resulting margins on sale

- Describe any wholesaler or retailer margins involved and how this compares with rivals

- Communicate any further planned products / development and when you expect them to reach market / bear fruit.

- Include any background information relevant to the products or services.

Example text, Medical Instruments:

The MelanoScanner

We have developed a medical instrument device for the detection of melanoma (skin cancers): the MelanoScanner, which has just been awarded the Queen's prize for innovation.

The MelanoScanner detects potential melanoma by measuring tiny temperature differences, caused by increased blood flow, between normal skin and a malignant melanoma.

It is a small, hand held portable device, between 15 to 25 centimetres wide that looks much like a hand held barcode and connects, much like a mouse, to a computer with the company's simple diagnostic software.

Any computer can be used and the programme is small in size.

The need being served

Melanoma is the most common form of cancer in the UK and the death toll from the disease is rapidly rising even though it can be successfully and easily treated if detected early.

The MelanoScanner allows for the first time for practical screening to be undertaken in a GP's surgery to a high degree of accuracy (over 95%) without the need to refer the patient to an expert dermatological surgeon for screening – which is not practical as they are scarce.

Pricing strategy

As there are no direct product comparisons we relied on same-type products to determine our pricing strategy and policy.

GP's have a number of instruments that they use and have been adopted almost universally by every GP in the country and around the western world. These instruments typically range between £5,000 and £12,000 per unit and this has been shown to be an affordable price within their specific budget for instruments.

In addition to this reference, we carried out a basic telephone survey of 300 GPs to ask them directly if they would buy such a product if available, and what would they be willing to pay. 98% of our sample said they would buy it and had the resources currently to pay for it – they were willing to pay between £3,000 and £5,000 for it.

The price has therefore been set at £4,500 (excluding VAT) to ensure we do not forsake profit, and to ensure that demand is a little slower so we can meet it. The price can easily be reduced if we needed but not readily increased.

Production costs and gross margins

Because the investment in our product is primarily in the technology, the physical cost of production is actually very low.

	Cost	% of Sales Price
Circuit board	35.00	
Plastic Mouldings	5.00	
CD with software	2.00	
Packaging Materials	2.50	
Assembly & Packing	1.00	
Total Unit Production Cost	**45.50**	**1%**
Selling Price (ex VAT)	**4,500.00**	**100%**
Gross Margin per Unit	**4,454.50**	**99%**
Reseller Commission	45.00	1%
Margin after Sales & Dist.	**4,409.50**	**98%**

The reseller will control Warehousing and distribution, and will meet these costs from their fixed price per unit commission.

Intellectual property rights

Our MelanoScanner has been patented internationally and the patent has been approved. The effective filling date was July 2002.

The MelanoScanner trademark has been filed and granted as a community trademark in Europe, the USA and Australia.

Research and development will continue as a major part of our business and we have budgeted accordingly in our financial plans.

The market

This section should describe the market you will be operating in – generally and specifically in terms of which sectors you will be targeting, what is the size of each sector, and what are the main current products being offered to that sector.

- Market overview.
- Market size and segmentation. What is the size of the market and how can this be segmented or grouped into sectors? Which segments, or sectors, will you specifically be targeting?
- Market growth trends.
- Other key market characteristics.
- Main competitors / products currently targeting these segments.

This section overlaps with the next section on competitive business strategy and you may choose to amalgamate them.

Competitive business strategy

Competitive market strategy

How is the company going to compete in the market? Will it compete on price, service, quality, convenience, new features and benefits, by targeting a very specific area of the market (niche), etc? Is this difference really important to the target customer / buyer?

To demonstrate that you have analysed your competitive environment, you should show a summary analysis using the Five Forces model and then a SWOT matrix:

1. Analysis of industry structure (Porter's Five Forces)

- Threat of new entrants to the market – what do we believe is the threat of new players entering the market, are there any barriers to entry or exit such as large investment etc.

- Threat of substitute products – the threat of different products filling the same need.

- Power of buyers – are the buyers of products very powerful and able to depress prices.

- Power of suppliers - what is the bargaining power of the suppliers to the business.

- Rivalry amongst existing players – how intense is this and how strong are they - for example in some markets rivals are willing to sacrifice profitability to gain market share. How profitable are the companies in the market - do they make good margins, good turnover, etc?

2. SWOT Analysis – this is a summary of your company's internal strengths and weaknesses, and the external opportunities and threats it faces in the market and its competitive environment.

Include any background information relevant to the products or services.

Example:

This analysis of our competitive environment sets our competitive strategy in context.

Analysis of Industry Structure – Industry Forces (External)

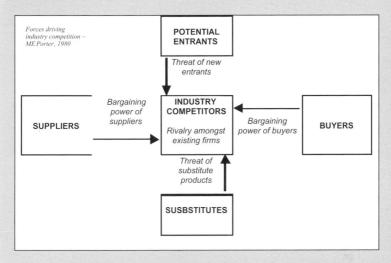

Power of suppliers: The power of our suppliers is weak as there are large numbers of suppliers and intense competition amongst them.

Threat of new entrants: The barriers to entry into this sector are high and we have overcome them through our patented technologies. Because of the modest profits characteristic in the industry using old technologies, the threat of new entrants is low.

Power of buyers: The power of buyers in this industry is very high. A relatively small number of customers control the market. However, because of our superior technology, we will be able to mitigate against this power.

Threat of substitute products: At present there is no known or likely prospect of products that can substitute for existing products in this market sector. The threat of substitutes is low.

Rivalry amongst existing firms: The market is characterised by seven major players and rivalry amongst them is strong. This has in recent times led to heavy price competition.

SWOT Analysis (Internal & External)

The internal strengths and weaknesses of the company, and the external opportunities and threats it faces, can be summarised as follows:

STRENGTHS	OPPORTUNITIES
Superior technology Professional management Low cost base Ability to expand production swiftly Low production lead times Low capital consumption as contract producer funds production	Growing market sector Undifferentiated rival products Consumer dissatisfaction New consumers entering the market
WEAKNESSES	THREATS
Low resources Lack of market experience Dependence on contractors	Contract producer could change terms Potential war could impact on spending Sustained price competition would erode margins

Our strengths will allow us to exploit the opportunities in the market: Our new technology is better placed than that of rivals to take advantage of the existing dissatisfaction amongst consumers and to attract the new customers entering the market. Our low cost base allows us to sustain price-promotional activity, and our ability to meet swift demand growth will ensure we will not squander created demand.

We are mitigating against weaknesses and threats: Through our low fixed cost base, our partnerships with expert organisations, and our retention of all intellectual property rights and know-how that can if necessary be transferred to new contractors. We are also less vulnerable to price competition because of the lower costs involved in the production of our technologically different products.

Marketing plan

This section should explain the major marketing activities that the company plans to undertake.

The document may well be directed towards broader strategy but even so should include major budgets.

- What is the core strategy for marketing your products?

- How are your target customers going to be made aware of your products? What mediums of communication will be used to reach your target consumer?

- Will there be any marketing effort aimed at any intermediaries you may have – such a wholesalers?

- Will you make substantial use of PR (public/press relations) in your marketing effort – are the products newsworthy or is another news story being created to support the products? (For example your company launching an educational website offering free advice to consumers on matters that have a relationship with your product)

- State how much this will cost and break down the costs between categories

- Introduce any agencies that will be used to assist you and confirm that they have been able to produce a practical action plan with the budget

- Explain what you expect the marketing effort to achieve and how you plan to monitor and control the effort to ensure it is effective

Sales and distribution

This section explains the strategy, structures and processes you will use to sell your product to customers, and intermediaries, and how you will physically deliver the product to them.

- State to whom you are selling the products, state specific segments of the market

- Explain how are you going to make the product available to customers sell the product to each of these segments – how are you going to make it convenient and accessible for your customers to buy your products

- Describe the retailer and intermediary margin structures for each sales channel you use through to the final consumer – and compare this to rivals

- If you need a sales force, will you develop this in-house or have you identified a sales organisation you can contract / partner with?

- Where will your products be warehoused? How will your products physically reach your customers? Will you employ a warehousing and distribution company, or will you contract with the Sales & Distribution outfit that offer the entire package?

- If you do enter a contract arrangement with sales & distribution, what are the terms of the agreement? Who will own the stock? Who will invoice and receive the funds?

- When and how will customer invoicing be done?

- What settlement terms are offered?

Production strategy and structures

This section will explain what strategy you have adopted for production and describe the structures that will be involved and their state of readiness. The level of detail will depend on the stage of your business.

- Explain what your production strategy will be – will you build a production plant, contract a production plant, contract entire production out, or license the technology?

- Describe where production will take place and if contracting out, who will undertake this.

- Describe the physical production process.

- Explain all the costs of production, stating the costs of each major component, to arrive at total production costs per product unit.

- If you are using your own production facility, describe what the fixed costs of the facility will be and differentiate these from the variable costs of production (e.g. materials).

- If you are building a plant state how much capital investment is required.

- Describe any quality assurance procedures you have in place.

- State the production 'lead-time': how long it takes to make a product from scratch – including the time taken from ordering of any components, etc.

- Explain what policies you have towards stock holding and component reordering – this is important to ensure continuity of supply but also to ensure that stock does not consume too much working capital – and that sufficient capital to fund stock has been planned for.

- State what your production capacity will be: how many products can you make, per month or year.

Financing requirements and deal structure

This section should explain to investors:

- How much money you need to execute the plan?
- What do you expect the sources of this money to be, e.g. Business Angels, Venture Capitalists, Bank Finance, or a mixture?
- Specifically how will that money be used?
- What is on offer, in terms of ownership (shares) in the company, for the money? Is 20% or 40% of the company's equity available for this investment?
- Details behind any banking facility or other forms of finance you expect (if any).
- What do you expect investors to receive in return for them risking their money?
- How do you expect investors to get their investment and return and when. Will this be through a trade sale, a flotation, or a management buy-out?

Example:

Finance Requirement

There is financing requirement of £650,000, which will be sought from Business Angel Investors. The equity offered will be 20%. The company has no loans or overdrafts and at this stage does not plan any.

In terms of financial structure, the shareholding structure of the company will be as follows:

Shareholders	Pre – Financing Stake	Post – Financing Stake
CEO (Founder)	50%	40%
Other Managers	30%	24%
Current Investors	20%	16%
New Investors		20%
Total	100%	100%

The investment is expected to qualify for full EIS relief for both individuals and VCT's.

The investment will be used as follows:

Investment Area	Proportion	Amount
Marketing	30%	£ 200,000
Working Capital (inc. contingency)	55%	£ 350,000
Development	15%	£ 100,000
Total	**100%**	**£ 650,000**

Cash projections

As we stated previously, the company anticipates its first sales to be achieved in 18 months time – though this could be sooner.

Forecast Cash Balance for the next three years (first year by month):

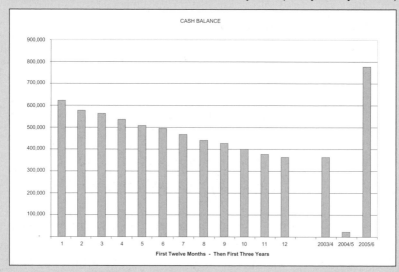

The company will have a basic monthly cash-burn of £23,000 per month, equivalent to £280,000 per year. The average cash burn before sales in year two is expected to rise to £35,000 per month – provided our milestones are achieved, otherwise cash consumption will be contained at year 1 levels.

Though we expect to achieve sales in 18 months, through controlling the cash burn in an event of a delay the company could support a further 9 month delay without having to return for more funding.

Overleaf are illustrative projections for the three years following financing.

Exit route

These funds will be used to take the product to market, at which stage we could continue to supply at lower levels without further funding or may decide to undertake a second round of financing to expand more aggressively.

Our planned an exit route available through an AIM flotation in the 4th or 5th year.

It is expected that within five years the company will achieve sales in excess of £20,000,000 and to be on a fast rising sales curve with the potential substantially higher sales growth as other catalysts in our product portfolio gradually reaches the market.

Key financial data and financial projections

All potential investors will expect to see a set of financial statements and illustrative projections for the project.

Cash Flow projection – this is a statement of your cash position and the sources and uses of cash going forward. Cash management is probably the most important aspect of financial management as the company becomes established and grows. Certain growth policies consume more cash than they generate, so detailed cash projections are vital.

- Profit & Loss projection – this is a statement of the company's trading activities.
- Balance Sheet projection – this is a statement of the company's assets and liabilities, starting with the current position.

We have found that investors like to see a graph of the cash balance, with the first year or eighteen months on a monthly basis, to illustrate to them that cash management has been carefully thought out and the rate at which the business consumes cash.

The projections should be in the way of full statements for the next three years, and then for high potential businesses an indication should be given of the headline figures for revenues and profit up to a further two years out – five years in total. This will provide investors with information on the potential upside of the business, which may not be clear from the three-year projection.

The statements should be accompanied by 'Notes to the Accounts' covering the assumptions under which the statements have been constructed, including:

- The assumptions behind the sales forecasts, perhaps related to market share or sales per store, etc. What logic has been used to arrive at this figure, as it was clearly not pulled out of the air?

- Assumptions behind costs, including the costs of production, offices, staffing, etc., and how these are constructed.

- Any policies adopted, such as on the depreciation of assets, the number of days credit given to customers, the period of time taken to pay your creditors, etc.

- The detail behind any loan or other overdraft facilities and expected interest rates.

- Other major budgets, including marketing, legal fees, accounting fees, etc.

The figures should demonstrate to the investor that you understand the major financial implications of your business plan, that the assumptions are reasonable, and that you have not been over optimistic.

It is important to highlight what contingency plans you have in the event of things not happening exactly as planned. Will the business fail if there is a month's delay in the timetable, or can it tolerate a year's delay through careful adjustment and control?

Appendix

List here what is included in the Appendix which follows.

We suggest it should include:

- Full director and key management CV's

- Full list of business advisors, including accountants

- Copies of any intellectual property – trademarks, patents, designs

- Copies of relevant letters / agreements indicating success – including any orders pending

- Copies of any commissioned market research or other reports not published

- Full illustrative financial projections

- Audited accounts if business has been going for some time

- Copy of the shareholder agreement
- Copies of any loan or other material agreements, including director loans
- Sample sales & marketing material, including brochures and product diagrams

A shareholders' agreement

One of the things you will need to consider unless you are the sole shareholder is a shareholder's agreement. Sort it out early to avoid conflict later.

SHAREHOLDER AGREEMENT

XYZ Co Ltd

Co Reg No: 12345678910

This agreement is made between the shareholders of the company and its directors to stipulate and clarify key issues in the running of the company and its relationship to, and the rights of its' shareholders above the legal requirements of the Companies Act 1985. It is a confidential internal company document and not available for public inspection. It complements the Memorandum and Articles of Association and covers only the shareholders who have signed up to it.

The directors and shareholders agree that without the written permission of shareholders representing 75% of the ordinary equity of the company, or as specifically stated otherwise in this agreement, that:

1. The Directors shall not:

- Open any new bank accounts
- Enter any new loan agreements, debentures or provide any guarantees or indemnities
- Deviate materially from the business plan or enter any new area of business
- Transfer, lease, assign, grant any license over any company property other than the sale of current assets in the normal course of trading
- Establish any subsidiary
- Authorise any increase in the authorised share capital of the company

- Agree the sale or takeover of the business
- Authorise any share option schemes or revise director emoluments

2. The Directors shall:

- Hold a monthly board meeting, with a maximum of 50 days between meetings, and a minimum of 10 board meetings per calendar year.

- At each board meeting, the time, date and place for the next meeting shall be agreed and each director and investor representative shall be notified at least 14 days prior to it.

- Circulate an agenda a week in advance of the meeting, including minutes from the last board meeting for approval. The agenda will include a review of trading activities and financial status, as well as any other material issues that are proposed for inclusion by directors and / or shareholders representing 5% of issued shares. Proposed agenda items should be proposed to the chairman at least 14 days prior to the meeting.

- Present a brief monthly management report, including a set of management accounts, covering progress in relation to plan, prospects for the business, and highlighting any key or material issues faced by the company.

3. Banking arrangements/transfer of funds

- The Company shall have 3 authorised signatories to all bank accounts, who must be directors, and shall be registered by the directors with the company's banks.

- In the normal running of the business one 'cheque book' / register of payments shall be used and kept by the Financial Director who will usually make routine payments.

- Any cheques or transfers in excess of £1,000 shall be required to be signed / authorised by two signatories, and any over £5,000 must additionally be approved by the board.

4. Share issues and sale of shares by the company or shareholders:

- Transfer of shares from an existing shareholder. Any transfer, other than within family members, or as a result of bereavement, or as a gift, must be approved by the board under the 75% rule.

Such consent shall not be unreasonably withheld.

- Any sale of shares must be approved, such consent will not be reasonably withheld, and existing shareholders shall have first refusal to purchase the shares under the same terms. Any issue / sale of shares by the company shall be offered to the existing shareholders under the same terms and they will have a pre-emption right to purchase such shares.

5. In the event of shareholder incapacity, or worse

- The shareholder shall nominate a representative, or nominate a member of the board, or the chairman, to vote on matters relating to the company on his / her behalf in the event of their incapacity until he/she issues written instructions to the contrary or legal clarity is established between his estate and its benefactors. In the event of no such representative being available, then a spouse, or next of kin, shall be asked to act. They shall have the right to attend board meetings. This representative shall not be held liable by any party to this agreement, or any party acting in behalf of the shareholders benefactors, for any consequences of their decision-making.

- The board and all shareholders will accept the representative's authority to vote on any matters of company policy.

- The normal management of the company shall continue to run under the remaining board based on normal board decision-making process. The directors shall be reasonable and consider the interests of the absent shareholder and act in good faith. They shall not be liable if decisions made were not to the maximum benefit of the absent shareholder.

6. Removal of directors

In addition to the provisions under the Articles of Association, a director may be removed from the office of director if:

- 2 other directors or major shareholders propose his / her removal in writing, this shall immediately be put to a vote and confirmed by a simple majority of over 50%.

- OR by the unanimous decision of the other board members providing there are at least four members on the board.

- Under such circumstances the severance rights in the directors service contract shall apply, as will their rights as shareholders under this agreement.

Minority protection

To change the following rights shall require a unanimous vote by all shareholders holding 5% or more of the issued equity of the company who are party to this agreement, and a majority of at least 75% of the voting equity of the company.

7. Right to appoint a non-executive director or investor representative

- Any investor, holding 5% or more of the company's issued shareholder capital shall have the right to appoint a non-executive director to the board, or to have a non-voting representative present at board meetings. The Board of Directors, acting unanimously, shall have the right to veto the appointment of any individual.

8. Dividend policy

- It is not expected that the company will make a dividend for the next three years. After that any shareholder, or shareholders acting as one through written authority, representing at least 5% of the ordinary voting equity of the company shall have the right to insist that at least 10% of profits available for distribution (within the definitions of the Companies Act 1985) in the accounting period, are distributed by way of cash dividends within 6 months of the end of that accounting period – providing it is lawful to do so.

9. Shareholder and director confidentially obligations.

To keep all matters relating to the company confidential except where disclosure is required by law, or as part of the process of seeking personal advice on the investment from professional advisers, whom the shareholder warrants will ensure confidentiality.

We agree to be bound by this agreement:
Director / Shareholder Name: Signature: Date:

Witnessed by the Company Secretary:
Company Secretary: Signature: Date:

An original copy should be given to every shareholder / director party to this agreement, plus one kept by the company secretary or the company's lawyers in the company file.

Debt vs investment

However, before you start chasing down and mauling business advisers, don't forget good old-fashioned debt financing that banks provide.

Investment

Pros

- No interest payments.
- No obligation to pay dividends.
- More money to invest back into the business.
- Investors may have expertise and knowledge to bring.
- Investment dollars actually increase the borrowing power of the company because banks look for equity before they loan money and many government programs want to match what the owners have in the company.
- Accepting investment dollars spreads the risk of failure to others shoulders.

Cons

- Less independence for owners.
- Risks of disagreements.
- Owner's share of company is diluted.

Debt

Pros

- Interest payments may be a tax deduction.
- No loss of ownership.
- Easier to obtain a loan then to get through the maze of the VC world.

Cons

- Interest! The payments must be made and it can affect your cash flow.

4 Networking

"Women share with men the need for personal success, even the taste of power, and no longer are we willing to satisfy those needs through the achievements of surrogates, whether husbands, children, or merely role models."

Elizabeth Dole

"There is no occasion for women to consider themselves subordinate or inferior to men."

Mohandas K. Gandhi

- Women's attitude to business networking.
- Advice on improving your business networking skills.
- So, how do you avoid having to be interested in rugby and golf?
- Relativity and dry powder.

Successful people are not self-made and self-sufficient. So don't be too shy or proud to network and ask for assistance.

Our anecdotal research found that even the most basic aspects of networking are missing from many women's repertoires. So here are a series of pointers distilled from the interviews we conducted.

Get a mentor

Without fail many successful people will say they had a mentor who had been there and achieved success; someone of experience and skill who has no personal vested conflict with seeing you succeed and who is a little like a non-executive chairman of 'You plc'.

They have the time to help you, even if by email. They have the contacts to put you in touch with others. They have the skills to know what they are talking about. They are successful in their own right. They uplift, rather than tread you down. They are someone you get on with and there is a bond.

Finding that person is not easy. There may be several people who you use for different aspects, but build those links. The relationship is similar to tutor-student in some regards.

Organisations such as www.tie-uk.org for instance specialise in providing mentors (free service) to its entrepeneur members.

If after reading this chapter you think, 'yes but that's all just good common sense though' then we've done a good job, and secondly, don't assume that good sense is that common.

Learn the parts of networking

Yes, we know, how do you go to networking events when you have to look after the kids and do the cooking? Well if that is you, then don't drop the 'non-essential' networking. Make arrangements for a nanny or family or friends to share those family responsibilities you have. One woman I have working for me says, 'but my husband and son expect their food'. Well, tell them what you want and buy them a cookbook!

What you need to do	Tips so you can do it
Do you know how to get a business card? Many women we spoke to were simply too unsure or shy or not 'ballsy' enough.	Practice at home so you rehearse the act of saying, 'actually that's interesting, may I have your card and I may send you something of interest by post '. This way the person does not feel threatened you're going to phone or ask to meet them (time consuming), but you're simply going to post. Of course you could then email, or call depending on how 'hungry' you were and how you think they might receive that call. (But read the principles of relativity and dry powder below).
Learn to move on. You can't network if you're with the same person all night.	One technique to leave the deadly grasp of the nervous loner who himself dare not let you out of his or her tractor beam for fear they themselves would have to network, is simply to say, 'well it was very nice to meet you, please do let me take your card'. That way, they know you're interested and not simply bored. Don't offend. People remember and word can spread. There are numerous stories I hear that 'ABC is someone not to speak to he gets bored, starts looking over your shoulder while you're speaking to him.' A reputation like that can mean people avoid interacting with you, for fear you'll do the same to them. Another 'leave them technique' is to look them in the eye (always make firm eye contact when saying goodbye), speak with an enthusiastic tone, and say, 'would you excuse me a moment, there is someone I

	need to speak to. Look, it was a pleasure to meet you. And I wonder if I can take your card and post you something of interest'.
Follow through: the principle of 'relativity'.	If you've met someone of interest you would like to stay in touch with, then depending on how busy/important they are your options are to call or email with a coffee request, but specify what you'd like to talk about (what's in it for them?).
	I hate calls when all the other person wants is help with some business issue. (Except the readers of this book – email me – as what's in it for me is that you bought the book!)
	But if the person is of far greater business importance than you (e.g. Richard Branson), then don't bug them with a call, reminding them you met them and would like to go for a coffee. Instead, it's a good idea to add them to your newsletter or email list for sending a regular (monthly/quarterly) newsletter or product sample with a cover letter. (Remind them where you met, as it needs to get through their PA who needs to know you're not a random person on the street.)
	That way, they don't need to reply. (People hate presumptuous pests who are relatively smaller than them on the business league and constantly want replies.)
	Equally, at least they are on your contact list and if you did need to use them for a big favour or a contact for a major issue, then you could (subject to the principle of 'dry powder' – next).
The principle of dry powder.	If you have met a relatively important business person, and assuming you have some contact with them via further bumping into each other or through your sending regular correspondence, then there may come a time where you think you could use their help. Keeping your powder dry means not bugging them for trivial things but a major one.
	Don't ask them for something you could get elsewhere as you can't keep going back to them for help as they'll get annoyed.

	There is a friend who works with a colleague of mine. He'll come into my office and ask me if I know the best way to set up a company. Now I know he wants my help for a hundred things, but to ask me something which he could find out himself, suggests either he is lazy or trying to hard to strike up conversation.
Be grateful.	If you have had help, thank the person concerned. Show your appreciation through a card. That extra step goes a long way in showing you're not like the others.
Don't rush it. I'm not your best friend.	Avoid trying too hard to be the other person's best friend – eg I've experienced it through the other guy trying to make personal jokes etc. If there is a bond, it will develop.
The principle of reciprocity.	How can you help them? Even the most powerful people need help with something. Listen to their conversation for clues. This is more important if on the principle of relativity you are down the food chain. The lower you are relative to them, the more important it is to build a bond by being useful.
	But it has to be genuine. Don't do it unless you really like this person/their business and want to help. Don't do it for reward. Do it even if you would if you had nothing to gain. The reason? If ever you need help, at least you did something for them. Behave like a host not a guest; introduce people to each other.
	Or as the cynical Sicilian saying goes, 'I don't do favours, I collect debts'.
Cards – do it properly.	At Christmas, don't just get a hundred cards and sign your name on each. Write a personal message. If it's not worth the trouble, don't insult them by sending anything else.
Right-hand man/woman.	For the really big VIP, make contact with their assistant at the party. That is usually a good way in. Whilst the rest are drooling at the VIP's feet, you can follow-up later via the card you got from their assistant.
	Remember, power of contact resides with the gate-keeper.
Newsletter/regular communication.	It is helpful to have a regular email/postal communication with the person you want.

	to stay in touch with. With that form of communication they are not being hassled by you expecting them to return a call.
	In my experience people will often pass on your newsletter to relevant people and that can make a big business advantage.
	If you don't have a regular communication, sending a copy of the odd article that the person may not have seen (i.e. not from the FT), and that may be of interest to them can be a useful alternative. Simply include a personal note (not asking for any reply) with a copy of your card and where you met. A simple note like 'Dear Jill, I thought this may be of interest. You'll recall we met at XYZ where we discussed ABD'.
	In my experience if nothing else, it may get you onto an invite list for some other function.
It does not matter if you do not know now why they may be useful.	You never know when you may change career or business or who people, who at first sight might seem useless to your business, may know.
Elevator pitch.	If you're asked 'what is it you do' can you say in 30 seconds what it is and include in there something sufficiently interesting that the listener may want to follow up with a further question? e.g. 'I run a XYZ business. We started last year, but we've just got our 20th customer this week and I'm excited about it.'
	People want to help people who are not being arrogant (you mentioned you were a start-up so that lets the other person know the level you are at to better enable them to assist).
	You exhibited enthusiasm: at networking events we all love someone with a bit of spark – god knows there are enough people who are so nervous at these things they look like they think it is a chore.
Interested in them and a bit about you.	If you're networking you have to make a genuine effort to listen, make eye contact and be interested in the speaker. Sounds obvious? Well, why do so few people do it then? But at the right point, you also need to know when to mention what you do and your experiences.

Tools of networking.	Have the tools of networking. That means a pen and small writing pad and business cards. I know it is easy to forget them if you have a dozen handbags and suits. So, keep a set in each single one always there after a meeting, ready for the next event.
	I also recommend an electronic business card scanner. We recommend CardScan (check the web). You can scan business cards in, keep a note of where you met the person and never lose a contact. You can search such databases and so when you need to send one contact the details of another – it is easy to do.
	Manage a database of contacts. (I also keep a separate one for media.) And make a note on it of what you sent to which person, so you don't re-send, but also so you work through efficiently that all the relevant people have got your communications.
Gap fillers.	Silence? Have some useful questions and anecdotes handy. Worse case scenario, 'are you busy, travelling much at the moment?' and that will usually open up into what the person is working on, what they do, their personality.
Get out there.	We have one friend who has an insurance business – a very successful one. But he felt he wasn't networking enough. At events if he said I am an insurance broker they would think he is only a salesman. Whereas his company only insures the largest businesses.
	One thing we advised him was to have a personal business card without his company name at all. That way he did not look like a salesman, but his email address would show someone where to go. Mystery adds class. The card was to be in black raised ink and on bonded card so more expensive looking than other cards to convey he was successful – which he was.
	Finally, if asked what he did, he was to say, 'I own a risk and insurance company covering medium and large corporates'. That way, the other guy knows he is not small scale.
	We also told him to get onto some business network boards and invite lists

	by checking them on the web, to get his name out there.
Spheres of influence.	When a senior woman media executive running the WorldWide TV operations for a media giant asked us over lunch how to get onto more boards we gave some sample pointers: 1. Look at an agency specialising in non-executive directors. 2. Write evidence for parliamentary select committees on media (any member of the public can and the evidence is published) that adds weight to your expertise and also you're doing a public service too. 3. Build influence through voluntary work (judging competitions etc) in neighbouring spheres – in her case, financial or business groups.
Invest.	The suit you wear for your networking is an investment. Make sure it costs at least double, and looks twice as good as, your regular office attire.

Existing business networks

Women's networks

British Association of Women Entrepreneurs

The British Association of Women Entrepreneurs (BAWE) is a non-profit professional organisation for UK based women business owners and is affiliated to the world association of women business owners (FCEM). Founded in 1954, BAWE encourages the personal development of member entrepreneurs and provides opportunities for them to expand their business.

DAWN

DAWN is the hub where dynamic professional and entrepreneurial Asian women connect, engage and explore ideas and opportunities to expand their horizons.

The Association of Women in Property

A dynamic forum for the professional development of women in the property and construction industry – to enhance business opportunities, exchange views, network and gain knowledge.

Business and Professional Women UK

Business and Professional Women UK (BPW) is a non-party-political lobbying organisation which gives women the opportunity to make a difference by influencing policy decisions. Members are given opportunities for self-development, which can help their self-confidence and career. Members can also receive the encouragement, training and information to apply for public appointments.

Entrepreneurs networks

The Indus Entrepreneurs

Non-profit global network of entrepreneurs and professionals

TiE, a not-for-profit global network of entrepreneurs and professionals, was founded in 1992 in Silicon Valley, California, USA. Although its birth name, The Indus Entrepreneurs, signifies the ethnic South Asian or Indus roots of the founders, TiE stands for Talent, Ideas and Enterprise. It is an open and inclusive organisation that has rapidly grown to more than forty chapters in nine countries. TiE endeavours to cultivate and nurture the ecosystems of entrepreneurship and free-market economies everywhere, as it sees this to be the single most powerful instrument of prosperity. The Indus Entrepreneurs, (TiE) is an organisation of industry professionals who share the common interests of promoting and fostering entrepreneurial efforts.

The members of TiE come from a variety of corporate and academic backgrounds and are united in their efforts to provide a dynamic and vibrant environment in which entrepreneurs can share their experiences and draw from a common pool of knowledge and experience.

In today's fast paced world of competitive business, the qualities recognised in an entrepreneur are highly sought after. The ability to make quick decisions, take calculated risks, recognise and nurture potential markets and develop a strategy and vision for a product are all essential aspects of being an entrepreneur.

As a member of TiE you will be able to recognise and develop such talent. You will have the opportunity to network and gain from formal and informal conversations with a multitude of business talent.

A Q&A with the director of TiE UK, Finoula Pender

In your experience are women entrepreneurs qualitatively different from male ones?

Women are far more subtle and less formal in their approach to business. However, the key motivation for self employment remains the same for both men and women i.e. the need for independence and control over ones destiny.

What advice would you give women entrepreneurs specific to their gender?

Join key networking organisations such as TiE UK. Gender is important but not the sole explanatory factor in differences between women and men. There are big differences in finance and business networks, access to start up finances, relationships with leaders. I would encourage women to join a few key networking organisations, which encourage networking amongst like minded people irrespective of gender.

Do men club together?

If an idea is good and sound, then men and women will react in the same way.

Do men elbow out women?

The sexes do not experience the business world in the same ways (whether as a client, supplier, manager or boss). Men still don't take women seriously in the world of business, but this is becoming less the norm. Expectations of what a women can achieve are often misguided.

Do men intimidate women entrepreneurs?

Sometimes. This comes down to general levels of confidence and women on the whole tend to have lower levels of confidence than her male counterpart. This in itself however is not a massive problem as confidence is something that can be improved and encouraged whether that be through networking and taking advantage of a good mentoring schemes.

Are women from Venus when it comes to business?

NO! Just ask Anita Ruddock et al. Women are subtle and less formal and excel in crucial areas such as networking and mentoring, both of which are imperative to building a successful business.

A Q&A with an entrepreneur network attendee, Nilam Patel*

In your experience are women entrepreneurs qualitatively different from male ones?

Eighteen years ago when I was first introduced to the financial services industry I definitely thought that being a female in this sector had it's disadvantages, let alone being an Asian! Working for a leading high street bank, women were expected to be front desk dollies pursuing roles such as cashiers and personal bankers and there was no encouragement to either study further to enhance your promotion prospects nor the opportunity to join the male dominated work regions of loans and securities.

I'm told that this no longer is the case but I left the bank many years ago so cannot comment. My experience of the insurance industry, however, is completely

*(no relation to the authors)

the opposite to that of the bank. Mind you, I joined this sector in the new millennium so surely you'd expect things to have progressed?

Now, I could see opportunities and it was up to you how you played it. Maybe working for the world's leading risk management firm made all the difference. I'm not sure. One thing I did notice however, was that these sectors have a naturally heavy proportion of men to women, whether it's for traditional reasons or because women just find this sector very tedious and uninteresting!

Yes... I think being female definitely has it's advantages and as much as I hate having to confess to it, I think women have the edge when it comes to building rapport as they are naturally warm human beings!!! We do have a competitive advantage and as my male colleagues often used to say to me ..."insurance is a dull enough subject anyway so give the MD a choice of who he would like to chat to, he'd obviously chose a woman! " (maybe most of the time not always!!) Having said that, using your competitive advantage is not the easy route to a deal, as at the end of the day, even men can see pass the flutter of long eye lashes! But it does help....

What advice would you give women entrepreneurs specific to their gender?

I'm in no position to give advice but my age and experience have definitely taught me that it is a man's world and for our ideas to be taken seriously, we need to get the foundations right. Have a vision, think through your ideas, make a business plan and be able to demonstrate your vision step by step. Keep the emotions out of it!

Do men club together?

Men do tend to club together in business, as I secretly believe they feel threatened by us! They are all fine and supportive whilst your climbing up the ladder and asking for their assistance but the minute you equal or exceed them, they start to resent you. I know I shouldn't generalise but I base this on what I have seen and my own experiences.

As a woman, if you succeed you did it because you are female and have the legs and the tits! Your talent, intelligence or hard work does not even come into the equation thus it is with these sweeping statements, at whatever level, that I have seen men club together. Too often, I've seen and heard men who still think that it is a woman's duty to make the teas and coffees at strategy meetings, even if it is the woman who is chairing the whole thing! And if they have moved on with the times, it doesn't stop them from still making a comment!

But there is a distinct change with the ages.... as although the boys from the old school still tend to club together, there is a noticeable change in the younger generation. In my experience, I have also seen a difference based on ethnicity and demography – and it all boils down to male pride.

Do men elbow out women?

Smarter men have come to realise that they do need to keep on the right side of a woman so as much as they would like to push us away, they don't. It's not worth the risk. More and more women these days are very assertive so I guess this gives out the warning signals from the onset ... 'Just cos I'm a woman, don't think I'm weak and vulnerable. I can give as good as I get so don't mess with me!'

Do men intimidate women entrepreneurs?

Whether in business or otherwise, there is always an element of intimidation and patronising involved. They just can't help themselves!!! Again, I think it comes from the traditional territory and male ego.

Are women from Venus when it comes to business?

Not sure if they are from Venus or rather I'm afraid to make a sweeping statement simply because the few enterprising women I have met have not been at all inspirational, so they were obviously lacking in something. No doubt, I met with the wrong type and in contrast to this, I've witnessed many men transform some of the weirdest of ideas into sound businesses. Perhaps women spend far too long analysing things rather than taking the plunge?

Business or not, women are from Venus, however, this should not be seen as a weakness. Women have their own qualities and attributes that differ from men and though the application varies, it can still result in a successful business. Successful women do not let emotions get in the way, as they know it doesn't make sound business sense!

5 Pitching for business

"When, however, one reads of a witch being ducked, of a woman possessed by devils, of a wise woman selling herbs, or even a very remarkable man who had a mother, then I think we are on the track of a lost novelist, a suppressed poet. . . indeed, I would venture to guess that Anon, who wrote so many poems without signing them, was often a woman."

Virginia Woolf

"Some leaders are born women."

Anon

> • The weaker sex?
> • A gender gap in pitching.
> • Improving on your pitching.

Are women naturally inclined to be less aggressive in asking for money, in asking for what their business needs and wants? Disarming prospective investors with their shyness may well leave them with little to show for their efforts.

Well, whatever the reality, the most important thing is that we know what types of information we should be armed with about our own businesses. That way we add extra confidence. We avoid nightmare situations of appearing uninformed. And when the opportunity arises to grab a quick 30 seconds with that rich investor, whether at a drinks party or in a lift, we have the facts to promote our business and grab that investment.

Below are some examples of the tools you'll need – more so as women, according to our research, are weaker on this than men – including conversations to have and approaches to take.

New opportunity approach

"Hello, this is **[your name]** with **[your company]**. You and I haven't spoken before, but we have been working with **[specific industry]** for the last **[number]** years. One of the chief concerns we are hearing (*lately*) from other **[job titles]** is their frustration (*difficulty*) with **[the job title's critical issue/need]**. We have been able to help our customers address this issue. Would you like to know how?"

Menu approach

"This is [your name] with [your company]. You and I haven't spoken before, but we have been working with [specific industry] for the last [number] years. The top three issues (*concerns*) we are hearing (*lately*) from other [job titles] are:

- [job title's first critical business issue/need]
- [job title's second critical business issue/need]
- [job title's third critical business issue/need]

We have helped companies like: [first reference company], [second reference company] and [third reference company] address some of these issues. Would you be curious to learn how?"

Customer referral approach

"This is [your name] with [your company]. You and I haven't spoken before, but [reference person's name], [reference person's title] at [reference person's company] suggested that I give you a call. We were able to help [her or him] address [her or his] [frustration or difficulty] with [reference person's critical business issue/need]. Would you be interested to know how?"

Competitive points list

Differentiator	My company	Competitor A	Competitor B
Years in business current ownership			
Overall financial strength			
Customers served			
Key customer segment			
Training/ certification			
Experience/ expertise			
Evaluation/trial opportunity			
Warranty/return policy			
Reference story			
Key product/ service difference			

Example

"It doesn't surprise me that you've talked with **[Customer Name]**. *They've done some good work, but let me tell you how we'd approach your project a bit differently. We specialise in developing solutions for rapidly growing medium and large businesses like yours, while* **[Customer Name]** *focuses more on small business projects. On average they're working with three or four times as many clients as we are. This means that they have to rely on outsourced development and deliver less-customised solutions. We also realise that a situation like yours might require a pilot installation, which we're very willing to work with you on. I'd be happy to prepare a detailed analysis of how our service compares to our major competitors on a project such as yours."*

Product/service benefit statement

Anxiety question

"How would you feel if your largest customer called and told you they were going to switch more of their business to a competitor? Their reason was that they couldn't reorder quickly enough on your hottest seasonal toys, which meant that they lost revenue and disappointed their customers. They mentioned that your competitor is able to provide this online reordering capability. How do you feel?"

Capability question

"What if there was a way, when your customer's inventory systems showed that their stock was getting low on a hot Tailspin Toy item, that their system could automatically place a repeat order over the internet...and your ordering and manufacturing systems would be automatically updated, too...all in real-time?"

Feature statement (feature becomes a benefit)

"Our web distribution solution can give you that capability."

Process steps for sales in small businesses

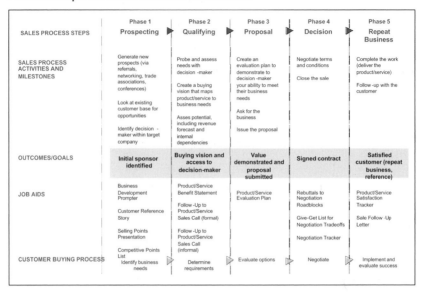

Process steps for sales to consumers

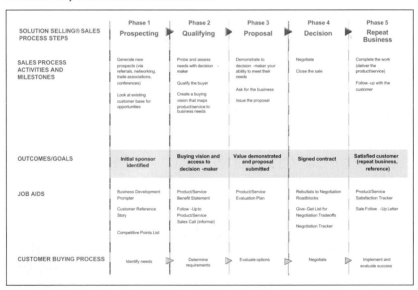

So what do we need to know? Well, opposite is a list of 'request for information' from the outstanding Tom's Law website (www.tomslaw.com), which a good investor should ask. If you have the answers ready, you appear better prepared to pitch – remember here we're talking about getting investors into the business as well as getting clients.

Request for information

Proposed investment in

[NAME OF COMPANY]

by

[NAME OF INVESTOR]

Request for Information

Proposed investment in [NAME OF THE COMPANY]

("the Company")

	CODE
This request for information is being made as part of the evaluation of the Company by [NAME OF INVESTOR] **("the Investor")**	

References in this request to "the Company" are to the Company and each of its subsidiary undertakings.

This request for information is not exhaustive and supplemental requests for information may be made. We suggest that you retain photocopies of any documents sent to us, so that in due course they can be incorporated, where applicable, in any formal disclosure letter to Investor.

Please supply the following copy documents and information in relation to the Company and its business and identify replies by using the same numerical reference system. Where a full understanding of the position cannot be obtained from the copy documents alone please also provide an explanation. We suggest that you supply responses as and when the information is available rather than waiting until all the information has been collected.

1. **Constitution**
1.1 Certificate of Incorporation and any Certificate of Incorporation on Change of Name.
1.2 Memorandum and articles of association, together with relevant resolutions and agreements.
1.3 Written confirmation of:
    (a) authorised share capital (including classes and denominations);
    (b) issued and paid up share capital (including classes and denominations);
    (c) changes in the issued share capital in the last 6 years;
    (d) name and address of each shareholder together with the number and class of shares held by each of them. Where shares are held on trust, please give the name and address of the beneficial owner and supply a copy of the declaration of trust;
    (e) names and addresses of the directors and secretary;

(f) accounting reference date; and

(g) where and when the statutory and minute books may be inspected.

1.4 Any Shareholders' or similar agreements.

1.5 Agreements granting options over or the right to call for the issue of any share or loan capital of the Company (other than to employees which are dealt with later).

1.6 Details of all subsidiaries and other corporate bodies in which the Company holds or owns any shares or other securities or loan stock or other forms of debentures or where the Company has entered into any agreement relating to the same. Please supply copies of all documentation which relate to any such bodies corporate to which the Company is party.

1.7 Details of when dormant subsidiaries last traded.

2. Accounts

2.1 Audited accounts for the last three years.

2.2 Management accounts since the last audited accounts.

2.3 The current business plans and to the extent they are not contained in the current business plan, current budgets and forecasts and the underlying assumptions.

3. Finance

Details of:

(a) the Company's bank accounts (including name and address of bank branch) and copies of all facility and loan arrangements with the Company's bankers or other financiers;

(b) all debenture stocks, loan stocks, loan notes or other debt instruments issued by the Company and copies of all relevant documents;

(c) consultants' commissions;

(d) any mortgages, charges or debentures over the Company's undertaking, assets or share capital and supply copies of the charging documents;

(e) any guarantees, indemnities, or counter-indemnities given by the Company and supply copies of the relevant documents;

(f) all grants and allowances made to the Company during the past six years;

(g) any current, proposed or projected capital commitments;

(h) any hire purchase, lease, rental, conditional sale or other similar credit agreements;

(i) any contingent liabilities;

(j) any debts owed to or from any group company; and

(k) an aged list of debtors showing debts considered bad or doubtful.

4. Taxation

4.1 Details of all VAT arrangements, including details of any VAT group of which the Company is a member.

4.2	Details of tax losses.

4.3 Details of PAYE/NI returns and of any potential liabilities.

5. Premises

5.1 A list of all premises owned, leased, occupied or in which any other interest is held by the Company and in relation to all such premises:

(a) the full postal address, title number and a full description of its use and the tenure held by the Company;

(b) a list of all the occupiers of the premises;

(c) copies of any valuations of the premises which have been made within the last 3 years; and

(d) particulars of all rents, service charges and other outgoings accrued due but not yet paid or received.

5.2 List of any properties previously leased, occupied or used by the Company and/or in respect of which the Company is or may be liable.

6. Trading Matters

Details of, together with copies of all related documentation:

6.1 any long term, unusual, non-routine, onerous or other material contracts or commitments and any current tender which, if accepted, would create such a contract or commitment;

6.2 all licences, permissions, authorisations and consents

6.3 necessary or which the Company knows will be necessary for the carrying on of its business;

6.4 contracts made with major suppliers (i.e. those accounting for more than 5 per cent of goods or services supplied) and value of purchases from them in each of the last 3 years;

6.5 complaints by or disputes with (either current or in the past years) any major supplier or customer; and

6.6 current insurance cover, specifying the nature and amount of cover, annual premiums and next renewal date together with details of significant claims made during the last twelve months.

7. Litigation

7.1 Details of any significant litigation, arbitration or dispute resolution procedure in which the Company is involved and which may have a material affect on the Company.

7.2 Details of any argument, dispute, claim or other facts or circumstances which might give rise to any significant litigation or other dispute resolution procedures which may have a material affect on the Company.

7.3 Details of any notices or communications received by the Company which indicates any material liability or potential material liability on the part of the Company or any obligation or restriction being placed on the Company which may have a materially adverse affect on its business.

7.4	Details of any investigation, finding or decision of any competent court or regulatory authority or body in relation to the Company.	

8. Employees

8.1 An up-to-date list of all persons currently employed by the Company ("the Employees") showing:

    (a) name;

    (b) date of birth;

    (c) date of commencement of employment;

    (d) job title;

    (e) normal working hours;

    (f) current annual salary (including date of last review and details of any proposed review or increase);

    (g) commission and bonus arrangements;

    (h) benefits;

    (i) notice period;

    (j) grade of employee;

    (k) disciplinary action taken during the last 3 years; and

    (l) job status temporary, permanent, (full time or part time).

8.2 Copies of:

    (a) all service agreements, contracts for services and consultancy agreements with directors and senior employees;

    (b) all standard terms of employment;

    (c) all terms and conditions of employment where they differ from the standard terms;

    (d) all staff handbooks;

    (e) disciplinary rules and procedures;

    (f) equal opportunities policies;

    (g) harassment (sex and race) policies;

    (h) all relevant agreements; and

    (i) all documentation confirming compliance with the Working Time Regulations 1998.

8.3 Details of:

    (a) any share option or profit sharing schemes or other employee incentive schemes;

    (b) all disputes, negotiations or claims in respect of any past or present director, officer or employee of the Company or any trade union or other similar body;

    (c) any complaint or grievance about discrimination raised by any past or present employee within the last 6 months;

    (d) any complaint or grievance relating to the Working Time Regulations 1998;

    (e) the maternity/paternity policy relating to Employees; and

    (f) personal commitments given to (or agreements reached with) individual Employees with depart from or vary standard terms of employment.

(g)   Details of all pension or retirement benefit schemes or similar arrangements to which the Company is a party or in which the Company participates or is otherwise involved, whether such scheme is legally enforceable or ex gratia.

9.   Connected persons

9.1   Details of any contracts or arrangements to which the Company is party and in which any of its shareholders, directors or persons related to or otherwise connected with them are or have been interested, whether directly or indirectly.

9.2   Details of all business activities or interests of the directors of the Company (or persons related to or otherwise connected with them) where these compete with or are material to the Company or its business.

10.   Environmental matters

10.1   Details of any:

(a)   trade effluent or waste substances discharged or disposed of;

(b)   hazardous substances handled or kept;

(c)   pollution discharged into the atmosphere, water or land by the Company.

10.2   Copies of:

(a)   all consents, approvals or licences obtained by the Company or which the Company knows will be necessary in connection with water abstraction, waste disposal, hazardous substances or any other environmental matters; and

(b)   any notices or correspondence received from a local authority or government department threatening any environmental enquiry, investigation or enforcement against the Company.

10.3   Details of:

(a)   any complaint from members of the public, adjoining landowners or pressure groups or organisations concerning environmental matters;

(b)   any claim or prosecution concerning environmental matters or product liability;

(c)   claims under any policy of insurance for any product liability or environmental matter;

(d)   internal environmental audit procedures and any environmental audits, surveys, reports or investigations;

(e)   capital expenditure or increased operating expenditure known or likely to be required over the next 3 years in relation or anticipated to environmental matters;

(f)   any known, notified or suspected contamination in, on or under any of the Company's properties;

(g)   previous uses of any of the Company's properties; and

(h)	any properties disposed of by the Company which were known, notified or suspected of being contaminated, with details of that contamination.		

11. Health & Safety

11.1 Copies of:

    (a)   the Company's written statement of health and safety policy;

    (b)   the organisation and arrangements for carrying out the Company's health and safety policy.

11.2 Copies of any forms, notices or correspondence sent to or received from a local authority, government department or the Health & Safety Executive concerning health and safety matters arising as a result of carrying on the Company.

11.3 Details of:

    (a)   any claim or prosecution relating to the Company concerning health and safety matters;

    (b)   any complaint from any person, group or body (not being or representing any employee of the Company) threatening any health and safety enquiry, investigation or enforcement in connection with the Company;

    (c)   claims under any policy of insurance for health and safety matters;

    (d)   any health and safety audits, survey, reports or investigations; and

    (e)   agreements or arrangements with trade unions or other bodies relevant to health and safety matters.

11.4 Details of any of the following hazardous substances/hazards handled, kept or present at the Company's premises: asbestos; lead; ionising radiation; highly flammable liquids and liquified petroleum gases; biological agents; or micro-organisms.

11.5 Details of any "construction work" as defined by Regulation 2, Construction (Design & Management) Regulations 1994 undertaken after 31 March 1995.

Source: Tom's Law (www.tomslaw.com)

Objection clinic

Of course one of the other reasons women may well lack the confidence to pitch is lack of confidence from going through an 'objection clinic'. If you can think of every objection an investor might have to your business and can then have answers in your mind, can you imagine how much more confident you will be?

Opposite is a useful template for just that – again, courtesy of the outstanding Tom's Law (www.tomslaw.com).

Business Plan Evaluation

Company: _____

I. Written Business Plan (30%)

In rating each of the below, please consider the following questions:

Is this area covered in adequate detail?

Does the plan show clear understanding of the elements that should be addressed?

Are the assumptions realistic and reasonable?

Are the risks identified and the ability to manage those risks conveyed?

(Using the rating system: 1 = poor, 2 = fair, 3 = good, 4 = very good, 5 = excellent)

Please evaluate the written business plan on the following aspects:

1.   Executive Summary (5%)

(Clear, exciting and effective as a stand-alone Overview of the plan)

| 1 | 2 | 3 | 4 | 5 |

Comments/Questions

2.   Company Overview (5%)

(Business purpose, history, genesis of concept, current status, overall strategy and objectives)

| 1 | 2 | 3 | 4 | 5 |

Comments/Questions

3.   Products or Services (15%)

(Description, features, benefits, pricing, current stage of development, proprietary position)

| 1 | 2 | 3 | 4 | 5 |

Comments/Questions

4.   Market and Marketing Strategy (20%)

(Description of market, competitive analysis, needs identification, market acceptance, unique capabilities, sales/promotion)

	1	2	3	4	5

Comments/Questions

5.   Operations (15%)

(Plan for production/delivery of product or services, product cost, margins, operating complexity, resources required)

	1	2	3	4	5

Comments/Questions

6.   Management (20%)

(Backgrounds of key individuals, ability to execute strategy, personnel needs, organisational structure, role of any non-student executive, which students will execute plan)

	1	2	3	4	5

Comments/Questions

7.   Summary Financials (10%)

(Presented in summary form and are easy to read and understand. Consistent with plan and effective in capturing final performance; Monthly for year, Quarterly for years 2-3, Annually for years 4-5).

a.	Cash Flow Statement	1	2	3	4	5
b.	Income Statement	1	2	3	4	5
c.	Balance Sheet	1	2	3	4	5
d.	Funds Required/Uses	1	2	3	4	5
e.	Assumptions/Trends/ Comparatives	1	2	3	4	5

Comments/Questions

8. **Offering (10%)**
(Proposal/terms to investors – indicates how much needed, the ROI, the structure of the deal and possible exit strategies)
1   2   3   4   5
Comments/Questions
Additional Comments

Business Plan Evaluation

Company: _____

II. Viability of Company (30%)

In rating each of the below, please consider the following questions:
Do you believe that the business idea presented has a chance to be successful?
Do you think that the company has a sustainable competitive advantage with this business idea?
Would you as a venture capitalist invest in this new business?
(Using the rating system: 1 = poor, 2 = fair, 3 = good, 4 = very good, 5 = excellent)
1.   Market Opportunity (20%)
(There is a clear market need presented as well as a way to take advantage of that need.)
1   2   3   4   5
2.   Distinctive Competence (20%)
(The company provides something novel/unique/special that gives it a competitive advantage in its market.)
1   2   3   4   5

3. **Management Capability (20%)**				
(This team can effectively develop this company and handle the risks associated with the venture.)				
1	2	3	4	5

4. **Financial Understanding (20%)**				
(This team has a solid understanding of the financial requirements of the business)				
1	2	3	4	5

5. **Investment Potential (20%)**				
(The business represents a real investment opportunity in which you would consider investing)				
1	2	3	4	5

Company Strengths

Company Weaknesses

Additional Comments

Business Plan Evaluation

Company: _____

III. Presentation (30%)

In rating each of the below, please consider the following questions:

Does he presentation make a compelling case for the business idea?

Is the presentation aligned with the written report?

(Using the rating system: 1 = poor, 2 = fair, 3 = good, 4 = very good, 5 = excellent)

1. Formal Presentation (50%)

a.	Materials presented in clear, logical and/or sequential and interesting form.	1	2	3	4	5
b.	Ability to relate need for the company with meaningful examples, and practical questions	1	2	3	4	5
c.	Ability to maintain judges' interest.	1	2	3	4	5
d.	Quality of Visual Aids.	1	2	3	4	5

2. Questions and Answers (50%)

a.	Ability to understand judges' inquiries	1	2	3	4	5
b.	Appropriately respond to judges' inquiries with substantive answers.	1	2	3	4	5
c.	Use of time allocated (minimal redundancy)	1	2	3	4	5
d.	Poise and confidence (think effectively on their feet.)	1	2	3	4	5

Strengths of Presentation

Weaknesses of Presentation

Business Plan Evaluation

Company: _____

IV. Ranking (10%)

Please rank all presentations.

Please use your comments and the strengths and weaknesses of the company and the presentation to determine an appropriate ranking

Ranking:

1. _____ (10 points)

2. _____ (7 points)

3. _____ (3 points)

4. _____ (0 points)

Source: Tom's Law (www.tomslaw.com)

Top advice

Below are just some of the useful pointers from various entrepreneurs and business people on pitching:

- Do what works for you in terms of confidence whether rehearsing, power dressing, over-preparing etc.

- Picture the passion for your business before you pitch. Confidence is about belief in self and product.

- Know your financials inside out at the top of your head. There is no point saying, 'ummm, I have those figures somewhere'. If you don't know them, why should someone give you money?

- Remember they have to like you, want to work with you and you with them. Sometimes you may not want their money.

- No-one owes you a living – don't be pushy for money.

- Don't be a victim. Don't go in there apologising for your business or expecting to fail.

- Make them believe in the business. A classic mistake is to feel inferior because you don't have a huge business yet.

6 True stories

"If you are truly determined, you will succeed."

Penny Streeter

- Prominent women in business.
- Facts and figures.
- Case studies from the UN.

There is no getting away from the fact that we all love hearing stories of success. How did they do it? If they can do it, so can I. I am not the only one facing the same difficulties as some of the most successful businesswomen.

So sit back and be inspired.

Penny Streeter – Ambition 24Hours

If you were to list the qualities needed to become a successful entrepreneur, determination and self-motivation would come pretty high up on the list. If you looked around for someone who embodies such virtues, you would be hard-pressed to find anyone to top Penny Streeter, founder of Ambition 24Hours.

Defying the odds, South African-born Penny, a single mother, has overcome lack of finance and negative attitudes to build up a company that, in less than 10 years, has an annual turnover of £60m.

But for Penny Streeter, the adversity she faced did not dent her belief that she could start up on her own and develop her idea into a world-class, multi-million pound business.

Streeter started up Ambition 24Hours, an employment agency for medical staff, in 1996. Initially, it was just Penny and her mother dealing with requests for locum doctors, nurses and care assistants. With the service offered 24 hours a day, as the company name suggests, Penny says she took calls at all times, often dealing with requests while in the supermarket.

This 24-hour service was necessary, as Streeter spotted a gap in the market that she felt she could exploit. She believed that there was a strong demand for agency staff during the weekend, when most agencies closed down.

However, with successive bank managers looking down their noses at her business plan, Streeter had to build up her firm without any funding at all. To make ends meet, she worked weekends as a children's entertainer. It was crucial in the early stages, providing cash to buy adverts to recruit medical staff to the books.

Looking back at her early struggles, it seems slightly astonishing that Streeter has built up Ambition 24Hours into a business that has an annual turnover of over £60m, around 13,500 healthcare staff on its books and 19 branch offices in the UK.

But when you learn that Penny still works 12-hour days, it becomes clear that adversity and knock-backs are mere irritations to this driven entrepreneur.

"I've always been very driven to succeed. When I started the business, I was divorced, with very young children to support, so I had to succeed," she said.

"We had all the usual problems of any start-up – no money, no time, no market awareness of the business. We overcame these by being absolutely focused and driven to succeed, with a 'siege mentality' to costs – we did not spend any money on anything that was not essential, with a very clear contribution on ROI.

We relied very much on our own resources, with no outside help, so we made mistakes, but we never made the same ones twice.

Ultimately, you have to rely on yourself; to be prepared to make the big decisions, although now we have an excellent management team."

Penny's success has made her a popular figure in the media, prompting helpful coverage in newspapers and TV. She has also won awards, but characteristically, this has not quenched her thirst for further success.

Giving advice to budding entrepreneurs she says:

"The key is to find out what customers really want, identify a niche market where you can differentiate from your competitors, working harder and more intelligently than the competition, focus on growth and the bottom line, regard obstacles as learning opportunities and remember that if you are truly determined, you will succeed."

Anita Roddick – The Body Shop

If anyone has come to business via an unconventional route it is Anita Roddick, founder of The Body Shop.

Her many jobs before opening the first Body Shop included clipping newspapers for the *International Herald Tribune* in Paris, teaching for a short time in England and working for the United Nations in Geneva.

After that she hit what she called the 'Hippy trail' and toured Tahiti, New Hebrides, New Caledonia, Reunion, Madagascar, Mauritius, Australia, and South Africa. She married Gordon Roddick in 1971 and the couple ran a restaurant and hotel in Littlehampton.

When Gordon was away in 1976, Anita took out a £6,000 loan to open the first Body Shop. It was situated, somewhat ironically, next to a funeral parlour in Brighton sparking a dispute between the owner and Anita. *The Brighton Evening Argus* ran the story on the dispute between the funeral parlour owners who were upset about a new cosmetics boutique which had opened up next door.

It wasn't the nature of the business they were getting hot under the collar about, but its name. They thought the green shop front emblazoned with the words The Body Shop in gold leaf might put off prospective customers.

"They wanted me to change my shop front which I had just spent £870 of my £4,000 loan on," recalls Roddick. "My smart move was to call the Argus and tell them I was being threatened by Mafia undertakers who wanted to close me down."

The press loved it. The story of the beleaguered single mum with the house in hock trying to support her two kids with a bootstrapping start-up worked a treat. The small splash made The Body Shop a *cause celebre*, won plenty of local support and won an important battle to get the business off the ground.

But although the battles got much bigger as Roddick grew her business into the multinational retailer it is today, anyone with even a passing familiarity with the Body Shop story will instantly recognise the defining characteristics of its fiery feisty founder in those early days of the business: 'Ethical Anita' versus the big bad world.

Her philosophy of profits with principles, and green image caught on in an age when environmental concerns came to the fore. It caught on to such an extent that there are now over 1,800 shops in 49 countries, achieving retail sales of £700m pounds last year from 77 million customers choosing from a range of over 600 products and more than 400 accessories.

This success has brought financial rewards to the Roddicks. In 1993, Anita was the 5th richest woman in Britain. The couple's fortune is valued by *The Sunday Times* at about £68m.

In 1999, The Body Shop brand was voted the second most trusted brand in the UK by the Consumers Association and the previous year *The Financial Times* ranked The Body Shop the 27th most respected company in the world.

But as The Body Shop became a global brand and more preoccupied with commercial realities, Anita's radicalism was seen by insiders as more of a liability than an asset. In 2002 she stepped down as the co-chair of The Body Shop and decided to take a backseat at the company she set up more than 25 years ago.

Martha Lane Fox – lastminute.com

A last minute change of heart has made Martha Lane Fox's massive fortune. At first she turned down the opportunity to launch blockbuster internet company lastminute.com, but former colleague Brent Hoberman finally persuaded Martha, 26, to join him in his new venture. "I can't take any credit for the idea for lastminute," Martha admits, "when Brent came up with the idea I thought it was terrible. I told him no one would want to buy things at the last minute over the internet."

But Brent, 30, managed to persuade Martha that the idea was worth a shot. "Whenever Brent travels he tries to get upgraded and when he is booking a hotel he likes to phone around until someone offers him a cheap deal," she says. "He believed that a similar proposal would work on the internet and he was right."

The story of lastminute.com is one of the most publicised dotcom stories around. The company was floated on the London Stock Exchange and New York's NASDAQ on 14th March 2000. Within days the initial price of 380p had climbed to a peak of 555p. At one point, Lane Fox was worth over £50m. After its first day as a public company lastminute.com was valued at £733m, placing it ahead of Debenhams and Iceland.

It soon went badly wrong. By March 2001 the share price was in the 30s, and Lane Fox and co-founder Brent Hoberman were widely pilloried by the press – the same press who had been talking them up a few short months earlier. The company was making losses with no clear sign of blackness on the horizon and private shareholders were not slow to vent their anger – at one point naming her the most hated woman in Britain.

Unlike companies such as Boo and Clickmango, lastminute.com kept going and expanding and are now probably the second most recognised e-tailer in the UK after Amazon. Their losses have now shrunk, and in March 2004 they bought rival company Online Travel.

Martha has said that the best advice she received was from Hoberman, who said to think big and act fast, as reported in the *Media Guardian* (March 25th, 2002). The market moves so quickly she claims that it is vital to get on with things as soon as you get that earth-shattering idea. She goes on: "Taking risks is a good thing if you feel like it. People should be prepared to go with their gut instinct if they feel it's the right thing to do. If you want to leave your job and go and do something else, then do it."

After university, Martha joined a management consultancy called Spectrum, where she met her future partner Brent. She spent several months in Korea working on a pay TV project for Samsung. She also carried out a study for the Department of Trade and Industry on use of the internet and new technology, but after three years at Spectrum she decided she needed more experience before starting her own business. She moved to Carlton Communications and worked on developing their pay TV channels before linking up again with Brent.

Perween Warsi – S&A Foods

As a young mother in the 1980s, Perween Warsi dreamt about running a business. Over fifteen years later, Warsi has built up a food manufacturer supplying ready-made meals to UK supermarkets and pubs, as well as exporting to Europe.

The company – named S&A Foods after her two sons Sadiq and Abid – turns over about £100m a year and employs 1,400 people in four factories in the north of England.

Company legend has it that Warsi set up her business after becoming fed up with the quality of Indian foods in British supermarkets.

Determination matched her ambition – day after day she would beg the supermarkets to trial her food. After six months, Asda finally agreed to a blind tasting of Warsi's foods alongside other samples.

In 1987, with the aim of finding more money to invest in the business, S&A Foods joined the Hughes Food Group. Three years later saw the Warsi family fighting to regain control after Hughes Food went belly-up.

After a successful management buyout, Warsi began diversifying into Thai, Malaysian, Chinese and American food. However, the loss of control has not gone forgotten – Warsi plans to "keep the business in the family" rather than risk a float on the stock market.

She says her secret ingredient has been an investment in product development. The company launches 300 food products a year and is constantly experimenting in its test kitchen.

Warsi has to battle with stiff competition. In recent years, British food manufacturers have become bright stars in an otherwise gloomy manufacturing sector. Some 7,000 new food products are tested in the UK each year, a fair reflection of the pace of change and competition in the sector.

Some suspect that food giants, such as Nabisco and Northern Foods, may be eyeing some of the Asian specialists as takeover targets. Companies like S&A are vulnerable because they do not have brand awareness among consumers. Someone buying chicken fajitas from Sainsbury's, for example, would never know from the packaging that the food was made by S&A.

Warsi's success to date, including a CBE for services to business, has been remarkable for a woman who never went to university and only came to the UK in 1975 after marrying her husband.

Nicola Horlick – SGAM

Nicola Horlick is long celebrated for her ability to combine a high-octane City career with bringing up a large family and a host of charity work.

As one of the City's highest-profile executives with asset management company SGAM, Horlick has been responsible for the assets of a catalogue of blue chip clients, whizzing across the country and overseeing £6.6bn of assets.

Once included on a list of the world's 100 most powerful women, her lock-in contract at SGAM, the company she co-founded, has secured her a rumoured personal purse of £20m.

Accruing these millions has not involved the sacrifice of a conventional family life. After her marriage to a fellow financial executive, Horlick never felt that material possessions "were more important than a baby. I was always a maternal person".

The couple have had six children but, five years ago, lost their eldest daughter to leukaemia. Ever since, Horlick has used her name, reputation and entrepreneurial efforts to raise money for specialist hospitals.

She also found an outlet for her grief by writing the book 'Can You Really Have It All?'. In it, she claimed the answer was a resounding 'Yes!' and that women made better managers than men.

The financial press were already interested in Horlick. Back in 1997, as the new managing director of Deutsche Morgan Grenfell and facing a possible suspension, the high-flying executive flew with a posse of journalists to Frankfurt, where she door-stepped her employers.

In August 2003 she announced that she would be moving to the role of special adviser to the group president. Although undoubtedly taxing, her new job does not involve the long hours and motorway miles she used to chalk up.

This retreat from day-to-day market activity comes soon after an accusation by a major client that Horlick's fund management was becoming, perhaps, "too much for her", a claim she called "ridiculous".

By the time she set up her own firm a year later, Horlick didn't dispute the media's depiction of her as a glittering example of ball-breaking, jam-making, all-round achievement.

Friends say her role model is Lady Thatcher, and Horlick admits to having political ambitions she wishes to fulfil. Having once flirted with the Labour Party, she now sees the Conservatives as what one friend calls the "sort of failing business she could help to turn around".

With such prospects before her, Nicola Horlick is adamant that she has "no intention of retiring at 42". If life in the feminine fast lane is the juggling act described by Cherie, it seems this enduring high-flyer is only too happy to add another ball.

Linda Bennett – LK Bennett

Shoe-obsessed retailer Linda Bennett, became the latest woman to be named Veuve Clicquot Business Woman of the Year in 2004. Organisers of the award said they picked the 39 year old as her shops satisfy a growing demand for quintessentially English fashion.

Linda Bennett, founder of LK Bennett, began her career designing handbags and quickly won orders from leading fashion retailers. This success prompted her to launch her own collection of LK Bennett shoes, and in 1990 she took out a loan to lease a small shop. 14 years on, Linda has a loyal customer base and 45 outlets.

The shops sell her own LK Bennett range of women's shoes, clothes and accessories.

Bennett's parents provided her with the perfect traits to get ahead – her father was a businessman and her mother a sculptor.

"I think I gained business acumen and creativity from them," she told *PA News*. Her love of fashion is a definite plus for her line of work. Linda does admit she is "mad" about shoes – storing up a hoard of around 200 pairs.

Not such a surprise for a woman who studied footwear design at Cordwainers College in Hackney, East London, and went onto gain experience at French and German design studios.

To build up the business in the early years she was not afraid of walking the floor at her own stores, and she still retains a hands-on approach to the business.

Bennett tries to remain accessible to her 400 staff and encourages feedback from her stores. She is also not just a retailer – among her diverse skills she has also designed clothes and accessories.

She said: "I believe it is important to be tenacious in business and not to give up on an idea."

"I am also very lucky in that I enjoy what I do and I think I have carved out a niche so that people now buy the brand."

As a result of her efforts she now has stores in the UK, Europe, The Middle East and the US.

Dawn Gibbins – Flowcrete

Dawn Gibbins wanted the builder's bum banned. Not because the ever-present crack in the trade offended Veuve Clicquot's Business Woman of the Year in 2003, but because back problems so prevalent in construction concerned her. It was also a nifty way to promote the self-levelling, fast-laying commercial floor screed her father created.

The woman who set up international commercial floor specialists Flowcrete in 1982 with her inventor father has changed the rules in a conservative and macho industry. Her methods and constant innovations have brought a considerable amount of recognition and generated a £25m turnover.

Yet it wasn't until 1990 that the company really took shape. Its growth up to then had been decidedly modest following the contract it secured with Mars on formation for a sugar-resistant floor. Gibbin's father Peter was a man with a reputation as an innovator, but not someone who realised the value of his work.

Like many small businesses Flowcrete was R&D oriented and vastly undercharged for its services, but it's a mark of the company's work that Mars, among other blue chips the world over, is still a client. A £40,000 turnover in 1982 rose to £600,000 in 1985 and finally the landmark £1m in 1990. However, the progress wasn't enough.

Her husband screamed at her one weekend that she was unstructured and too spontaneous, she claims. It was the jolt Gibbins needed. She decided knowledge was power and enrolled at business school and on a series of short courses, including time management to give her the much needed structure.

Incredibly, the company only got its first business plan eight years in, as part of the process for securing a SMART award. One of the first key moves of Gibbins' new approach was to recruit her husband from Shell – a man with responsibility £28m of the corporation's money and a £5m marketing budget. At Flowcrete he got a £50,000 ad spend.

She also gave the company a specific mission – to be the UK's leading flooring company. Six years later it was. The bar has been raised now and it competes for the title on a world scale. To achieve this Gibbins recognised her strengths in HR, marketing and product innovation, tasked her husband with international dealmaking and radically changed the culture. No longer did long hours necessarily mean productivity. More important is a positive attitude.

Fortunes changed dramatically, and while she's now happy with her 200 staff, it hasn't gone unnoticed that the 25 person team in Asia has outperformed the 75 in Europe and 100 in the UK on the company's bottom line. Asia added £750,000, Europe brought £300,000 and the UK achieved £600,000. This confirmed that the business model has evolved to such an extent that the UK base now carries baggage despite a constant war on waste. This means one thing to Gibbins: "1990 was a key stage for us. I feel we're on the cusp of another evolutionary change now," she asserts. "I feel I'm on a launch pad. We can be the world leader."

Dee Edwards – Habbo Ltd

Dee Edwards used her experience in the internet field to launch Habbo Ltd, a youth brand built on a graphical chat and gaming environment for teenagers. The company is backed by Electric Mother Ventures, a Scandinavian venture capitalist, and has seen financing of £1m. It has turned over £1m from the first year of trading.

Edwards believed the internet business could be made successful by using technology to run a business effectively and leveraging the different way people were changing their communications. She felt few companies were doing this effectively and wanted to prove it could be done.

Edwards' background is in business to business marketing and internet business strategy. She joined David Bowen, the *Independent on Sunday's* former business editor in setting up the internet publishing company Net Profit. After helping to build the company into a credible and trustworthy brand, she moved onto the internet business consultancy Razorfish where she focused on new business and conceptualisation. The idea of Habbo Ltd was born while she was entrepreneur in residence at the internet incubator, Brainspark plc.

The idea for her business came when she met with a development company in Finland who were creating innovative multi-user environments and felt that there was a potential to work together to create a new type of business and a new type of brand. It was a natural progression for her to start her own online business after building up so much experience in the industry.

She says the single most important thing that has helped her business to succeed is "truly understanding people's needs and addressing them in a unique manner is the only way to succeed."

Sarah Tremellen – Bravissimo

When Sarah Tremellen set out for Cambridge to study biology the furthest thing from her mind was the mail order lingerie business. But now, ten years later, she's the director of Bravissimo, a company which provides lingerie for larger women.

The company, which started in a living room in 1994, expects to turn over something in the region of £7m this year and has 35 employees, the majority of them women. The company now offers a range of lingerie, including over 50 different bras in a whole host of different styles and a range of swimwear.

After a short flirtation with academia, Tremellen travelled the world before settling in a marketing career. But it was while on maternity leave, she had married and got pregnant earlier than anticipated, that her career really took off.

It is rare that getting pregnant is the stepping stone to an entrepreneurial career, but for Tremellen it prompted the realisation that it was practically impossible for the larger busted woman to get her hands on a stylish and comfortable bra. There simply wasn't anyone out there catering to this market.

Her lack of business experience didn't put her off. From the outset she always had big ambitions for the business. Tremellen and a friend decided to take an eight-week small business course run over consecutive weekends. At the end of the course participants were required to produce a business plan and present it to a panel, which happened to comprise the local bank manager. Her presentation won her a £10,000 bank loan and, with the £3,000 each that she and her partner put into the business, Bravissimo was born.

Since then the business has been entirely self-financing, and while it took three and a half years to make a profit, it never incurred huge losses.

Once they got off the ground, nothing prepared them for their early success. The company caught the imagination of the news media and within three weeks the *Daily Mail* ran a two-page spread on Bravissimo as a pioneering "woman to woman" UK based company. In the first three days of the article's publication, the company received over 1000 calls.

The most difficult move came in the form of its move into high street retailing. In 1999 the company opened a retail store in Ealing, West London, close to the company's headquarters. With no prior experience of a retail environment, and a staff taken largely from existing Bravissimo employees, it was a gamble.

But the Ealing shop has proved a success and pointed the way forward for ten more across the UK, the second one opening in Manchester.

From its first beginnings, Bravissimo has been an unconventional route to success. Who would consider getting pregnant a path to business success? Tremellen herself admits that success is quite often down to a relaxed attitude, building solid foundations and a cautious approach to expansion.

The future certainly seems rosy. The company registered 300% growth in year one and 200% in its second year of operation and since then it's grown by 70% year on year.

Stories from the United Nations

Marina J. Kornava

JSC StroyFinPartnership (Moscow)

Medium-sized enterprise (raw materials and food products supply)

Vision of entrepreneurship

"Development of SMEs, with the support of the Government based on an honest and civilised code of entrepreneurship. We could build our partnership relations only by such a means. The principle idea of my vision is: let's do things together in order to achieve high results."

How I became an entrepreneur

"I obtained a high degree in economics, having graduated from the Moscow Plekhanov Economic Academy. I started my career, working as the chief of the Gostorg Trade Department. I then worked as the Leading Economist in a Municipal Department. Having spent several years abroad, including China, India, Japan, Mongolia, North and South Korea, I established my own company, which, at a later stage was transformed into a holding structure. It has been developing successfully over the last five years."

Message for the 21st century

"As a business woman, I believe that my mission is to contribute to the creation of jobs and raising living standards in our country, which is an economy in transition. Modern businesses should improve all possible aspects of a woman's life. The 21st century should be seen under the sign of woman. My wish for all women worldwide is: do not hide your talents within the walls of your houses, but enter the world and share your experiences with others."

Geppa Vera Vitalevna

Vera Geppa Fashion Centre (Kursk)

Small-sized enterprise (design and manufacturing clothing, organising fashion shows and training designers)

Vision of entrepreneurship

"Entrepreneurship is only a tool for implementation of your ideas, which have to lead towards the development of the following: qualitative growth and increase or extension of production. I believe that such an entrepreneurship is optimal, because: it invites for co-operation of a large number of talented people and provides an opportunity for realisation of their talents; provides an opportunity for expanding your production sphere, which could lead to a solution of important social problems, reduction of unemployment and creation of new jobs; and increases the tax base and income of the country and, consequently, contributes to a higher economic growth."

How I became an entrepreneur

"In 1987, after it was allowed to start-up individual business activities, I got an idea to create a fashion salon to realise my dream. My plan was focused on small-scale production. However, as people became acquainted with my products, I got orders from other persons, even from large companies. I also obtained a lot of suggestions. It was necessary to enlarge my salon. Step-by-step, I created a small-scale enterprise, followed by the establishment of the 'Vera Geppa' Fashion House, and then, in 1999, 'Vera Geppa' Fashion Centre. Fashion is a very complicated and comprehensive activity, which requires the development of different skills from creativity to manufacturing and from education to special marketing knowledge. All these activities are subject to a specific rhythm understandable only to the artist. It is practically impossible to prepare a sound business-plan for investors, because the economic efficiency of such activities at the start of the process is very low. During the initial stage, any fashion house hardly deserves its name, and economic gains may come only at a later stage. It is even more true for those persons who started up their entrepreneurial activities without any external financial support."

Message for the 21st century

"Entrepreneurship of the 21st century should not only become a successful commercial undertaking of the entrepreneur, but it should also add a social value. In my opinion, only such a kind of entrepreneurship adds to a country's economic strength and contributes in the development of a socially responsible market economy."

Suchkova Natalia Sergeevna

KROTBERS Holding Company (Kasimov)

Large-sized enterprise (holding company in constructing materials, metallurgy, agro-products, trade and catering)

Vision of entrepreneurship

"Entrepreneurial activities should be oriented towards the creation of state-of-the-art technologies, favourable social conditions for employees and investing in human resources development."

How I became an entrepreneur

"In 1989, the KROTBERS construction material manufacturing company was established. Today, the KROTBERS Holding Company incorporates a multi-sectoral modern structure with various production capabilities."

Message for the 21st century

"Let us raise the economy of the Russian to the level of the leading European States."

Vasilieva Valentina Ivanova

ZARNITSA Joint Stock Company (Moscow)

Large-sized enterprise (light-industry)

Vision of entrepreneurship

"Organising effectively the work of the enterprise. Equipping the enterprise with modern equipment. Manufacturing goods that are under a great public demand. Increasing profit with the aim of improving the welfare of employees; their social status; and living standards."

How I became an entrepreneur

"After graduating from the Moscow Technological Institute for Light Industry, I started my career as a foreman, and then the Director of Tailoring and Dressmaking Establishment. For three years I was mastering managing employees and the enterprise, and then decided to try to work in the field of science. I began to work as a research worker in the Scientific Research Institute for Clothing Industry. While working in the sphere of science, I became very interested in manufacturing of goods. Thus, I started my career in 1968 at the factory named Krasny Voin (today it is called the Joint Stock Company ZARNITSA) as the Chief Engineer. That time, I realized that I wanted and could do much more. In 1984, I became the General Director of this enterprise. It was very interesting for me to manage this enterprise, to create highly trained personnel, to install new equipment and to improve the social base of the company. In 1992, our enterprise was one of the first in Moscow, which manufactured excellent products and had a wide network with other manufacturers."

Message for the 21st century

"We entered the 21st century. Each of us, summing her life experience in the 20th century, tried to look forward, to dream and to reason about what is awaiting us in the new century. For the Russians, the 20th century was full of anxiety, wars and hopes for a better future. We lived, struggled against the fascism and won in the name of life, our Motherland, in the name of opportunity for all of us to work for the prosperity of our Motherland. Many hopes and dreams didn't come true in the 20th century; it brought quite a number of disappointments to all of us. Looking forward into the 21st century, we wish that all local wars would stop. We wish all peoples of our Planet to live in peace and friendship. We must not allow new world wars with the use of nuclear weapons to break out. Production and usage of nuclear weapons must be banned forever. We hope, that the day, when the stability in the development of our society will come, is not so distant. We hope that industry and economy will develop, and this will be the basis for the restoration of the greatness and might of our Motherland. To solve these problems, it is necessary to contribute to the development of the creative personality of people, to their spiritual development. Women can really do much for these purposes. Let the whole world work in the name of Humanity!"

Kusmina Tatiana Sergeevna

Restaurant Youth, Dance-Club Northern Lights, Billiard Club 10ft, Hairdresser's Saloon, Parking Place (Nizhni Novgorod)

Medium-sized enterprises (decorative-applied arts, choreography, music, folklore ensemble, fitness-club, model agency)

Vision of entrepreneurship

"Business is a kind of activity that allows to realise the capacity and desires of an individual. For this to happen certain significant conditions have to be in place: low taxes; possibility of getting short-term credits with an acceptable interest rate; partnership relationship with the authorities; and a great capacity for work."

How I became an entrepreneur

"I organised my enterprise with a team of alliances. In 1991, I got a credit under a guarantee of one of my enterprises and rented the building of the Culture Centre for Youth with a total area of 3,200 square meters. Having decorated the premises of the building, I opened public services and studios enumerated above. Then I constructed a parking place and bought, through an auction, a shop with total area of 565 square meters. As a result, I have become the 82nd proprietor of the city of Nizhni Novgorod."

Message for the 21st century

"In the 21st century, I wish women freedom, independence and self-confidence. Nobody, but ourselves will make us happy. And of course, I wish women to be loved, darling and healthy. Let prosperity, kindness and welfare enter each house. Let kindness and warmth of women's hearts bring happiness to the whole world."

Matveeva Liudmila Borisovna

CEREMUSHKI Joint Stock Company (Moscow)

Large-sized enterprise (light industry, manufacturing corsets)

Vision of entrepreneurship

"Entrepreneurship is an activity, which is something connected with making risky decisions in order to get high and systematic income. This implies: to have a certain aim and to do everything for it's achievement; to be able to a find solution in any situation; to foresee and promptly react to existing economic and market situations and to be the master of the circumstances, rather than to obey them."

How I became an entrepreneur

"I started my career as a foreman. Since then I have been specialising in the manufacturing of goods in the light industry, and my work experience has made it possible for me to be competent in many matters. Now, I am working as the General Director of a large enterprise in the light industry. I think that I made such a career, owning to my purposefulness, vigorousness, diligence, desire to look into each matter, willpower, strong character, healthy ambitions and, of course, optimism."

Message for the 21st century

"I would like the 21st century to enter into the history of every country as the greatest and brightest epoch. Let the new century to be the time of great discovering and inventions. Looking back at the achievements of the 20th century, we could live our lives with all the best and the kindness that was in that century. I wish the 21st century to give people an opportunity to realise all their knowledge and abilities, and let warmth, prosperity and happiness enter into each house!"

Kananina Liudmila Ivanovna

Knitted Surface Joint Stock Company (Moscow)

Medium-sized enterprise (manufacturing of knitted carpet surfaces)

Vision of entrepreneurship

"I think that the State support for entrepreneurship is of a great importance. This includes: timely allocation of credits; efficient system of taxation; stimulating the development of entrepreneurship; and encouragement of successful entrepreneurs."

How I became an entrepreneur

"After graduating from the Moscow Textile Institute, I started my working career as a foremen's assistant in a weaving shop of a factory. After that, I changed many posts, starting from an engineer of a physic-mechanical testing laboratory, a deputy chief engineer, chief engineer of a carpet integrated plant all the way up to the General Director of the Knitted Surface Joint Stock Company. The great role in my professional growth and my transformation into a leader of a large enterprise played my constant participation in public work: three times I was elected as a Deputy of the City's Council of People's Deputies: I was also the Member of the Presidium of Moscow City's Peace Foundation, and I am a Member of the Directors' Council in the Women's Union of Russia. I have always strived to improve my professional standards, so, I attended lectures at the Courses of Qualification Improvement. At the moment I am also a Member of the Business Women Club."

Message for the 21st century

"I wish generations of the 21st century to review the spiritual values of the Russian Nation, to eradicate poverty and corruption. I wish Russia to become a highly industrial state capable of providing the working population with jobs, to ensure a further economic progress and high living standards for her people. I wish future generations to raise a galaxy of clever and talented leaders, who will be patriots of their country, capable of making Russia into a leading country of the world."

Kosorukova Galina Andreevna

Joint Stock Company RADUGA (Moscow)

Large-sized enterprise (manufacturing of men's and women's overcoats, dairy processing)

Vision of entrepreneurship

"The market economy in Russia is just beginning to develop. One of the main elements of the market economy is entrepreneurship that gives birth to market competition. In its essence, entrepreneurship is the process of search and development of new forms of management and of new means to meet public needs. Entrepreneurship also includes readiness to take a risk with the aim of getting high profit. But first of all, entrepreneurship is the ability to actively react to market changes, to take liberty of making quick decisions. On her way to success, an entrepreneur must promptly react to lucky opportunities granted by the market, she must also be in a constant search of new markets for her goods and services, to be open to new perspectives and to overcome difficulties."

How I became an entrepreneur

"I was working in the light industry branch for more than 40 years. I started my working experience from the post of an electric sewing-machine operator, went through all stages of production up to the post of the General Director, and I was working in this position for more than 20 years. I obtained the title of Honoured Worker of the Textile and Light Industry of the Russian Federation. I am rewarded also with the orders for Servicing the Country of the 1st and 2nd Degree."

Message for the 21st century

"I wish women entrepreneurs not to stop at the achieved results, but always strive for perfection, believe in your own strength, carry women's gentleness, humanity and beauty into the world of business. Try to give people and yourselves joy and gratification with your work."

7 Media coverage

> - Ways for women to get media coverage.
> - A couple of journalists tell all.
> - A woman in business tells it as it is.

PR is the lifeblood of any business. We can't all be Donald Trump, Richard Branson...or Martha Stewart, but having raised finance, one thing that will not be impressive is if you spend more than you need to on customer acquisition.

Why do you think Trump and Branson generate free column inches through PR? Ego. Okay, partly, but also because editorial (i.e. non-paid) coverage creates a greater impact. Money can't buy it, and it adds to brand image. If they're talking about you – then you must be important or good!

Many business people either lack the charm or swarm to pull it off, or they underestimate its importance. So in this chapter we cover some of the top key tips. Why short punchy tips? Come on...you're busy. You want to read it, digest it and execute it.

I've advised some very large financial services companies on generating low cost high impact coverage. It's not the kind of advice they can get from PR firms. Why? Because I just said low cost of course! So here goes:

Be timely

I have been fortunate in being on the receiving end of PR as a columnist for the *Financial Times* and as a co-presenter on Bloomberg TV. That teaches you a lot when you have to jump over the fence and advise others.

One classic mistake from new businesses was trying to come up with stories that had nothing to do with what is happening now. For god's sake, buy a calendar.

Be an expert

The media want to quote experts. Write a book, an article, get onto speaking platforms (contact the organisers with your biography and a short 100 word pitch on why you're a leading authority in your field) and contact journalists.

Buy or build a database of journalists

Come on it's easy, but so many small businesses don't do it: who writes in national and local papers about your sector? Pick up the papers, find their names, work out their email (it doesn't take a rocket scientist e.g. firstname.secondname@company.co.uk or some variation) and then add them to your list to send occasional emails to with news.

Get into the little black book

Bookers on TV shows (those whose job it is to book guests) are underpaid, overworked and just want a helping hand. Find out their names, addresses (easy) and email (easy) and post and email them about your company and the latest press release. How do you get their names? Come on, you're an entrepreneur. Watch the programme you want to be on, find out who the producer is from the credits, call the TV company for the booker and send the same material to the producer too.

Once you're on the computer system it's shocking how often you will be called on.

Be good

Okay, I have done hundreds of TV slots from BBC, to CNBC, to CNN globally. So listen up. If you want to be invited on over and over again do the following:

1. Prepare beforehand – I mean 1 hour for a 3 minute slot. Work out what they might ask, plan bullet points, short responses and memorise key facts – people love punchy facts and figures.

2. Use the 'I didn't know that' trick. If you have a fact that would make the audience say, 'I didn't know that' then they will be interested and the booker will have you on again. Remember it is not the same as 'I don't care'. For instance, instead of just saying your company hit a profit of £100,000, say you're more profitable than 10 FTSE 100 companies (on the basis that at the time of writing 10 FTSE 100 companies are loss-making).

3. Get angry or at least persuasive. Don't just talk. Be passionate. Passion excites. It wakes people up. Get mad beforehand. Women are probably not naturally inclined to be as aggressive as testosterone ridden men, but passionate – of course they are!

4. It's all about the angles. I as a journalist would get lots of companies pitching their ideas for TV or print coverage but few had an 'angle' – look at it from the viewer's perspective – why should they care about your company?

5. Sound authoritative and confident – practice it. Wearing the right clothes will help.

6. Get to the studio early – that way you can get used to it.

7. Look smart.

8. Be calm. Visualise the interview beforehand. Pretend it is a chat with a friend. Think about how good it is for your company. Think about how cool it is to be on TV. *Don't* think about what could go wrong, other than if anything does, you can be cool and laugh it off as you would if chatting to a mate in a bar.

9. Don't be high maintenance – make them like you at the TV/Radio station.

10. Email us – seriously – if you need help and we'll chat!

Advice from a PR expert and a business woman

We asked PR expert, Kully Dhadda, Managing Director, Flame Public Relations (www.flamepr.com) to give us the low-down on how women entrepreneurs can get their message across. She should know – she is a woman entrepreneur.

"For most people who run companies, the prospect of coming home from work and seeing their business featured on the national evening news, is a concept which exceeds their wildest dreams. Yet write-ups and interviews in the high profile media should be a regular occurrence for any good business or commentator with expertise, needless to say the rewards can impact every aspect of your company or career.

For all the women business leaders I have come across, the creation of their business, venture or project has been a real heart-and-soul experience, and so when someone like me comes along and says 'we have managed to secure a live interview on breakfast television' the look of shock and disbelief, which eventually glazes over into fear and trepidation, is a real picture.

Thankfully, with some media coaching and a few more interviews, the experience becomes a positively delightful and even joyful one. In fact once they have tasted the limelight women tend to want to understand more about how to court positive publicity and create opportunities to secure exposure. They are far more methodical about taking PR to the core of their operations and enshrining provisions for it into every phase of development in their business. It's at this stage that they begin to develop a hunger for knowledge about what drives the editorial news agenda and how they can capitalise on it. The flame of fame has been lit!

During my fifteen years as a journalist at the BBC, I had a vague awareness of the inability of PR companies to penetrate the media, which explains why so many of them fail to deliver the coverage they have promised to their clients. As I was preparing to leave the BBC and venture into the world of PR, I was a little concerned that I had never actually worked in PR, and was about to set up a business, but the PR practitioners I had been in touch with rapidly reassured me that my lack of experience was a positive advantage as I was untainted by bad practice.

It was completely true. Within days of leaving journalism my clients were on the national and international television and print media. However the sheer scale of bad practice in the PR world had not struck me until I had actually left the BBC and begun to pitch for business.

The tales of woe are in abundance, it rapidly became clear to me that there are many operators out there who portray themselves as experts in the media, but have little knowledge, substance or experience about the news making machine. A good company will secure publicity to the commercial value of several multiples of what their client has spent, within months of being taken on.

Needless to say the ramifications for their business have been phenomenal to say the least.

So how does one go about finding a good PR expert? Without a doubt my strongest asset is the depth of experience I have acquired through working at the BBC, and one of the most banded about phrases people churn out when talking about good PR is 'it's all about contacts', but it isn't just contacts.

No one can deny that contacts are a vital ingredient, and if you do want to talk contacts, then working for the BBC, which undoubtedly is broadcaster *par excellence*, has indeed equipped me with some of the best contacts in the business. However, contacts can only be useful if you know how to work them.

In my experience there is nothing that can beat working as a journalist in news, either in front of camera or behind, in preparing for PR. When I worked as a reporter and presenter at the BBC, I discovered and developed the real art of extracting gems of information from interviewees, and the job of a good PR person is to identify those gems and help clients to promote themselves.

So to the sixty four million dollar question, how is the news agenda created? And more importantly – how can you get yourself in the press, for all the right reasons! The editorial agenda is often perceived as a dark art in the PR world, as no one really understands its key drivers, which is why PR people find it so difficult to secure publicity for their clients.

This is where my days on breakfast television have been so helpful, as we would have to predict twenty four hours in advance which stories and issues would be making the news the following day. Broadly speaking, there are two key themes that drive the news agenda, controversy is the one that is most well known, but the other less obvious one is innovation, and it is this area that is most satisfying from a PR perspective.

It is our strong grasp of the concept of innovation, that has helped Flame Public Relations to become one of the fastest growing companies in the UK. Our powerful blend of strategic insight, strong connections and creativity, deliver campaigns, which change perceptions and drive real business growth. Our skill and expertise in penetrating the media, helps deliver your message to key stakeholders effectively, enhancing their brand and raising their profile. Whether it's the mass media or a niche audience that is sought, our detailed strategies are designed to help deliver results, and create maximum impact.

It is our quest for innovation that is the single most important influential factor behind our success. The question we ask ourselves every time we take on a new project or client is 'Where is the magic?'. Every company, every organisation has a uniqueness that distinguishes it above everything and everyone else in its sphere of reference. This is indeed a voyage of discovery that involves delving deep into the soul of a business, and it is only through this immersion process that successful, creative, high profile campaigns are born.

Getting women leaders to talk about their magic is a much slower process, but the moment they experience the sparkle of a creative campaign, they are far more driven to strengthen their media profile. One of the most satisfying aspects of advising women, is coaching women who are media virgins, and developing their public persona. The end result is that they can often be far more media savvy than their male counterparts. Once women have been trained the world can literally be their oyster!!

The opportunities for women commentators are limitless, almost all the high profile broadcasters and print media will freely admit that their coverage is lacking in diversity. Sometimes I will get calls from the BBC asking specifically for a female voice on a conventional male subject, simply to demonstrate their diversity.

The business press in particular perpetually struggles with this concept, as almost all the commentators put up by organisations and large institutions tend to be male. Hence when a female commentator has been a success it is often noted, and the opportunities for a repeat interview are far greater if she is pro-actively marketed again. Diversity is a real challenge for everyone in the media world, and whilst many outlets have made considerable progress in this area, there is still a long way to go.

Behind every good woman there has to be a carefully thought through PR strategy, but finding the right company to do the job can be a very challenging experience. However there are some helpful questions you can ask which should give you a good idea about how competent the company is.

A popular misconception about PR is that a sector specific expert is best. Journalists working in the high profile end of news have to demonstrate an ability to cover any news story that is presented to them with authority, and if they have worked in business news, they should be able to place clients in any sector. The media hierarchy is such that all trade press monitor stories in the high profile media, and will cover stories they have missed. So there is enormous mileage in taking on a top-tier journalist.

This does come with one important caveat: former journalists are not guaranteed success stories in PR. They have to be prepared to pitch, and pitch regularly, which involves combining the skills of journalism with sales and marketing, and believe you me there are plenty of stories around about journalists who haven't been able to secure the exposure their clients deserve, and this is often down to their lack of ability to sell.

When PR representatives pitch to journalists it is one of the most sophisticated marketing experiences I have ever encountered. Undoubtedly at Flame our roots in journalism have strengthened our hand through our in-depth knowledge of the audience profile of each programme and publication we pitch to.

This knowledge helps us to shape and mould the presentation, and also each press release we send out, so that it is relevant to the readership, or viewers of the publications and programmes being pitched to. Just like you and I like to be communicated to personally, and made to feel we are special, journalists are the same. So don't be fooled by anyone who tells you they will be sending out the best press release on the planet, in sufficiently large quantities to cause serious environmental concerns – this is not about playing big, but playing smart.

One of the big advantages of not coming into the business via the conventional PR route is that Flame PR is run like a newsroom, designed to deliver results. This means working to the deadlines of the journalists and broadcasters, which ultimately involves working early mornings, late nights or weekends – the opportunities can come at the most unsociable times.

Sometimes I will have done half a days work by 9am. The media is twenty four hours, especially in the digital age and consumers are hungry for information and expect real-time news at the touch of a button. For your representative to be totally effective they must be aware of this.

Unlike my competitors I have always had a rather unusual approach to beauty parades; many of my competitors will spend days preparing their pitch and cancel all engagements to ensure they are across every bit of detail about the business almost to the point of being anal. I will go into a pitch with an open mind, wanting to genuinely understand the business and work through the magic of the business or campaign, whilst all the time preparing in my own mind how I am going to sell this to journalists. Well does it work? Here is what the clients think."

Russell Scott, Asha

"Good PR is all about the chemistry between the client and the agency. If the chemistry is wrong between both parties the task of PR becomes a very straight forward, rather dull, but functional media relations exercise with poor results. However if the chemistry is strong it opens an avenue of mutual understanding, passion and creativity which builds and inspires brands, products or people.

This ultimately impacts on the business in a myriad of ways, customers, investors etc. When we put the proposition out to tender for Asha's restaurants we saw eight agencies. They were all given the same brief. Seven out of the eight agencies came back with very cold, formal, functional strategies. Why? Well they just did not see what the project was other then a restaurant roll-out of Indian food. They did not want to understand any more (No further information was ever asked for!!)

Flame PR was the only agency which immediately grasped the key principles of the project. I was also drawn to Flame's positive, passionate and exciting approach to this project which allowed both parties to develop trust and openness to go forward.

Within weeks of that meeting Asha's received big write-ups in the FT, Times, Express and several BBC Radio stations, followed almost instantly by coverage in a plethora of trade press. The global ricochet meant the story became headline news in places like India and beyond.

The PR/client relationship continues to be an enriching experience, as Flame continues to get inside the business, it is able to add value at every stage by shifting the focus of communication as the business evolves. One cannot put a price on the depth of this sort of relationship."

"So as you pursue your dreams, don't forget to share your magic with your key stakeholders through strategic communication, it will magnify your success and profits in a profound way."

Use a wire

As PR newswire put it:

"The beauty of wire distribution in the internet age is that you get both opt-in readers and passive readers. Opt-in readers are journalists and others who ask to receive press releases from wire services. Passive readers are people who just happen to stumble upon a press release as part of normal web surfing."

Wire service distribution will get your release on websites such as Yahoo!, News Alert, CBS MarketWatch and DallasNews.com (The Dallas Morning News) for a flat fee. Most importantly, it's free eyeballs. Most wire services will promise that they have a whole bunch of journalists signed up to receive press releases in certain subjects, but not all services can promise wide distribution to websites.

I can tell you from experience that press releases on wire services do catch journalists' eyes. Many of us utilise personalised homepages such as MyYahoo! Press releases are distributed in general news categories such as 'Internet News' and 'Telecommunications News'. The press releases become intermingled with actual news stories and blend into the normal news reading cycle. And press releases, because they're classified as news contents on these sites, can end up in news search results.

Use a professional press release

Even if you do it yourself rather than hire a PR – use the layout they use. Here it is in the terms PR Newswire prefer:

FOR IMMEDIATE RELEASE

These words should appear in the upper left-hand margin with all letters capitalised.

Headline

This should be a sentence that gives the essence of what the press release is about. Articles, prepositions, conjunctions of three letter words or fewer should be lowercased.

Dateline

This should be the city your press release is issued from and the date you are mailing your release.

Lead paragraph

A strong introductory paragraph should grasp the readers attention and should contain the information most relevant to your message such as the five W's (who, what, when, where, why). This paragraph should summarise the press release and include a hook to get your audience interested in reading more.

Body

The main body of your press release is where your message should fully develop. Many companies choose to use a strategy called the inverted pyramid, which is written with the most important information and quotes first.

Company boilerplate

Your press release should end with a short paragraph that describes your company, products, service and a short company history. If you are filing a joint press release include a boilerplate for both companies.

Contact information

Name, phone, email.

Remember, remember

Everything you say or do is public relations. Some even say there is no such thing as bad publicity…except your obituary. Equally as Napoleon said, "four hostile newspapers are more to be feared than a thousand bayonets". He also recognised a "great reputation is a great noise, the more there is of it, the further does it swell. Land, monuments, national, all fall, but the noise remains, and will reach to other generations".

Reputation, PR, marketing and branding are all related. You cannot get a reputation on what you are going to do. If you make a promise that is your brand and you have to deliver on your brand promise. As Socrates said, "one of the best ways to get a good reputation is to endeavour to be what you desire to appear".

Good for us that newspapers cannot differentiate between bicycle accidents and the collapse of a nation. If women in business, however small the business, can make a noise and get coverage then it lets them compete with the bigger crowd for that moment.

Marketing plan

A sample business plan:

Market summary

Market: past, present, and future

Review changes in the market, which can include:

- Market share
- Leadership
- Players
- Competition
- Market shifts
- Costs
- Pricing

Market cycle

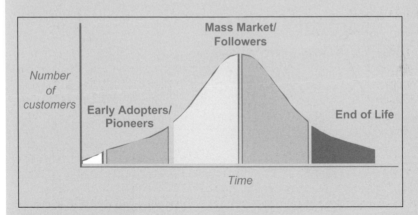

Product definition

Describe the product or service being marketed.

Competitive landscape

Provide an overview of product competitors.

Competitors

-
-
-

Competitors' strengths

-
-
-

Competitors' weaknesses

-
-
-

Product comparison

Position each competitor's product against the new product.

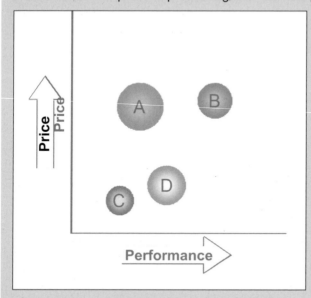

Positioning

Positioning of product or service

Distinctly define the product in its market and against its competition over time.

Consumer promise

Summarise the benefit of the product or service to the consumer.

Communication strategies

Messaging by audience

List marketing messages for different audiences.

Target-consumer demographics

List the demographics for the targeted consumer groups.

Launch strategies

Launch plan

Discuss launch plan if the product is being announced.

Promotion budget

Supply backup material with detailed budget information for review.

Promotional schedule

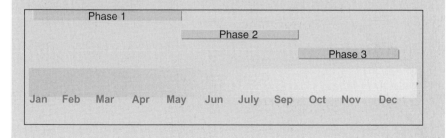

Public relations strategy and execution

Discuss:

- PR strategies.
- PR plan highlights.
- Backup PR plan, including editorial calendars, speaking engagements, conference schedules, etc.

Advertising strategy and execution

Give:

- Overview of strategy.
- Overview of media and timing.
- Overview of spending on advertising.

Other promotion

Direct marketing

Give:

- Overview of strategy, vehicles and timing.
- Overview of response targets, goals and budget.

Third-party marketing

Describe co-marketing arrangements with other companies.

Marketing programmes

Describe other promotional programmes.

Packaging and fulfilment

Product packaging

Discuss:

- Form-factor, pricing, look and strategy.
- Fulfilment issues for items not shipped directly with the product.

COGs

Summarise 'Cost of Goods' and high-level 'Bill of Materials'.

Pricing and policies

Pricing

Summarise specific pricing or pricing strategies, and compare to similar products.

Policies

Summarise policies relevant to understanding key pricing issues.

Distribution

Distribution strategy

Summarise the strategy for distribution.

Channels of distribution

Summarise the channels of distribution.

Distribution by channel

Illustrate what percentage of distribution will be contributed by each channel. A pie chart might be helpful.

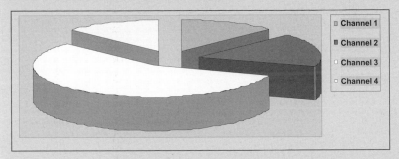

Vertical markets/segments

Discuss vertical market opportunities:

- Discuss specific market segment opportunities.
- Address distribution strategies for those markets or segments.
- Address use of third-party partners in distributing to vertical markets.

International

International distribution

Discuss:

- Distribution strategies.
- Issues specific to international distribution.

International pricing strategy

Explain the strategy for marketing within other countries.

Translation issues

Highlight requirements for local product variations.

Success metrics

List:

- First year goals.
- Additional year goals.
- Requirements for success.
- Measures of success/failure.

Schedule

18-month schedule highlights

Outline highlights of the first 18 months.

Timing

Identify timing dependencies critical to success.

Marketing schedule

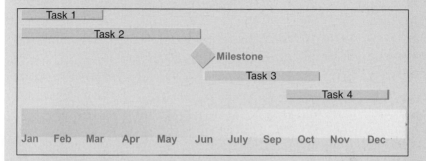

Channel strategy

Executive summary

Provide a high-level overview of channel strategy to executives.

Background

Provide information about why this channel strategy is required.

Objectives

Provide objectives that need to be achieved.

Overview

Provide a brief overview of strategy and plan.

Business objectives

Define business objectives and alignment with strategic objectives.

Objective A

Insert objective here.

Objective B

Insert objective here.

Channel schema

Overview

Describe channel schema.
Insert channel schema here.

Channels assessment

Channels available

Insert list of all available channels here.

Example:

Direct marketing

Paid advertising

- Radio
- Television
- Internet

Print

- Newspapers
- Magazines
- 'Shoppers'
- Business telephone directory
- Residential telephone directory
- Chamber of Commerce directory
- Posters

Direct mail

- Letters
- Newsletters
- Pamphlets
- Postcards
- Coupons
- Envelope stuffers

Telemarketing

- Customer service
- Direct marketing
- Inquiry handling

One-on-one selling

- Presentation materials
- Personal letters

Retail

Retail chains:

- Tesco
- Sainsburys
- Waitrose

Department stores:

- Debenhams
- John Lewis
- House of Fraser

Wholesalers

Channels economic analysis

Provide a high-level analysis.

Cost per transaction

Total Channel Expense/Number of Transactions. Examples of channel expenses include direct selling expenses (sales representative salaries, commissions, and indirect expenses such as travel) and distributor costs (broker/agent commission, distributor margin, indirect channel marketing, and promotion cost).

Channel profitability ratio

Total Expense/Total Revenue

Channel capacity

Channel Selling Unit Capacity x Number of Units

For example:

Telemarketing: 100 telemarketers x 10 units per day = 1,000 units per day capacity

Sales force: 100 sales reps x 1,000 units per week = 10,000 units per week capacity

Retail outlet: 1,000 outlets x 100 units per day = 100,000 units per day capacity

Channel productivity

Channel Selling Unit Productivity x Number of Units x Rate per Unit

For example:

Telemarketing: 100 telemarketers x 10 units per day x £10 per unit = £10,000/day

Sales force: 100 sales reps x 1,000 units per week x £10 per unit = £1,000,000/week

Retail outlet: 1,000 outlets x 100 units per day x £10 per unit = £1,000,000/day

Comparative income statement

Insert Comparative Income Statement table here. The table helps you understand the overall value of using the specific channel.

Example:

	Channel A	Channel B	Channel C
Sales: Cost of goods sold Gross profit			
Operating expenses: Selling, general and administrative R&D Nonrecurring expenses Operating profit			
Taxes			
Net profit			

Channel pros and cons

Insert channel pros and cons table here.

Example:

Channel	Pros	Cons
Channel A		
Channel B		
Channel C		

Competitors' channel assessment

Insert competitors' channel schema with competitive assessment here, one schema per competitor.

Competitor A

Insert competitor's channel schema with competitive assessment here.

Competitor B

Insert competitor's channel schema with competitive assessment here.

Summary

Summarise overall weaknesses and strengths of your competitors' channel strategies.

Preferred channel analysis

Channel selection matrix

Insert channel selection matrix here.

Preferred channel schema

Insert channel schema with identification of preferred types of channels here.

Strategic objectives alignment

Define how the recommended channel selection will align with strategic objectives.

Advantages

List the advantages of using the preferred channel.

Disadvantages

List the disadvantages of using the preferred channel.

Cost

List the cost of using the preferred channel.

Risks

Identify the risks of using the preferred channel, and identify any mitigation strategies.

Tactical plan

Include activities and timing of channel selection and management that need to occur over the next several months. The plan determines how many channel partners you want to engage and when you want to engage them.

Insert channel marketing tactical calendar/plan here.

Preferred channel positioning

Insert positioning statement here. The statement helps you determine how to competitively position your company, your products, and your sales support to the channel partners. This step helps you decide what to highlight in your initial conversations with channel partners and guides overall contract development and negotiations.

Budget

Provide highlights of how much money you want to spend on channel activities. This determination must take into account different pricing and discounting scenarios, revenue and sales forecasts for both the overall business and the specific channels, and the overall marketing budget.

Insert budget here.

Example:

Budget for Distribution Channels	
Channel training	£0.00
Channel promotions and incentives	£0.00
Channel commissions/bonuses	£0.00
Channel management	£0.00
Customer acquisition and retention	£0.00
Channel communication	£0.00
Other	£0.00

Pricing, discount, and promotional guidelines

Provide pricing, discount, and promotional guidelines. These are mostly the same for all products within the organisation. Include legal, cost, branding, and other guidelines for pricing, discount, and promotions. Determining your guidelines for these activities is critical for negotiations with and management of your channel partners.

Insert channel schema with pricing here.

Channel functions

Outline the functions you expect the channel to provide. Include more discounts for more functions.

Insert channel schema with functions by channel type here.

Communications plan for [audience name]

1. Communication, buying, and selling processes

The following diagram depicts the relationships among the communication, buying, and selling processes used with and by [audience name]. In the row beginning with 'Awareness', the communication process outlines the key communication objectives that must be met to facilitate progress in the buying and selling processes.

> You might need to modify the buying or selling process to reflect your company's or your audience's process.

Communication process

Awareness	Credibility		Interest	Preference	Selection	Loyalty
	Lead generation					

Buying process (this might need to be modified)

Identify the need	Identify alternative sources	Evaluate alternative sources	Select a short list of alternatives	Conduct a technical evaluation	Purchase	Renewal

Sales process (this might need to be modified)

	Identify opportunity	Qualify opportunity	Plan the solution	Propose solution	Provide due diligence	Close sale	Manage account

2. Communication process and the evolution of messaging

As your company moves through the communication process, you must evolve your messages to map to the information requirements of your audience. In general, as you move through the communication process, your messages should provide more detail and substantiation about your business and products. Understanding the messages that are required to support the later stages of the buying and selling processes makes it possible for you to create better messages in the earlier stages of the process. The following table summarises how and when you can evolve the essence, or the net 'takeaway', from your messages.

Communication process – net takeaway from [your company name] messages

Awareness	Credibility	Interest	Preference	Selection	Loyalty
	Lead generation				

[Your company] is in the [business type] business.

[Your company]'s business is validated by the industry and your customers.

[Your company] has a vision for and commitment to the [business type] business.

[Your company] has specific offerings and capabilities that meet customers' specific needs.

[Your company] has strong capabilities that make it competitive in the [business type] business.

You made the right choice in selecting [your company].

[Your company] delivered on its promise.

[Audience 1] buying process

Identify the need	Identify alternative sources	Evaluate alternative sources	Select a short list of alternatives	Conduct a technical evaluation	Purchase	Renewal

[Your company's] sales process

Identify opportunity	Qualify opportunity	Plan the solution	Propose the solution	Provide due diligence	Close sale	Manage account

3. Communication vehicle options

The types of communication vehicles that you use to support different stages of the buying and selling processes are dictated by the corresponding communication objectives. In the row beginning with 'Awareness', the following table outlines the key communication vehicles that support each communication objective. Not all communication vehicles are required for you to relay your message to the market effectively. It is important to understand fully how your audience finds information and to select the most appropriate communication vehicles based on your audience's preferred sources for information.

In conjunction with the preceding table, which outlines the evolution of messaging throughout the communication process, marketing communications specialists can use the following table to determine how best to focus messages in each communication vehicle.

Communication process—sample communication vehicles					
Awareness	**Credibility**	**Interest**	**Preference**	**Selection**	**Loyalty**
Press briefing or tour, or both	Press mentions	Business White Papers	Data sheets and other product collateral	Proposal templates, invoices, and other company documents	"Thank you" and "just checking in" contact by email, phone or other modes
Press releases and associated materials	Analyst quotes, references and mentions	Press articles	Feature and functionality presentations, videos and other types of demonstration	Customer references	Internet marketing
Analyst briefing or tour, or both	Customer and partner quotes and references	Analyst papers and presentations	Printed customer success stories	E-commerce website	
Company informational website	Company or product overview collateral	Conference speaker presentations	Capabilities brochure		
Industry event trade show floor participation	Company or product overview slide presentation	Competitive positioning advertising	Return on investment (ROI) tools		
Awareness advertising	Product overview demonstration on web	Direct marketing	Technical white papers		
Public relations	Press and analyst article reprints	Internet marketing	Direct-response advertising		
Internet marketing			Direct marketing		

8 The glass cliff aka the poison chalice aka the double-edged sword

"If you want anything said, ask a man. If you want something done, ask a woman."

Margaret Thatcher

> - Getting to the top.
> - Staying there.
> - Is it worth it?
> - Alternatives to being a woman in business.

What is the glass cliff? This is where women are promoted. What's wrong with that? Wait. It's promotion into a risky precarious position.

Remember how we celebrated when the CEO of Hewlett-Packard was announced as Carly Fiorina? And then numerous business surveys named her the most powerful woman in business. But as she was ousted from that position, was it just one of those things that happen in business or are we being paranoid to say she broke through the glass ceiling only to end up on the glass cliff?

Negotiating challenges for women leaders

In 2003, Martha Lagace wrote a piece in the Harvard Business School magazine about the differences between women and men on various business issues.

"Women don't have a problem developing an effective leadership style. What they do struggle with more than men, however, is claiming the authority to lead,' according to Hannah Riley Bowles and Kathleen L. McGinn. The gender gap in leadership is the focus of 'Claiming Authority: Negotiating Challenges for Women Leaders,' a chapter in the book Psychology of Leadership: Some New Approaches, edited by David Messick and Roderick Kramer (Lawrence Erlbaum Press).

Q: What are the root causes of these differences in negotiation success?

Riley Bowles*: 'What some studies do is look at salary and control for a whole bunch of things: How many years of experience the subjects had, what program they were from, what industry they went into, what job function they had, how many interviews they got, how many job offers they got, et cetera. And then you still find a gap. In the past, people thought, if there is still a gap and you've controlled for all these factors that might explain why people would get different salaries, it must be just: 'Discrimination. How else would you possibly explain it?'*

'Instead of waiting for the tectonic plates of society to shift, we would rather ask what we can do in the interim. How can we change the situation through negotiation?'

We're not saying gender discrimination doesn't exist. But we are saying, you know, there's a behavioural explanation to this as well.

When we think about what might make women walk into a negotiation with, say, lower expectations than men, one of the explanations for that comes from social psychology. It's called the entitlement effect.

That research shows that in conditions of ambiguity, if you bring men and women into the lab and you say either one of two things: 'Work until you think you've earned the $10 we just gave you,' or 'Work and then tell us how much you think you deserve,' the women work longer hours with fewer errors for comparable pay, and pay themselves less for comparable work.'

Q: How should women put this knowledge into practice?

'Be more prepared to the extent that you can reduce gender triggers. There are situations in which you can reposition the bargaining in a way that is not gendered. For example, if I see an opportunity for leadership, and believe that in that position of leadership I can attain additional value for those who would be working with me, then I can face the negotiation not as grabbing everything for myself but rather as an opportunity to increase the value for a whole bunch of people. That tends to demasculinise the situation.'

'At a deeper level, power is the ability to get on the agenda what you want on the agenda. That has more to do with access to networks and resources.

And at a completely fundamental level, power is the ability to change what it is people should even be thinking about or asking for. That is a level at which, if women actually attain power, then these struggles of getting an extra $10,000 in salary are going to be obsolete.'"

Should you ask for the promotion? Should you take one that is offered? How do you get one?

In 2004, the US company, General Electric completed a study of its 135,000 professional workers and found that women quit at a higher rate: Annual voluntary turnover of the women is 8%, vs 6.5% for the men. (2,025 more women than men a year.)

Research firm Catalyst reports that 26% of professional women who are not yet in the most senior posts say they don't want those jobs. In addition, of the 108 women who have appeared on the FORTUNE 50 over the past five years, at least 20 have left their prestigious positions, like former Pepsi-Cola North America

CEO Brenda Barnes (who moved home to Illinois to focus on her family) and former Fidelity Personal Investments president Gail McGovern. Evidently it's not that women can't get high-level jobs.

Again as *Fortune Magazine* research explains, "Andrea Jung (No. 3) says that she has never asked for a promotion. Nor has Genentech COO Myrtle Potter (No. 29). Indeed, early in her career Potter rejected two bigger jobs outright. She figured that lateral moves would better develop her talents. 'Everyone thought I was crazy – well, not crazy, but naive,' says Potter. 'Today I tell young people that they need to develop themselves broadly." (She's probably right: Lack of line management experience is the No. 1 barrier to women reaching the top, according to Catalyst.) During her 12 years at Wal-Mart, Linda Dillman (No. 28) has never asked for a promotion either. 'Promotions have come to me before I felt I was ready,' she says. Last year, when Wal-Mart CFO Tom Schoewe and then CIO Kevin Turner told Dillman that they planned to elevate her to Turner's job, she replied, 'Tell me what you're going to do if I don'at take the job.' She recalls, Their jaws hit the table. They walked me through why I had to take the job. They said, 'We really didn't have a contingency plan.'" "

Maybe we jump and are not pushed?

Maybe it is not that promotion is not a poison chalice, but women in business are not good enough? It's worth considering. Shares in companies with more women directors tended to underperform relative to the FTSE average, as suggested by *The Times* in 2004. But is it cause or effect? Are women given such roles in the expectation of tough times ahead, so that they can be replaced by a man from the board a couple of years later? Is that what happened to Carly Fiorina? Did she step right into it? Was she just keeping the seat warm for a man?

It's not detailed research, but, taking the 12-month performance of the highest ranking female CEO led FTSE 100 company (Pearson) you find the company is in the top two-thirds by share price performance.

Job title or satisfaction?

Women in business seem to want different things to men. Again, *Fortune's* research, albeit, anecdotal shows some interesting findings:

"While a reluctance to toot their own horn may hinder some women from rising as quickly as men, paradoxically it may also be one of their biggest sources of strength."

Jim Collins, author of the leadership bible *Good to Great*, observes that many women on the FORTUNE 50 share traits with the outstanding leaders he's written about, such as Kimberly-Clark's Darwin Smith and Fannie Mae's David Maxwell. (He has only written about men, by the way.)

"Any number of the greatest leaders, when offered the CEO position, responded, 'I'm not qualified' or something like that," Collins says. "It's not that they lacked ambition or were weak. They were willful, but they were always questioning themselves. They were their own hardest graders."

Of course, some women reject the offer of greater power at work because they're not willing to make personal sacrifices. Jamie Gorelick, formerly vice chairman of Fannie Mae, recalls that a few years ago CEO Frank Raines invited her to be considered for the COO job. She declined. "I just don't want that pace in my life," says Gorelick, who has a 15 year old son and a 10 year old daughter. Seeking flexibility and more variety in her work, she quit Fannie Mae this year and joined law firm Wilmer Cutler & Pickering. "The dirty little secret," Gorelick adds, "is that women demand a lot more satisfaction in their lives than men do."

Who's at home?

So who's at home then…assuming someone needs to be? That is another side of the double-edged sword.

Fortune describes one case-study:

When Anne Stevens wakes up at 4:15am to exercise, her husband Bill makes coffee and breakfast for her. She leaves the house at 6:15am, heading for the firing line of Ford Motor's turnaround effort. As head of North American vehicle operations, she is under severe pressure to reduce costs and raise quality at the 29 manufacturing plants in her division. While she's doing battle, Bill is home tending the gardens, running errands, managing the social calendar, planning the weekend and playing golf. When Anne gets home, Bill is waiting. Okay, not with her slippers, newspaper and pipe. But he does have dinner on the table. He's capable of a killer beef Wellington, though on weeknights he keeps things simple, with chicken or pasta salad. Although he'd love some scintillating conversation, he usually lets Anne flop in front of Wheel of Fortune or Jeopardy! and fall asleep. "We have a good arrangement," says Bill. "Anne works her tail off during the week. The weekends are our time.... I am the domestic executive assistant."

Domestic arrangements

In the plight to juggle a career and a family, 2.6 million women have a mere 34 minutes a day to do as they please. A further 2 million have just 47 minutes a day.

ICM Poll for Sainsburys Bank, 2004

Women, on average, do about 70% of the household work (Baxter, 2000). Only one third of women regard this as unfair.

Quoted in *Organisational Behaviour and Gender*, Ashgate, 2003 (2nd edition)

Traditional gender ideologies concerning who does what in the household continue to apply to both working class and middle class women.

Quoted in *Organisational Behaviour and Gender*, Ashgate, 2003 (2nd edition)

Women still do the majority of the household chores, despite their increased participation in the labour market. Women spend nearly 3 hours a day on average on housework (excluding shopping and childcare). This compares with the one hour 40 minutes spent by men.

UK 2000 Time Use Survey, Office for National Statistics, January 2003

Working age women with dependent children are less likely than those without to be economically active: 68% compared with 76% in spring 2003 in the UK. Conversely, men with dependent children are more likely than those without, to be in the labour force. The age of their children has no impact. Around 93% of men with dependent children are in the labour force regardless of the age of their youngest child.

Labour Force Survey, Office for National Statistics, 2003

Work-life balance

54% of women start a business so they can choose what hours they work, compared to only 35% of men.

Figures extracted from On the move: Women & Men Business Owners in the United Kingdom, IBM, February 2002

21% of women state family commitments as a reason for becoming self-employed (2% men).

Women as Entrepreneurs in Sweden and the UK, The Women's Unit, Cabinet Office, 2001

Women want flexibility in service provision to match their busy lifestyle.

Women in Business, The Barriers Start to Fall, Barclays, 2000

Twice as many women (as men) had volunteered in sports (6% compared with 3%).

Sports and Leisure Module, General Household Survey, 2002/2003

Men in full time work have more free time on a weekday than women who work full time. Men spend more time than women watching TV or a video, or listening to the radio. In contrast, women spend more time socialising than men.

UK Time Use Survey, Office for National Statistics, 2000

Earn it quick then

Okay, if you want to earn it quick – according to the US Department of Labour – these are jobs you should consider...not businesses but professions.

Top 10 jobs with highest earnings for women

Earnings gap Btwn women & men	% women in occupation	Occupation	
$1,105	9.5%	46.7%	1. Pharmacists
$974	27.3%	33.1%	2. Lawyers
$933	11.8%	10.1%	3. Engineers
$907	16.0%	28.9%	4. Computer systems analysts, scientists
$859	17.3%	37.8%	5. Teachers: college, university
$852	37.6%	27.2%	6. Physicians
$819	23.8%	59.7%	7. Administrators: education
$808	no available	67.4%	8. Physical therapists
$800	35.6%	36.5%	9. Managers: marketing, advertising, public relations
$790	26.8%	48.4%	10. Management analysts

Career planning – how much or how little?

So how much should we plan our business careers? Of course conventional wisdom is that women should plan even more intensely than men. However, Condoleezza Rice, the most powerful woman on the planet in 2005 puts it slightly differently:

"I never sat down and thought, 'I'll major in political science and Soviet studies, get a Ph.D., become a professor, serve in the first Bush administration, become provost at Stanford, and then become National Security Advisor'. Not planning has permitted me to accept the twists and turns."

Fortune Magazine 2003

Lists: who you calling arm-candy?

For those who like business power lists, here are just a selection of powerful women in business according to various publications at the time of writing:

(From *Fortune* Magazine) Doreen Toben, EVP and CFO, Verizon (No. 25); Amy Pascal, Chairman, Columbia Pictures (No. 26); Pam Strobel, EVP, Exelon, and CEO, Exelan Energy Development (No. 29); Susan Arnold, President, Personal Beauty & Feminine Care, Procter & Gamble (No. 32); Mary Kay Haben, Group VP, Kraft Foods North America (No. 33); Deb Henretta, President, Global Baby Care, Procter & Gamble (No. 34); Kathi Siefert, EVP, Kimberly-Clark (No. 38); Sallie Krawcheck, Chairman & CEO, Sanford C. Bernstein (No. 42); and Fran Keeth, President and CEO, Shell Chemicals, Royal Dutch Petroleum (No. 49).

The 25 most powerful women in banking 2004 by *US Banker*

1) **MARJORIE MAGNER,** Chairman & CEO, Global Consumer Group, **Citigroup**

2) **PEYTON PATTERSON,** Chairman, President & CEO, **NewAlliance Bancshares**

3) **AMY BRINKLEY,** Chief Risk Officer, **Bank of America**

4) **CECE SUTTON,** Evp, Head of Retail Banking, **Wachovia**

5) **COLLEEN KVETKO,** President, CEO & Chairman, **Fifth Third Bank, Florida**

6) **PATRICIA MOSS,** President & CEO, **Cascade Bancorp**

7) **DOREEN WOO HO,** President, Consumer Credit Group, **Wells Fargo**

8) **JILL DENHAM,** Vice Chair, Retail Markets, **CIBC**

9) **AVID MODJTABAI,** Evp & Head of Internet Services Group, **Wells Fargo**

10) **ELIZABETH JAMES,** Vice Chairman & CIO, **Synovus Financial**

11) **CONSTANCE LAU,** President & CEO, **American Savings Bank**

12) **SUSAN PITTMAN HORTON,** President, CEO & Chairman, **Wheatland Bank**

13) **JEAN DAVIS,** Snr Evp & Division Head for IT, eCommerce & Operations, **Wachovia**

14) **CATHY BESSANT,** Chief Marketing Officer, **Bank of America**

15) **PAMELA MONTPELIER,** President & CEO, **Strata Bank**

16) **DINA DUBLON,** Evp & CFO, **JPMorgan Chase**

17) **MARY LYNN LENZ,** President & CEO, **Slade's Ferry Bank**

18) **MAURA MARKUS,** President, Citibank N.A Retail Distribution Group, **Citigroup**

19) **BARBARA DESOER,** Chief Technology, Service & Fulfillment Exec, **Bank of America**

20) **KATHLEEN BEECHEM,** Evp, **U.S. Bancorp**

21) **CAROL NELSON,** President & CEO, **Cascade Financial**

22) **MELANIE DRESSEL,** President & CEO, **Columbia Banking System**

23) **LEEANNE LINDERMAN,** Evp, **Zions First National Bank**

24) **ROSE PATTEN,** Snr Evp, HR & Head, Office of Strategic Management, **BMO Financial**

25) **SUSAN SMITH,** Evp & CFO, **Metropolitan National Bank**

Not business...politics then?

Looking to the US, and according to *Fortune*, "Women account for 14% of the US Senate, for example, and 14% of the House of Representatives. (Women's reluctance to promote themselves is a main factor: Women are far less likely than men to 'self-identify' – that is, decide to run for office on their own rather than at the invitation of their party.) But, says Nancy Pelosi, the House Democratic leader, 'I think we'll achieve parity in Congress before we see it in corporate America. That's because the decisions aren't made by the powers that be [but rather by the voters]. It's open season, and women have more control over the outcome."

According to a 2002 study of 4,200 teenagers by Simmons College and the Committee of 200, a women's group, only 9% of girls (vs 15% of boys) anticipate careers in business. Meanwhile, business schools are struggling to attract more female students. Women make up 36% of MBA students, vs 47% of medical school and 49% of law school students. Judy Rodin, president of the University of Pennsylvania, reports that young women on her campus are saying, "'You women worked too hard. You're too strung out.' It's the single most worrisome thing to me. They might not want to fill the pipeline." Says Judy Olian, the dean of Penn State's Smeal College of Business: "In our lifetime and in our daughters' lifetime, given the numbers, there's no way there can be parity."

And what are the prospects in corporate America? Will women ever hold half of the top-level jobs (EVP and above) in major companies, vs. 8% today? Will 250 female CEOs populate the FORTUNE 500, vs eight now? Yes, declares Fiorina: "I'm willing to put money down!" Yes, says eBay's Whitman – "in 50 years, when I'm 97." Yes, says Shelly Lazarus (No. 16), the CEO of Ogilvy & Mather – though, she admits, "I'm on the lunatic fringe of optimism."

Okay, some of it is good, some bad. What now?

We asked diversity expert Tracey Carr (CEO of Eve-olution) what next?

Eve-olution is a diversity consultancy specialising in gender. The organisation was established in 2001 when, in November of that year, it ran its first Creative Female Leader programme, which is an open, two day residential course – attended by senior women leaders from Britain and Europe from all industries and professions.

Today Eve-olution works with FTSE companies and public sector bodies offering an end-to-end solution from strategic consulting all the way through to bespoke solutions such as the Leading Edge programme, (a gender-specific leadership programme currently being rolled out at Barclays), cultural diversity programmes and 'Mars & Venus at Work' workshops.

The Mars & Venus at Work workshops were established in 2004 and they came about, primarily, as a result of having developed and run women's leadership programmes and listening to the feedback from the women themselves. The women felt that whilst they had benefitted tremendously from the leadership programmes, they felt that it was only one side of the coin and that something needed to be done to work at changing the predominantly male-dominated cultures that they were, and are still, working in.

Over the last 4-5 years Tracey Carr has developed close working relationships with diversity directors, particularly in the City and particularly in investment banking. As a result of discussions and conversations with leading diversity practitioners it became clear that whilst a lot of organisations had rolled out general diversity awareness programmes, there was nothing that was specifically designed to look at culture from a gender perspective.

Finally, Eve-olution regularly do a survey called 'Women Leaders Speak Out' and research has consistently shown that people feel that there isn't enough money being spent on training men and women on how to work more effectively together.

With these three themes in mind, and working on the assumption that people seem to find it fairly easy to laugh about 'Men are from Mars, Women are from Venus' outside of work and hotly debate the topic at a dinner party, Tracey then came up with the idea of incorporating the general themes about gender differences into a workshop that was specifically designed for the City, on the basis that if people can laugh about these differences outside of work, then they ought to be able to laugh about them inside of work as well. "The theory being that if we can bring the conversation out of the closet, then we can also simultaneously raise awareness and if we can do that then hopefully we can move towards a less politically sensitive era."

"Eve-olution's design team were in research and development with the Mars & Venus concept for six months and took it to market in the middle of 2004. A Think Tank was held for high profile men and women from the City, specifically aimed at investment banking. The Think Tank session was really just an opportunity to present some ideas and to see how those ideas would be received. It became evident from that first session that men and women were starting in a completely different place with regard to their awareness around the subject. Most women seem to have high awareness, presumably this is because they've been thinking about it and talking about it for decades. There didn't seem to be the same level of awareness from the men."

"Feedback from the Think Tank session was good and many lessons were learned i.e. that because gender difference is such a politically sensitive subject we need to take people through the learning in the third person, i.e. it's not about the people in this room, it's about others out there who you may be managing or it's about selling to, or wanting to influence, the opposite sex. For some reason gender, unlike other cultures, seems to be more politically sensitive in that people feel that their own identity is being attacked."

"Another lesson learned from the initial Think Tank was that this was a subject that was going to be difficult to deliver, simply because since equal opportunities were introduced in the mid-1970s, corporations have been telling their workforce that men and women are the same. Unfortunately the interpretation of that statement is that men and women are the same, think the same, communicate the same way and therefore everybody gets treated the same. The end result of this thinking is that the only women who really make it to the very top of organisations are those who emulate the male work ethic."

"The rationale behind Mars & Venus is to bring the conversation out of the closet so that we can allow these differences to co-exist and that what we're saying is that men and women are different and that difference means equal. Moving away from the concept that equality means the same."

"As a result of the Think Tank, the workshop was fully developed, taking on board people's feedback. Incorporated into the fabric of the workshop are some role-plays because whilst a lot of people may know the information intellectually, it's quite another thing to actually experience what that means. Therefore the main fabric of the workshop incorporates different gendered cultural role-plays and, so whilst we are generalising and we realise we are generalising, we get them to practice a different gender style. That means that we encourage the men to take on a feminine way of communicating and we encourage the women to take on a male way of communicating. This is where delegates get the most benefit – getting them to have a look at gendered styles of communication, through negotiation, through influencing. This is the most difficult part of the workshop for the delegates but it's also the most beneficial. No matter how long we allow for role-play, the feedback is always that they would like more practical experience. In other words, there seems that there is a huge pent-up demand from people who know intellectually that men and women are different, but whilst they know it, they're not too sure what to do about it. So the workshops give people an opportunity to learn some new skills and practice some new ways of communicating and influencing, taking those differences into account."

"Pilots have now been completed with some of our key clients, such as Citigroup and Barclays. The workshops have been delivered for very senior staff and some of the comments that we've heard on the workshop have been extraordinary. For instance, one of the delegates commented 'I've been working in this organisation for 20 years and for the last 10 years I've been told that men and women are the same, so I've treated them the same. Now you're telling me that they're different, what do I do with this new information?'"

"It is also the responsibility of the organisation, whilst raising awareness, to be very clear about what are the objectives of the workshops and ultimately the strategy for the organisation. Fortunately, for our clients this has been a high priority workshop. It has therefore had top-level support, CEO support and board support. This is doubly important if a company is seeking to change the culture. Personally I believe that the Mars & Venus at Work workshops are an essential part of any change programme and any organisation that is serious about having a balanced workforce has to tackle people's perceptions."

"In the commercial world we really only trust conscious decision-making and a lot of our prejudices and our stereotypes are made at the adaptive conscious level. That means that we're all unconsciously discriminating as a result of rapid cognition. First impressions are generated by experiences, environment and history."

"Mars & Venus at Work goes some way towards showing people what's happening outside of their awareness and how to fix it. The way to fix it is to set up a set of associations that are positive around gender differences. Taking rapid cognition seriously and acknowledging the incredible power that first impressions play, requires that we take active steps to manage and control those impressions."

9 Being a bitch: tough business decisions

"Woman is the companion of man, gifted with equal mental capacity."

Mohandas K. Gandhi

- Leverage your assets.
- What's going to be tougher for a woman – so much for equality.

Actually, you don't need to be. We ran through the *Wall Street Journal's* top 50 women to check for two things. One, did they need to be a cold heartless bitch to make it and secondly, perhaps more importantly, for a bit of 'wow, I didn't know that inspiration'.

Name	Company	Achievement
1. Carly Fiorina Chief Executive	Hewlett-Packard (HPQ)	At the helm of H-P's controversial buyout of Compaq.
2. Margaret C. Whitman Chief Executive	eBay (EBAY)	Turned eBay from an online bazaar to an international powerhouse.
3. Andrea Jung Chairman	Avon Products (AVP)	Modernised Avon's business, boosted bottom line.
4. Michelle Peluso President, CEO	Travelocity	Tapped to run Travelocity at 32 after developing travel seller Site59.com.
5. Anne Mulcahy Chief Executive	Xerox (XRX)	Leading Xerox back from the brink of bankruptcy.
6. Rose Marie Bravo Chief Executive	Burberry Group	Revamped Burberry and is now the highest paid woman in European business.
7. Ann Fudge Chairman and CEO	Young & Rubicam	The only African-American woman to run a global advertising firm.
8. Patricia Russo Chairman and CEO	Lucent Technologies (LU)	The only woman to run a major telecommunications company.
9. Xie Qihua Chairwoman	Shanghai Baosteel	Heads China's largest iron and steel producer.
10. Debra A. Cafaro President and CEO	Ventas (VTR)	Took the health-care firm from insolvency to success.
11. Anne Lauvergeon Chief Executive	Areva	Plans to take her nuclear power and waste company public.

| 12. Ho Ching
Executive Director
and CEO | Temasek Holdings | CEO of Singapore's state investment company and also married to the Prime Minister. |
| 13. Marjorie Scardino | Pearson (PSO)
Chief Executive | Led Pearson through $7.1 billion in acquisitions to become the world's largest educational publisher. |

In line to lead

Name	Company	Achievement
1. Karen Katen President	Pfizer Global Pharmaceuticals (PFE)	Launched Pfizer's first blood-pressure pill and anti-inflammatory medicine, as well as Zoloft, Zithromax and Norvasc.
2. Marjorie Magner Chairman and CEO	Citigroup (C)	The first female MBA hired at New York Chemical Bank, she now oversees more than 150,000 employees in 54 countries.
3. Indra Nooyi President and CFO	PepsiCo (PEP)	One of the lead negotiators on the $13.8bn acquisition of Quaker Oats and its prized Gatorade brand.
4. Zoe Cruz Global Head of Fixed Income	Morgan Stanley (MWD)	Master of the bond world, she received $16.1m in compensation in 2003 – more than Morgan Stanley's CEO.
5. Brenda Barnes President and COO	Sara Lee (SLE)	She left the business world for her family six years ago, only to return as an example of the balance between work and family.
6. Sharon Allen Chairman	Deloitte & Touche	The highest ranking female in the accounting Big Four, and an advocate for women in the workplace.
7. Susan Arnold Vice Chairman	Procter & Gamble (PG)	She runs all the beauty brands and is part of a three-person pool to succeed the CEO.

8. Safra Catz Co-President	Oracle (ORCL)	Larry Ellison credits her with the idea behind the PeopleSoft hostile takeover.
9. Linda Cook Executive Director, Gas and Power, Royal Dutch/Shell Group	Shell Gas & Power	In charge of the next frontier for Shell – expanding its global natural gas and power business.
10. Gina Centrello President and Publisher	Random House Publishing Group	From proofreader of legal books to publisher of William Faulkner literature, she has climbed steadily.
11. Susan Desmond- Hellmann President, Product Development	Genentech (DNA)	An oncologist, she was the architect behind the company's cancer drug development.
12. Linda Dillman Executive Vice President	Wal-Mart Stores (WMT)	The power behind Wal-Mart's use of technology, presiding over a data-storage system second only to the Pentagon's in size.
13. Fumiko Hayashi President	BMW Tokyo	Made her way in Japan's male-dominated business world by selling so many cars she couldn't be denied.
14. Ann Moore Chairman and CEO	Time Inc.	Oversees 134 magazines that reach 300 million readers and is considered the most powerful figure in magazine publishing.
15. Sallie Krawcheck Chief Financial Officer	Citigroup (C)	Her latest promotion has Wall Street buzzing about whether it may lead to a higher role.
16. Jenny Ming President	Old Navy (GPS)	In just 10 years, has helped create one of America's biggest retail brands.
17. Vanessa Castagna CEO, Stores, Catalog, Internet	J.C. Penney (JCP)	A key player in Penney's turnaround after overhauling its merchandising process and centralising its buying operations.
18. Wu Xiaoling Deputy governor	People's Bank of China	Arguably the most influential woman in China's financial system.

19. Yang Mianmian President	Haier Group	Helped build Haier into the leading home-appliance maker in China.
20. Mellody Hobson President	Ariel Capital Management	Leads a firm that bills itself as the largest African-American money manager, with more than $18bn under management.
21. Naina Lal Kidwai Deputy CEO, India	HSBC	Has helped Indian companies raise billions at home and abroad.
22. Myrtle Potter President of Commercial Operations	Genentech (DNA)	Oversaw a major expansion at the biotech company, where revenue has almost doubled since she joined.
23. Doreen Toben Chief Financial Officer	Verizon Communications (VZ)	Executive at America's largest phone company, with 21 years' experience in different roles.
24. Yoon Song Yee Vice President	SK Telecom	At 28, she's the highest-ranking woman executive at South Korea's largest telecom service provider.

The inheritors

Name	Company	Achievement
1. Abigail P. Johnson President	Fidelity Management & Research Co.	She steered Fidelity through the share trading scandals. Now she's trying to reverse a market share slide at the nation's largest mutual fund company.
2. Ana Patricia Botin Chairwoman	Banco Espanol de Credito	A natural candidate to succeed her father at Banco Santander, she could become one of the most powerful women in global finance.
3. Shari Redstone President	National Amusements	Expected to have a growing influence at Viacom, the media conglomerate headed by her father.

4.	Maria Asuncion Aramburuzabala Vice Chairwoman	Grupo Modelo	Has successfully built upon the fortune left by her father, who founded Mexico's leading beer company, Grupo Modelo. She is Mexico's richest woman.
5.	Elizabeth Murdoch Chairman, CEO	Shine	Daughter of Rupert Murdoch, she is making it in the media world on her own and is poised to be an executive at News Corp.

The owners

Name	Company	Achievement
1. Oprah Winfrey	Harpo Inc.	Head of a successful media empire that includes her own TV show, O magazine and Oxygen, a women's cable network.
2. Kim Sung Joo	Sungjoo International, Sungjoo Design Tech & Distribution	Controls South Korea's two largest luxury goods retailers, with 90 outlets in the country.
3. Fredy Bush	Xinhua Financial Network	Built a China-based financial news service, which today distributes to more than 1,000 business clients globally.
4. Dolly Parton	Dollywood	Reigns over a rapidly expanding entertainment empire stretching from Florida to California with an estimated $200m annual revenue.

The grant giver

Name	Company	Achievement
1. Patty Stonesifer President and Co-Chairman	Bill and Melinda Gates Foundation	Manages the world's largest philanthropy, with assets of $27bn.

The watchdogs

Name	Company	Achievement
1. Elizabeth Grossman Acting Regional Attorney	Equal Employment Opportunity Commission	Led the lengthy sex-bias fight against Morgan Stanley, which resulted in a landmark $54m settlement.
2. Amy Butte Chief Financial Officer	NYSE	At 36, the youngest woman ever to become an executive vice president at the Big Board.
3. Linda Chatman Thomsen Deputy Director of Enforcement	SEC	Seen as a likely successor to the SEC's director of enforcement after overseeing the agency's probe of Enron.

Further proof

Carly Fiorina, Former Chief Executive, Hewlett-Packard

"Once installed at H-P, Ms. Fiorina immediately introduced a plan to centralise its dispersed corporate structure, cutting down its 83 business units to just a handful."

Margaret C. Whitman, Chief Executive, eBay

"Now, eBay has more than 7,600 employees and owns online marketplaces around the world through which $24 billion of merchandise was sold in 2003."

Andrea Jung, Chairman, Avon Products

"Since moving into the CEO suite five years ago, the tall, glamorous Ms. Jung – known for her signature three-strand pearl necklace and no-nonsense style – has impressed Wall Street with her strategic and marketing know-how. She has also increased the number of sales representatives to more than 4.4 million world-wide from about three million in 1999. And the company recently reported an 11% jump in third-quarter sales, fuelled by robust gains in Central and Eastern Europe and Latin America and a 15% jump in sales of beauty products."

Anne Mulcahy, Chief Executive, Xerox

"Ms. Mulcahy, 52 years old, was named president and chief operating officer of Xerox in May 2000. By the time she became CEO in July 2001, the company was in the middle of a government investigation into what turned out to be $1.4 billion of overstated earnings. Ms. Mulcahy, following Mr. Buffet advice, says she concluded that rebuilding relations with customers was key to saving Xerox. She

instituted a policy of meeting every week with some big customers, and she assigned each executive – even the general counsel – responsibility for Xerox's relationship with at least one of its top 500 accounts.

Ms. Mulcahy cut costs by outsourcing manufacturing and back-office operations, reducing employment to 60,000 today from 96,000."

Straight from the horse's mouth (no offence intended to our interviewees!)

Interview 1

We asked two women involved in business for their take on some of the issues in this chapter. Here is what they had to say – first up is Rakhee Patel of Tulsee.com, a company which produces ayurvedic eye drops.

1. Have you found any disadvantages by virtue of your gender in starting up in business?

Banks have always looked down on women starting up business. There is total lack of confidence being shown to women who wish to start a business. There is a bias towards men when it comes to interest charges, loans and general assistance given to women.

2. What strengths do you think you bring being a woman in business?

Organisational ability and long working hours without complaints are the strong points. This is as a result of looking after home and children. As a woman I also find that all of the administrative duties are carried out on a daily basis. The strongest attributes for a woman in business is that of time management whilst taking care of school runs, shopping for food and household chores.

3. What are your weakest traits by virtue of your gender do you think?

- Being too soft.
- Caring.
- Playing it 'safe' indirectly.
- Lack of self-esteem.

4. What top tips and lessons learnt would you give to a woman embarking on a new business?

- Find strength and confidence in the potency and critical value that a woman's qualities bring to the world.
- Distinguish between 'doing it' and 'being it', therefore bringing more inspiration and purpose to your leadership.

- Make a more effective contribution in your work and your life by harnessing the power of your own individual self.

- Live your passion through trust and reliance in your own intuition, wisdom and heart.

5. Do you think women are better at soft-skills, like communications, as opposed to hard-skills such as financial analysis?

Categorising women against men is not really the issue. It is a fact that men cannot multi-task.

While the woman is dealing with the financial side of running the house, she is also working, looking after the house, the kids, and basically, ensuring that the house is run efficiently. Ask a man if he could manage all of the above and he probably wouldn't know where to start!

Hence, a woman's skills, whether it is communications or financial, often start at home.

So, answering the question, I think women are better at both soft-skills such as communications and hard-skills like financial skills.

6. What would you do differently?

- Project myself in a more aggressive way whilst attending presentations.

- Be more enthusiastic during presentations.

- Be more assertive.

7. Regarding the product, do you think your choice of business line was affected by your gender?

Not really, my choice of business line has been attained with the help of my father. Having experience in the optics field and keeping in touch with past acquaintances have all helped tremendously in choosing a product such as herbal eye drops.

Interview 2

An interview with Sheetal Mehta, former Director VC Relations Microsoft, currently pursuing a PhD and creation of a Social Fund to take technology to Africa and the Middle East.

1. Have you found any disadvantages by virtue of your gender in starting up in business?

In countries like the Middle East where the perception is that women are treated poorly, I had no problems at all. In the US and in Europe, where women have more rights, I have always had to prove myself.

2. What strengths do you think you bring being a woman in business?

- A different way of thinking (i.e. using instinct sometimes and trusting my gut).
- Women are also better at team work and promoting others while men really prefer competition.

3. What is your weakest trait by virtue of your gender do you think?

Not aggressive enough.

4. What top tips and lessons learnt would you give to a woman embarking on a new business?

Be confident and always remain professional (dress, presentations and interactions).

5. When it comes to negotiating, do you think men are better? What do they do better?

I think it depends on the man....and it depends on the negotiations.

6. Do you think women are better at soft-skills, like communications, as opposed to hard skills like financial analysis?

I think women, when they are focussed, can be good at both.

7. What would you do differently?

Work with more professional women and learn from them – I have always only worked with men.

Negotiating and dealing with business partners

One of the toughest negotiations you are likely to have is with a business partner. They are your friend, but asking the tough questions is vital, and doing it early is very important. Overleaf are some of the key questions you as a shareholder with your partner, or as a representative of your company looking at a joint venture, should consider. It is a vital checklist in business provided by Tom's Law.

By having the checklist, not only do you know what to talk about, you also understand why it is important too. That not only avoids future conflicts, but ensures a more efficient, better planned business. Something which is important if the stereotype we're meant to believe about women in business as amateurs is true – and, of course, it isn't!

PLANNING JOINT VENTURES IN ENGLAND

1. Scope of the Joint Venture

1.1 What are the Joint Venturers' intentions from the outset? Is it intended to be a short term or a long term joint venture? What is the aim of the enterprise? For example, is it intended to sell the business after a number of years to an acquirer for the highest price, or to float the joint venture on a stock exchange or securities market? It may be that the joint venture is more successful than the parties envisage. It may even be necessary to specify that the company will not be floated (see "exit routes" below).

1.2 What are the objects of the joint venture company? This is important in that none of the parties to the joint venture will want the joint venture company to stray from the purpose envisaged by all or both of them at the outset. This will also help in focussing the parties' minds on the compatibility of their various aims. (Some parties may have very different aims from others, for example one party may be interested only in developing technology involved in the business, others only in financing the venture and not in developing the business. In some cases, the parties may not wish to maximise the profits available for distribution to the Joint Venturers.)

1.3 Should there be a non-competition clause (usually towards the back of the Shareholders Agreement) prohibiting the Shareholders from competing against the joint venture? If so, the scope of the joint venture becomes very important and the parties should focus on the precise area where the joint venture intends to carry on business, not only in terms of the type of activities but also the locations where they are carried on.

1.4 What contribution is each of the parties to the joint venture putting in to the business?

2. Financing

2.1 After the initial share capital is injected, how will the working capital of the joint venture company be funded? If disagreement arises over this and the company lacks funding, the business may effectively be frozen until the disagreement is resolved. Alternatively a shareholder who refused to contribute further capital can be diluted.

2.2 Debt equity ratio. Will the joint venture company take borrowings from banks, and is it necessary to specify in the agreement how the loans will be taken? i.e. whether they will be secured or unsecured, what charges will be given and the term i.e duration of the loan.

2.3 Are there to be shareholder loans? In many joint ventures the shareholders will themselves lend money to the joint venture company and the Shareholders Agreement would normally specify the amounts, interest rates etc.

2.4 Will the shareholders give guarantees to banks and other lenders? Frequently the parties will want to resist giving guarantees to banks, but if they do, whilst their liability to the bank will be joint and several, as between the shareholders, cross indemnities may need to be given in order to keep their liability pro rata to their shareholdings.

2.5 A contribution of assets by shareholders in return for shares is permitted for private companies, but valuation of the assets needs careful consideration.

3. Management

3.1 Who will "manage" the joint venture? What protections will there be for the shareholders? It is easier to achieve "negative control" in drafting the management provisions of a joint venture agreement, than to draft positive directions for the joint venture company.

(a) The easiest control to put into place is a list of actions on which unanimous decisions (or decisions by a specified majority) are required from the Shareholders, otherwise the action cannot be taken.

(b) The second level of control which is also easy to implement is a list of actions on which a unanimous decision (or a decision by a specified minority) is required from the Directors, without which the action cannot be implemented.

(c) A statement should normally be included in the joint venture agreement restricting the company to carrying on only the business (pursuing only the objects - see 1.2 above). This can be defined in the Joint Venture/Shareholders Agreement (or if the parties want more detail, can be set out in a business plan).

(d) Restrictions on what may be done at the level of day to day operational management, whilst protecting "pure investor" shareholders, can be unduly restrictive and are usually best omitted and left to trust. It is possible to provide for an executive board or an executive committee which will carry out day to day management decisions, but many investors are unhappy to delegate powers to such an executive committee.

4. Share Structure

4.1 In an English company the share rights are usually defined in the Articles of Association. It is possible to have preference shares, which normally participate in dividends on a preferential (frequently cumulative) basis. They can be made redeemable, frequently after a certain number of years, to give management time to produce enough profits to repay pure investor shareholders. Preference shares could also be made convertible, so that if the company defaults on its interest or redemption obligations, they automatically convert into ordinary shares, thus diluting the management (assuming that the management hold the ordinary shares). Another solution would be rather than converting the ordinary shares on a default they can be given increased voting rights enabling the preference shareholders if necessary to out vote the ordinary shares and change the board of directors.

4.2 Alternatively, debentures can be issued which are effectively debt instruments of the company and do not have the characteristics of share capital. Being debt instruments they are repayable. It may be important to the investor to have debt and not equity. From the Company's point of view the balance sheet will however look worse with debt rather than equity. Debt instruments can also be made convertible.

4.3 Different classes of shares may be issued and each shareholder or class of shareholder can be given a different class of shares. This can be used to ensure that one representative of each class of shares is present at shareholders meetings.

5. Earnings

5.1 How do the parties intend to take profits out of the joint venture? Is this intended to be by way of salaries, dividends, management charges, licence fees (royalties) or loan repayments.

5.2 Dividends: there are various ways in which the profitability of the joint venture company can be managed and this is of particular importance to the minority shareholders, who will not have control over the resolutions to declare dividends. This can be regulated either by having a clearly defined policy, for example to declare and pay maximum dividends; or by providing that only a stated percentage of after tax profits will be declared as a dividend; or that the declaration of dividends shall follow the company's business plan (which will have to be updated from time to time.

6. Deadlock

6.1 Do the parties want to have a 50:50 shareholding? It is possible, if desired, to create a position where the company cannot effectively carry on business unless the parties agree. This is done by providing that no resolution can be passed either at the level of the board of directors or at shareholder level, and thus no decision can be taken at all, unless each of the joint venturers votes in favour of the resolution.

6.2 If this is the case, then some mechanism should be built into the joint venture agreements providing for a means of breaking the deadlock. This is frequently done by triggering the exit route, i.e. the pre-emption or share transfer provisions of the agreements.

7. Exit Routes

7.1 What happens if one party wants to sell? Allied to the overall aim of the enterprise (see 1.1 above) is the question of the exit routes. An obligatory sale after a number of years would be unusual, but by no means illogical. This would give a very different flavour to the venture than the usual pre-emption provisions in the Shareholders Agreement. On the other hand the usual form of pre-emption provisions, if drafted in the way the parties want, may provide precisely the means of exiting which is desired.

7.2 The most common form of pre-emption clause provides for a selling shareholder to offer his shares to all the other shareholders, either at an offer price chosen by the seller or, if requested by one of the other shareholders, at a value certified by the auditors. (This can be a simple "fair value" or a specific valuation formula) If more than one shareholder accepts the offer, the seller must sell to them pro rata to their existing shareholdings, to preserve the status quo between the other shareholders. If the offer is not accepted the selling shareholder is free to sell to a third party at the offer price or the valuation price.

7.3 An alternative to the above is the so-called "Russian Roulette" or "Texas Shootout" clause (usually when there is only one other shareholder - these clauses tending to favour two party joint ventures), whereby the selling shareholder chooses a price and the other shareholder has the option of either buying the seller's shares at that price, or selling his own shares at that price - in other words it can go either way. This is intended to force the selling shareholder to choose a fair price.

7.4 A third alternative is what is called the "Drag along" which recognises that it is frequently difficult to find a buyer for a partial shareholding in a joint venture company. There are various versions of this clause, but a common one allows any shareholder who wishes to sell, to force a sale of all of the shares of the company to a third party. One version works by providing that the seller can contract to sell the whole company: however, the contract must be conditional and the condition is that within a specified time after signing the contract the selling shareholder must offer his own shares to all the other shareholders at the same price (scaled down on a pro rata basis) as that offered by the third party. If the other shareholders do not take this offer up the contract can be completed with the third party and the company can be sold. Other variations include "Tag along" which allows shareholders to force another shareholder who wishes to sell, to sell their shares also.

APPENDIX: SUMMARY NOTES ON :

SHARE CAPITAL STRUCTURE, TYPES OF SHARE CAPITAL, COMPLAINTS AND SOLUTIONS.

Share Capital Structure

1. Key percentages - 25.01% - 50.01% - 75%:
    (a) 75% will pass special and extraordinary resolutions therefore a 25.01% shareholding allows the blocking of special and extraordinary resolutions. The principal matters for which a special / extraordinary resolution are required are changing the name, the Memorandum or Articles of Association, reduction of share capital, purchase or redemption of a company's own shares, liquidation, variation of rights of a class of shareholders ("class rights").
    (b) 50.01% gives control for the purpose of passing all other resolutions including resolutions to appoint and remove Directors; ie control of the Board.

Different types of share capital

2. Cumulative/non-cumulative preference shares which frequently do not carry voting rights. Useful way of giving a shareholder a fixed preferential participation in profits, without participation in ordinary dividends, and often without voting rights.
3. Convertible preference shares give a right to convert, usually to ordinary shares having full voting rights.
4. Deferred shares with reduced voting/dividend rights. These can also be made convertible.
5. Redeemable shares, normally redeemable at the end of a fixed term. Encourage outside investors who will be more confident of a market for their shares.
6. Non-voting shares would normally carry voting rights in respect of a variation of class rights, which essentially means any alteration of their rights.
7. Ordinary shares usually carry full rights of participation in income and capital (ie. after any preference shares); normally carry voting control in general meetings.

Complaints

8. Most common complaints made by minority shareholders about management are:
    (a) They are excluded from management.
    (b) Little or no participation in profit sharing / excessive remuneration being paid to majority.
    (c) Information about company's affairs too limited (at law shareholders

have no legal rights to see board minutes or company's accounts except for annual audited accounts).

(d) Lack of involvement in important decisions.

(e) Inability to prevent their shareholding being diluted.

(f) No ability to sell shares.

(g) No market for their shares (the major disadvantage of investing in a private company).

(h) Majority are unfairly operating / involved in competing businesses.

(i) Bad management by the majority.

(j) Majority have used voting power to alter or interfere with minority's rights.

(k) Tax advantages are available to the majority which minority do not have: 75% shareholdings have right to surrender trading losses and use group relief provisions; 51% shareholder can surrender advance corporation tax downwards to subsidiary.

Solutions

9. (a) (Management involvement) Right to appoint nominated director or to be employed as director under service agreement / veto on certain management or policy decisions / specified quorum of Directors required for all/some decisions.

(b) (Profit Sharing) Service agreements for majority / service agreements for minority (such service agreements not to be varied without agreement of minority)/ entrenched dividend policy written into shareholders agreement / shareholders agreement can provide for any "remuneration" (widely defined) to be apportioned between majority and minority.

(c) (Information) Right to information in shareholders agreement / right for nominated director to disclose to his nominating shareholder.

(d) (Important decisions) Difficult to frame this in a positive manner, much easier to include "negative control" in shareholders agreement by listing decisions which cannot be taken without unanimous consent. Even so minority cannot force a decision, only prevent a decision.

(e) (Dilution) Usual to include power of veto on any decision to issue more shares so as to dilute. If dilution is contemplated and accepted in specific circumstances this can be incorporated in business plan / shareholders agreement.

(f) (Transfer of shares) There are a variety of shareholders agreement clauses dealing with pre-emption provisions which are well established. Usually involve a) right of first refusal in favour of other shareholders before sale of any shares to third party / put or call option in certain circumstances. Consider carefully fixed valuation formula (often based on accounts) / statement that price and terms to be same as offered to third party. See (g) below.

(g) (No market for shares) Restriction on majority from selling to outsider without forcing outsider to make an offer for minority's shares / controlled re-purchase by company of its own shares in contract in specific circumstances / create redeemable shares which minority can sell back to the company. Also worth noting that institutional investors will often buy out minority shareholders especially if substantial further investment contemplated.

(h) (Competing interests of majority) Restrictive covenants /

confidentiality undertakings / service agreements / express clauses in shareholders agreements.

(i) (Bad management) Restrictions on (inter alia): buying and selling assets only at best price / not dealing otherwise on arms length terms / insuring assets to full replacement value / other negative obligations.

(j) (Alteration of minority rights) These can be protected by a voting agreement if the rights are in the Articles or they can be entrenched in the shareholders agreement.

(k) (Tax advantages of majority) - these rights can be restricted by contract so as not to be possible / require minority's consent; if company is a close company, shareholders agreement can require distributions to be made to members.

Source: Tom's Law (www.tomslaw.com)

Women take on the suit

Rebellion against the collar and tie is the latest skirmish in the battle of the sexes. Men around the country are griping that women in the workplace are not forced to maintain the same sartorial standards. In March 2003, Matthew Thompson, an administrative assistant at Stockport's Jobcentre Plus, told an employment tribunal that it amounted to sexual discrimination.

So it seems the wheel of working fashion has come full circle.

Just over a century ago, it was professional women who were only too keen to ape their male colleagues. Since then, women have become increasingly adept at using the subtleties of dress to reinforce their own role in the workforce. "Fashion has to do with ideas, the way we live, what is happening," designer Coco Chanel once said.

In the late 19th century, middle class, educated women first began to wear suits as a symbol of their professionalism. In its earliest incarnation, the suit consisted of a tailored jacket and skirt, which didn't necessarily match. Later, they were both made of the same material.

In the 1890s, a suit made women look serious, and capable of doing a man's job. Early adopters, however, were ridiculed in the press. Male caricaturists portrayed the suits as sexless, shapeless clothes worn by unattractive women in spectacles. So much so that the Suffrage movement urged its members to wear their best clothes on the marches in 1908.

In the Victorian era the suit also helped to differentiate white-collar workers travelling home on the tram from prostitutes. Men were unaccustomed to seeing women unchaperoned on the street, but the suit sent out the right message. It meant a woman out on business – "hands off!"

Many of these professional women were journalists, book keepers, typists and employees of the telegraph service. Although they were rarely paid as much as men in the same job, their buying power did not go unnoticed.

Advertising to women began to flourish at the same time as the suit, tempting the new workforce with skincare, hair dye, medicines and make-up.

That other borrowed male garment – a pair of trousers – was not so quick to find its way into the woman's working wardrobe. Even though female munitions workers started wearing trousers during World War I, in peacetime trousers were strictly for leisure.

This taboo has taken time to die out. As recently as five years ago, most companies preferred female employees not to wear trousers as part of their corporate uniform. Richard Branson, for example, is said to prefer his female staff to wear skirts.

The trouser suit started to become socially acceptable in the late 1960s, when it was popularised by designer Yves Saint Laurent. But it was not until the late 1980s and early 1990s that it crossed over into the working wardrobe.

As women became more established and occupied powerful positions, they had the confidence to wear the trousers.

10 Baby, baby

"The great question that has never been answered, and which I have not yet been able to answer despite my thirty years of research into the feminine soul is 'what does a woman want?'"

Sigmund Freud

"The history of men's opposition to women's emancipation is more interesting perhaps than the story of that emancipation itself."

Virginia Woolf

- Is it a bird, is it a plane, no it's superwoman: the triple C.
- 'We'd promote you but you'll start having kids' – how to avoid the gender bias trap without suing everyone in sight: City women insights.
- How to sue everyone in sight: the employment lawyers insights.

Can you be a triple C?

Can you have career, cash and children? More than 250,000 British women with teenage children earn more than £50,000 a year, according to research from internet bank Egg. Nearly a third of these mums earn more than £100,000 and one in six British women with children under the age of 17 now earns more than her partner.

Egg surveyed 500 working mothers from all walks of life and found that their average annual income was £21,221.

According to figures from the Female FTSE Index report produced by the Cranfield Centre for Developing Women Business Leaders, the number of female-held directorships increased by nine to 110 in 2004. These 110 seats are held by 96 women. In 2004 they saw the biggest jump in new director appointments going to women with the numbers rising over the last four years from 13.4% in 2003 to a remarkable 17%. 69 of the UK's top 100 companies now have women directors.

As Head of Investment Business 3i, Baroness Sarah Hogg is the FTSE 100's only chairwoman. Dame Marjorie Scardino became the first – and currently only – female chief executive of a FTSE 100 company when she took over the running of the Pearson media group in 1997.

In July 2003, WH Smith plc announced the appointment of Kate Swann as Group Chief Executive. Swann is 38 and is married with two children. She met her husband when she was a schoolgirl working as a waitress while on holiday. She reportedly earned £1.29m in her first year in the job, including a £500,000 sign-on fee and £220,000 bonus.

Cranfield's listings show that companies with the highest percentage of women on the board include Centrica, with three women directors, and J. Sainsbury with two. In both companies women comprise a third of the non-executive directors. (Centrica has moved up from 10th place last year.) AstraZeneca comes third with four female directors making up 31% of its board. In joint fourth place are British Airways and Pearson with three women each making up a quarter of their boards.

Summary of females in the FTSE Indices

Clearly, kids and success are not incompatible:

	2004	2003	2002	2001	2000
Female held directorships	110	101	84	75	69
Female executive directorships	17	84	15	10	11
Female non-executive directors	93	84	69	65	60
Women holding FTSE directorships	96	88	75	68	60
Companies with at least one woman director	69	68	61	57	58
Companies with multiple women directors	29	22	17	15	12
Companies with two women directors	19	13	11	12	14
Companies with no women directors	31	32	39	43	42

Source: Cranfield

A raw deal for pregnant women

The Equal Opportunities Commission (EOC) warned that many pregnant women face discrimination and, in some extreme cases, unemployment, unless the Government takes action.

The EOC has criticised the Government for failing to provide the necessary support to families and employers or improve awareness over the issue of pregnancy discrimination in the work place.

Entitled 'Tip of the Iceberg', the report investigated discrimination against pregnant women at work and proposed a number of measures designed to promote equal opportunity.

Published in September 2004, the study also reviewed how responsibilities, costs of pregnancy and benefits are shared among employers, the state and individual mothers.

Julie Mellor, Chair of the EOC, said, "Every year around a thousand women in the England and Wales go so far as to take legal action claiming they were sacked because they were pregnant, and that is likely to be just the tip of the iceberg."

"Others face pay cuts, demotion, hostile treatments or are made to work in an unsafe environment. The impact on these women's lives and on the health of their baby can be disastrous."

Proposals for change are geared towards a better understanding of employment law and calls for more support from the Government.

These include a statement outlining rights and responsibilities, extensions to the three-month time limit for filing a pregnancy-related employment tribunal claim and better childcare and parental leave to reduce the difficulties of returning to work.

Mellor said, "It's not just families that benefit when pregnancy at work is managed successfully – it's in everyone's interests. Most families now rely on two incomes."

"Women make up nearly half of the workforce and make a major contribution to the success of individual businesses and the economy. We cannot afford to lose their skills and experience."

With 350,000 working women in the UK becoming pregnant each year, the effects on productivity within small businesses can be disastrous. However, the EOC argues that with the right Government legislation, such discrimination can be avoided.

Solutions suggested by the EOC include extra financial support to spread the cost of pregnancy and free mediation services to help employers and employees resolve disputes.

However, with more than a third of employers believing pregnancy poses undue cost burdens on their business, such proposals may be a lot harder to implement into the workplace.

Know your responsibilities

Many women know from bitter experience that they have been held back in the workplace through inflexible practices and outdated attitudes to family responsibilities.

Whilst only an employer with a penchant for law suits would ever put it as crudely as 'we'd promote you but you'll start having kids', ask many men responsible for employment decisions or speaking amongst other men and they will gradually disclose that it can be incredibly costly and inefficient to hire or promote a woman who will then not be participating in the workforce through maternity leave.

So guess what? Women may never be given the opportunity in the first place. Don't just take our word for it – studies confirm it. Before going into your rights, let's look at the reality.

Michelle Rimmer, a teacher from Liverpool who was made redundant without her knowledge whilst on maternity leave, received £20,000 compensation in a settlement with her employer who admitted discrimination on the grounds of pregnancy.

Julie Mellor, Chair of the EOC, said, "New research has shown around 30,000 working women are sacked, made redundant or leave their jobs due to pregnancy discrimination. This case highlights the need for better dialogue between employers and women when they go on maternity leave. Our investigation into pregnancy discrimination at work is calling for an end to discrimination. We are working with the Government, employers, trade unions and others to find ways of improving communication as part of a package of measures to help employers and women manage pregnancy at work successfully."

Of the 441,000 women that are pregnant at work each year, the EOC's research report reveals that:

- Overall, almost half of women who had worked while pregnant said they experienced some form of discrimination because of their pregnancy.
- Over a fifth said they lost out financially due to discrimination.
- 1 in 20 were put under pressure to hand in their notice when they announced their pregnancy.

The EOC has found that employers who have experienced pregnancy in the last three years are more positive about it than those who have not – indicating that fear of the unknown is part of the problem.

Carol Bonehill won a similar case of unfair dismissal due to pregnancy at the Employment Tribunal on 30th April 2003. After the birth of her second baby she was delighted to receive a congratulations card from her employer. However, enclosed with the card was a redundancy letter and her P45.

But it gets worse

You don't have to be pregnant to be 'up the duff'! The gender pay gap is defined as the percentage difference in hourly earnings between men and women. Figures published by the Office of National Statistics, show that the gap for full-time workers is 18%, and the gap between part-time workers is 40%. Both figures are now at their lowest since the Equal Pay Act came into force in 1975. At that time, the gap between men and women's hourly average earnings in full-time employment was 30%.

According to the Annual Survey of Hours and Earnings (ASHE), women who work full-time earn £412 on average per week, compared with £531 for men. The reason for this difference can be explained by the fact that men typically earn more per hour than women and also that women in full-time employment typically work on average two hours less per week than their male counterparts.

In April 2003, women's full-time average annual earnings passed the £20,000 barrier for the first time ever, and in 2004 they stood at £21,730. Men's full-time average annual earnings were £30,131 in 2004.

The largest pay gap (27.5%) is for skilled trades occupations. Next come managers and senior officials with a gap of 21.4% and finally process, plant and machine operatives at 18.3%. The smallest pay gap of all is in the highest paid sector, professional occupations, and is currently 3.5%.

It is against the law to pay women less than a man for the same or similar work and women have the right to find out how much male colleagues are being paid for doing the same job.

Virgin Money's 'Show Me the Money' study found that 45% of Britain's bosses admire workers who fight for more money.

Time management

Well, women pride themselves on being able to multi-task, if not parallel park! Fine then, but just in case women are better at parallel parking than the time management skills that come with multi-tasking (or for the boys sneaking a peek at this book) here are some top tips on time management. Why a list? So it can be read quickly and save time of course...keep up!

1. Planning time: set aside time each day to plan the day and prioritise tasks.
2. Chunk the big stuff: if it is a big difficult task, take a small part of it and start on that immediately. The feeling of power of having made a dent will give you momentum.

3. Delegate: find people to do the things which are not worth your time doing. If you don't know what that is – then work out how much your time is worth per hour. That should give you some idea of whether someone else should be doing some of those menial tasks. You could hire a part-time working parent to come in weekly to sort out bills, get a cleaner – whatever you need.

4. Split your day into time slots. Use a daily calendar, as you can find on Microsoft Outlook, to plan.

5. Get accurate: many people are bad time managers and bring on extra stress because they underestimate how long it will take to do a task. When you make your daily log of tasks, check how much time they actually took.

6. Make sure you are spending your time allocation correctly. When you analyse your log, are you spending 60% of your time on planning and development and 15% on routine tasks or is it the other way around? 25% should be spent on ongoing projects.

7. Allow more travel time: arriving late and unprepared to meetings? You might be scheduling too little time to get too and from meetings. If so, you're adding extra stress.

8. Phones: don't give your mobile number out to everyone, and don't take voice messages on it. You will spend your life checking them. Instead put a message on the phone that callers can only leave text messages only. It's surprising how many calls suddenly become unimportant enough not to leave a text message, saving you time not having to check your messages 100 times a day.

9. Use a message service: for your office phone use a 24/7 message taking service from a company like www.call2save.co.uk which takes messages and then emails or texts you, so you can be in charge of your time.

10. You, of course, have a daily to-do list. I add '1' for important tasks, '2' for not so important and '3' for can wait to quickly help prioritise.

11. Don't try to concentrate without a break for more than an hour – otherwise your creativity and productivity will decrease.

12. Business productivity needs you to eat healthily, sleep regularly and exercise. Okay, this one we're better at preaching than doing too!

13. Clear your desk at night, so in the morning you actually feel like coming to work.

14. Email: file messages for reference, delete, delegate or action. I use a purple flag for non-urgent ones needing longer replies and handle those on train journeys etc.

15. Reading: unsubscribe to things you do not read and skim read the rest. If it is information you may need, tear out the piece and keep it otherwise ditch it.

16. Blank screen? Need to write a report and don't know where to begin? Get a template from Microsoft Word online or from a Google search.

17. Use a phone on which you can get emails e.g. a Blackberry or similar

18. Use a phone, PDA in one so your phone has your appointments and synchronises with your email program so you don't have lots of papers.

19. Use websites such as www.streetmap.co.uk for printing directions and locations. Drag and drop locations into the PDA so you have all the numbers in case you need to call ahead if you are going to be late.

20. For travel, buy a light laptop with a built-in wireless modem.

21. Parkinson's Law: "Work expands to fill the time available."

22. The costliest expenditure is time.

We can't afford to take the attitude of Douglas Adams: "I love deadlines. I like the whooshing sound they make as they fly by." Equally, we do not want to be in a situation where we agree with the saying that 'if it weren't for the last minute, nothing would get done'.

At the end of the day remember: "Time flies like an arrow, fruit flies like a banana" (as Groucho Marx once said).

Halifax Bank of Scotland case study

According to the outstanding Aurora Women's Network (www.busygirl.com) founded by Glenda Stone, Halifax Bank of Scotland (HBOS) has '35 items of evidence' about attracting, retaining and advancing women. So what should you look for in an employer and how do you improve yours? Use these as a benchmark.

How do the organisation's core values relate to the advancement of women?

At HBOS we aim to have the best and most highly motivated workforce. It is important, therefore, that our colleagues are able to recognise a culture where everyone is encouraged to develop to their full potential. We want our colleagues to be strong advocates of our business strategy, our employment policies and our products. Committed colleagues are motivated colleagues, keen to provide our customers with the best financial solution to their financial needs.

Recruiting and retaining the best talent, not only meets our business needs, but is consistent with our values of fairness and respect, which we believe keeps HBOS at the vanguard of leading edge employers.

Why is the advancement of women, of economic importance to the organisation?

The Equality and Diversity Strategy is aligned with the objectives of HBOS and is formerly embedded within our stakeholder goals. Putting Equality and Diversity into practice will mean that the people inside our business will be a reflection of the people outside it – our customers. We believe it is our individual differences that give HBOS a creative edge but it requires everyone's commitment, co-operation and determination to make it succeed.

Women form the majority of our workforce

HBOS is committed to ensuring equality at work for women – in fact, women make up 64% of our workforce so just about everything we do impacts on them. Our whole approach towards Equality and Diversity is about achieving business excellence through valuing and respecting individual differences – whatever they are and benefitting from the advantages they bring. This ensures that we continuously work towards having the best and most highly motivated workforce, that we retain the best talent and that we continue to meet the needs of our business.

What evidence shows senior managers in the organisation support the advancement of women?

Social, moral, political and business drivers underpin our Equality and Diversity Strategy. We recognise that top-level support and commitment is key to its success and so we have ensured that the Strategy has management support from our Chief Executive downwards. It is based on a dual approach to not only benefit from a diverse workforce but also to capitalise on sales opportunities within diverse communities.

Support from the CEO – James Crosby

Our Chief Executive, James Crosby, personally chairs the Diversity Leadership Forum – an HBOS-wide co-ordinating body consisting of senior business and HR managers, tasked with driving our diversity vision.

What policies support women's advancement and what proves they aren't just rhetoric?

At HBOS, we are committed to creating a safe environment through our organisational policies which encourage openness, honesty and mutual respect, and where colleagues can constructively challenge and ask questions. We offer Equality of Opportunity for everyone to develop their skills and knowledge, and to enjoy fulfilling careers.

Ensuring our policies are not just a piece of paper

To ensure we maintain our portfolio of leading edge policies we externally benchmark. Our performance achieved Platinum Standard in the Opportunity Now Gender Equality benchmarking survey for 2004. This is the highest accreditation possible, scoring 96% – 18% above our sector norm.

What evidence demonstrates that the organisation truly values women's talent?

Our Equality and Diversity Strategy ensures that we value the talent of all our staff and we firmly believe that individual differences give HBOS a creative edge. As women form over 64% of our workforce we could not progress without our valuable female talent.

Women In Business

Our Women in Business team are currently unique in the retail banking sector – offering dedicated support to female entrepreneurs and business women. For full details visit our web pages at:

www.bankofscotland.co.uk/women

where we offer an invaluable range of materials to help women who are starting up or already run their own business. We've used our findings along with our expertise to pinpoint and provide the type of solutions and support women's businesses might need to succeed. The range of resources available include Facts and Figures, Top 10 Tips, Case Studies, Guides and Reports, Useful Links and Big Fish – an online magazine for women to help them develop their business potential.

How does the organisation progressively attract and position themselves with women?

Working on gender equality has enabled Halifax Bank Of Scotland to become more responsive to the needs of colleagues and customers. A portfolio of enhanced equality policies and more effective resourcing has increased our appeal to a wider range of applicants, which continually enhances our internal employee relations. At HBOS, we offer 'Standards of Excellence' which we have designed to ensure we attract the best colleagues, and that then, our colleagues receive the best. In particular, we have developed an excellent range of flexible options to support new parents, with a view to appealing to and therefore retaining more of our maternity leavers.

How does the organisation monitor equal pay, fair rewards & recognition?

At HBOS, providing equal pay for equal work is central to fair reward. We recognise that it is also one of the key factors affecting motivation and relationships at work. We believe that any doubts about the equity of our pay practices will result in reduced productivity and commitment, as well as potentially damaging our corporate reputation and stakeholder relationships.

Equal pay practices are therefore, an essential component of our colleague proposition to attract and maintain a motivated and valued workforce.

How does the organisation ensure women have real choices about work/life responsibilities?

HBOS is committed to ensuring a healthy work/life balance for all its colleagues and encourages them to agree flexible working arrangements informally with their line managers. We also have a formal flexible working policy that enhances the support and choice through which our colleagues may request a new working pattern or revised flexible arrangement.

Flexible working options

The range of flexible working arrangements vary by business area and include:

- Job share
- Reduced hours/part-time
- Home-working
- Flexible hours
- Staggered hours
- Career break
- Term-time working
- Compressed hours
- Annualised hours

We also have a wide range of flexible working options such as 9-day fortnights, 4-day weeks, home working and flexible work locations. A comprehensive Employee Assistance Programme also provides a confidential information and counselling service for our colleagues. A programme of continuous improvement to enhance services for people with a disability and to generate more business ownership is ongoing.

What parental & care support initiatives exist and how is their effectiveness monitored?

We understand the importance of providing proper care and support for our colleagues who make the decision to start a family or who already have children to ensure that they can successfully balance family life with a career, should they choose to do so.

Maternity provisions

The Company's maternity provisions exceed legal obligations and allow colleagues up to 52 weeks' maternity leave, irrespective of length of service. In addition, it includes a right to time off for ante natal care, maternity pay, as well as being able to return to the same job or similar. The company also recognises that whilst most women continue to work normally during pregnancy, it is important that a flexible and supportive approach is taken, therefore all women have the right to paid time off for ante natal care and requests for time off to attend classes may be made at the recommendation of a doctor, midwife or health visitor. If classes cannot be attended in the evening then reasonable paid time off should be allowed to enable attendance during the day, wherever possible.

Following the birth of their baby, colleagues can also take up to 13 weeks' Parental Leave, in addition to the leave detailed above. Colleagues may return to work on the same conditions, hours, level and salary as before yet, a flexible and supportive approach will be taken to accommodate any request from a colleague wishing to return on different terms to those before maternity leave.

Childcare Support Scheme

HBOS is committed to helping colleagues who have family responsibilities and recognise that for many working parents, balancing the demands of work and family responsibilities is not easy. Childcare is a very personal issue and the ultimate choice of childcare rests with each parent. The HBOS Childcare Support Scheme offers a free, confidential, practical and caring service to help colleagues resolve their childcare issues on an individual basis. There are two elements to the scheme:

- Childcare Matching Service.
- Family Advice and Information Helpline.

The scheme has been designed to help colleagues make an informed choice – safe in the knowledge that they have considered all the options and made the right choice for their family. Family Matters, an established provider of childcare support, operates the scheme on behalf of HBOS. Their team of specialist advisers will help colleagues understand the range of childcare available, guide them through the services and offer support and advice throughout the enquiry.

How is fair promotion guaranteed & access to dispute processes available without penalty?

HBOS is committed to the dignity at work and fair treatment of all colleagues. In particular, we are committed to ensuring that the following underpinning principles apply to all our employment policies and that they are adhered to. The following principles have been agreed with our unions, ACCORD and UNIFI:

- Promoting dignity at work within an open and non-hierarchical culture.
- Supporting the balance between work and personal life.
- An integrated approach, where appropriate, across the company as a whole.
- Simplicity and transparency.

HBOS will help in trying to resolve any grievance issue colleagues may have in connection with their employment and will undertake fair and objective investigation of any complaint.

What do the stats & trends show when it comes to attracting, retaining & advancing women?

HBOS are strongly committed to recruiting more women into the managerial positions within the banking sector. We have made immense progress in this area as ten years ago only 7% of women held senior management positions, now the figure stands at 27%.

Gender statistics

The following statistics demonstrate our open approach to the gender mix we have at HBOS. We are actively trying to improve upon the number of women in senior level positions through progressing and advancing their talent.

- 67% of our colleagues are female.
- 64% of colleagues at junior management level are female.
- 46% of colleagues at middle management level are female.
- 27% of colleagues at senior management level are female.
- 24% of our colleagues work part time.
- 93% of part-time colleagues are female.

What external awards & recognition have the organisation & their women employees received?

HBOS are extremely proud of the significant number of awards we have received in recognition of our commitment and work towards achieving a diverse workforce and a great environment for all our colleagues to work in.

Opportunity Now

With over 67,000 employees, HBOS has an award-winning diversity policy. Having been awarded the Gold Standard in Business in the Community's Opportunity Now benchmarking survey in 2001, 2002 and 2003, we are immensely proud of successfully achieving the highest level possible, Platinum, in 2004.

HBOS also won the Opportunity Now Private Sector Award for Gender Diversity in April 2005 with a submission comprised of HR activities and the Women in Business programme.

CBI/Real Business First Women Awards

The HBOS Women in Business team won the Corporate Award at the inaugural awards in June 2005.

How it looks – a state of the female working nation

Below are just some snippets from major UK employers on their statistics regarding women employees – to give us a flavour of the 'state of the nation'.

Accenture, United Kingdom
Stats & trends
Summary

We currently have over 29,000 women building their careers at Accenture globally. This represents around 26% of our total workforce. However, we realise that this figure is not sufficient and we are working to attract more female graduates to apply every year through female-targeted advertising and events at universities.

British American Tobacco, United Kingdom
Stats & trends
Summary

We are continuously developing new opportunities for female talent. Women are particularly encouraged to apply for senior positions.

Citigroup, United Kingdom
Stats & trends
Representation of women at senior management level is growing

Whilst, in line with many of our competitors in the financial sector, the Corporate and Investment Bank is predominately but not exclusively, male dominated, however, with almost 40% of our workforce female, Citigroup is keen to recognise and reward their contribution. Based on figures for 2002, the percentage of female senior managers (Directors and Managing Directors) stands at 12% with a further 28% holding middle-management roles.

Citigroup, United Kingdom
Stats & trends
Women are making their way on to the Boards in Europe & globally

Within the European Corporate and Investment Bank of Citigroup, 15% of the European equivalent of the board level members are women. These women represent the most senior levels of the company in the key roles such as Chief Financial Officer, Chief of Staff to the Operating Committee and Head of Corporate Communications.

Citigroup, United Kingdom
Stats & trends
Summary

In order to establish a baseline for GCIB diversity, benchmark with peers and track the firm's progress, diversity statistics are collected and distributed quarterly.

Deutsche Bank, United Kingdom
Stats & trends
Summary

Our efforts to attract, retain, develop and promote women are paying off. Women now make up 44.9% of the Bank's workforce.

HSBC Bank plc, United Kingdom
Stats & trends
Our statistics

Overall throughout HSBC, women represent 62% of our overall workforce with 75% being in clerical grades and 33% in management (as at December 2002).

IBM UK Limited, United Kingdom
Stats & trends
Women's participation in EMEA is continuing to grow

- 26% of the total population (Q4 2002).
- 33% of all new hires.
- 25% of all leavers.
- 18% increase in number of female executives between Q42001 and Q42002.

Microsoft Limited, United Kingdom
Stats & trends
Summary

Microsoft provides employees with statistical data about the allocation of female talent in the company. The aim is to increase the involvement of women at a senior management level. Moreover the company deploys recruitment strategies, which aim to broaden the diversity of the workforce.

Morgan Stanley, United Kingdom
Stats & trends
Summary

40% of our European work force are women as of June 1, 2003, 13% of Senior Management are women as of June 1, 2003, 19% of our Officer population are women as of June 1, 2003.

Shell International, United Kingdom

Stats & trends

Progress along diversity & inclusiveness journey

Shell's commitment to diversity and inclusiveness stemmed from a recommendation by a Shell Value Creation Team in 1997.

Shell International, United Kingdom

Stats & trends

Global diversity and inclusiveness targets

At the end of 2004, 9.4% of Shell's most senior 600 leaders were women. This has more than doubled from 4% in 1997, but is still behind our target of 20%.

Shell International, United Kingdom

Stats & trends

Summary

We aim to continuously improve female representation in our global top management level to minimum 20%. By the end of 2004, we have reached close to 10% globally.

Source: Aurora Women's Network

Ideas for your firm?

Want some ideas for what can be done for women in business? Just look at some of the things the 'best of breed' are up to:

"Citigroup encourages its female employees to market themselves and the company via media appearances. Lynne Fisher, Managing Director, Head of Diversity is a regular expert speaker at conferences promoting women in the workplace. Most recently Lynne was invited to lead a workshop at the Women & Equity Unit's 'Advancing Women in the Workplace Conference'. Lynne provided invaluable advice to participants on how to kick-start their gender diversity programme. Lynne has also been interviewed in the FT and has submitted articles for the Equal Opportunities Commission and the *MBA Career Guide,* whose circulation includes graduates at many of the top universities and business schools in the UK.

Cindy Ferrara, Managing Director, Equity Derivative Sales was shadowed by E-Financial Careers for an article portraying a typical day in the life of a senior female financial executive. Citigroup are also proud to be involved in a Channel Four documentary regarding the experiences of Kosser Sheikh, a young Muslim employee, during her recent Haj/pilgrimage to Mecca. We are particularly proud to be involved in this venture which demonstrates our commitment to our female minority employees and our support of them and their cultural and spiritual needs."

You have special protection during pregnancy and after childbirth

Pregnancy is not an illness and you do not suddenly become less capable of doing your job.

During maternity leave some things in your contract stay the same and some change. The changes are differ depending on what kind of maternity leave period you are in.

Pay

- You will be paid for time off to attend antenatal classes.

- You should continue to receive pay rises and most bonuses during ordinary maternity leave. Pension contributions will continue during this time.

- During maternity leave you will either be entitled to maternity pay (paid by your employer) or, depending on your earnings, to maternity allowance (paid by Social Security).

Keeping your job

- You cannot be dismissed because you are pregnant or for reasons connected with your pregnancy or maternity leave.

- You should be offered the same training and promotion opportunities as other staff while pregnant.

- You should be allowed to keep the same duties and responsibilities while pregnant.

- You must be allowed to return to your own job unless this is genuinely not possible (e.g. redundancy situation) when you should be offered a suitable alternative.

A safe pregnancy

- You and your baby must be protected from risks to your health at work.

- Your employer needs to carry out a health and safety risk assessment.

- You should not have to put up with, for example:
    - Unduly stressful work.
    - Working alone.
    - Working in awkward work positions.
    - Unnecessary travelling.

- You should have a suitable place where you can rest and later breast-feed.

- You are entitled to 26 weeks' ordinary maternity leave.

- Additional maternity leave is 26 weeks, which starts from the end of ordinary maternity leave. You will be entitled to take additional maternity leave if you have worked for your employer for 26 weeks by the 15th week before your baby is due.

The two main acts that give you rights during pregnancy and maternity are the Employment Rights Act 1996 (as amended by the Employment Act 2002) and the Sex Discrimination Act 1975.

Important information

- To receive the full extent of your rights, you must tell your employer (in writing if they request) that you are pregnant, preferably as soon as you know.

- Find out about your company's maternity policy. It may give you more than your basic rights.

- You can find detailed information about maternity rights at:
  www.tiger.gov.uk
  and from the Maternity Alliance on 020 7490 7638 or at:
  www.maternityalliance.org.uk

Visa International Service Association v Paul (2004 IRLR 42)(EAT)

Mrs Paul worked in the card design section of Visa's operating regulations services department. She took maternity leave in July 2000. Before doing so, she had expressed an interest in moving to the dispute resolution section within the same department. While Mrs Paul was on maternity leave, Visa re-organised the department, creating two new posts. The tribunal found that Mrs Paul was not told about the vacancies because she was on maternity leave.

Mrs Paul claimed that the failure to keep her informed about developments in her department while she was on maternity leave was sex discrimination and a breach of the implied term of good faith in her employment contract. She claimed that the breach was serious enough to justify her resigning and claiming constructive dismissal, and that that dismissal was automatically unfair under ERA s 99 because it was related to her maternity leave.

The Employment Tribunal (ET) agreed with Mrs Paul and found that Visa's failure to keep her informed of developments during her maternity leave was unlawful sex discrimination and also breached her contract of employment to such an extent that she could claim constructive dismissal. Because that dismissal was related to her maternity leave, it was automatically unfair. The Employment Appeals Tribunal (EAT) upheld the ET's decision.

Below are some further real-life examples of pregnancy issues.

Recruitment and promotion

"During my maternity leave a promotion came up. The job went to my maternity cover, whom I trained for my job, and when I return to work, I will be working for her. I knew nothing about the vacancy and was not given the opportunity to apply."

You will have a claim under the Sex Discrimination Act 1975 (SDA) if you can show that but for your absence on maternity leave you would have been informed about the vacancy and so have had the opportunity to apply for it. The fact that your maternity cover was less experienced will help to show that you were the more suitable candidate for the post. You will need to show that if you had been at work, you would have been aware of the vacancy, for example because it was publicised on the company intranet or advertised on a company notice board or newsletter to which you didn't have access because you were on maternity leave.

"Since being offered a job I have discovered that I am pregnant. I told my new employer and immediately the offer was withdrawn. Is this unlawful discrimination?"

Yes, it is unlawful if the withdrawal was because you are pregnant. There might be a dispute over whether or not there was a firm job offer if you do not have written confirmation. You will need precise notes of when and who made the offer. Other evidence might be relevant, such as whether you were asked questions about childcare, or family plans at interview. This might lead a tribunal to infer a discriminatory attitude to mothers, or mothers to be.

Dismissal for pregnancy/maternity related reasons

"I was appointed to a temporary post to cover for someone on maternity leave, with the possibility of staying on permanently. However, I have now been dismissed because I got pregnant. Is this sex discrimination?"

Yes. It is illegal to dismiss a woman because she is pregnant, even if the job is a temporary one.

"I have been dismissed before the end of my probationary period and I think it is owing to my pregnancy. I have been warned informally about arriving late, but after becoming pregnant I have been criticised unfairly for my work and have not been given any training to help me do the job."

This will be unlawful sex discrimination if you can show that your pregnancy was an effective (but not necessarily the only) reason why you were dismissed and were deprived of training. You might have to convince a tribunal that the criticisms about your timekeeping were unjustified or exaggerated and you should be prepared to rebut any allegations about the standard of your work and commitment. If your timekeeping was in fact poor and there were major criticisms of your work, which were justified, then you would not be able to claim that your treatment was discriminatory on the grounds of your pregnancy.

"I had an ectopic pregnancy and was dismissed while on certificated sick leave for my absence. Is this unlawful sex discrimination?"

Yes, it is, provided that you can show that your dismissal was as a result of this sickness absence and because of the nature of the illness. As an ectopic pregnancy is a condition unique to women and you have suffered a detriment by way of your dismissal, you would argue that this was automatically sex discrimination irrespective of how anyone else would be treated with the same length of sickness absence.

"I had a few problems before my maternity leave in adjusting to the new computer system which was installed. My employer says he won't have me back as they prefer the woman they took on to cover for me. Is this unlawful sex discrimination?"

Yes, it is unlawful since the job loss can be related specifically to your absence on maternity leave. If you had not been absent your employer would not have been in a position to replace you with someone he preferred.

"I miscarried in the twenty-third week of my pregnancy and because I have been off for a month on sick leave, my employer now says that I do not have the right to return."

Your entitlement to statutory maternity leave and your rights on return from maternity leave which are under the Employment Rights Act 1996 (ERA) come into play only if your baby is stillborn after the 24th week of pregnancy. However, the absence of any statutory entitlement to leave and rights on return does not provide the employer with a licence to dismiss you unfairly. You may well have an unfair dismissal claim under the ERA.

You do also have protection under the SDA against detrimental treatment which arises because of your pregnancy. You need to establish that your employer's treatment is directly related to the fact that you were pregnant and miscarried and that your absence was for those reasons. Try to find out how men and other women employees have been dealt with over sickness absence in terms of the amount of time off and the reason for their sickness absence.

Generally bad treatment at work

"Since I announced my pregnancy, my main duties have been given to others and I am left with mundane tasks. I have been denied an appraisal when my pay rise depends on my appraisal rating. I feel as though I am being pushed out of my job and the stress has made me ill. Where do I stand legally?"

Your treatment may amount to sex discrimination under the SDA's provisions, which cover access to work-related benefits and general treatment at work. It is unlawful under the SDA to remove your duties, deny you an appraisal and a pay rise if you can show that your pregnancy was a substantial cause of that treatment. You may have additional rights under the Equal Pay Act 1970 (EPA). Bad treatment like this can also give rise to a claim for unfair constructive dismissal.

"My employer keeps altering my hours of work and now I am not required unless called in. He is also making me take unpaid leave for antenatal visits. I won't be able to qualify for Statutory Maternity Pay because of the irregular pay and reduction in hours."

Changing your hours of work is unlawful if you can show that this was because of your pregnancy and not because of, say, a downturn in business. The ERA entitles you to reasonable time off with pay for antenatal visits. Denying you this could also be sex discrimination. If you take and win your case, you should request the amount you would have received in Statutory Maternity Pay along with other losses as part of your request for compensation.

Pregnancy and maternity related sickness

"I have been very ill with my pregnancy and have had a lot of time off, more than the company's sick scheme allows for. I have now been sacked because of this. What are my rights?"

Under the SDA it is unlawful to dismiss you for any reason connected with your pregnancy. This includes pregnancy-related sickness during your pregnancy. It does not matter if your dismissal was as a result of a contractual provision entitling the employer to dismiss employees after a number of weeks of continued absence. If your pregnancy and related illness are the cause of your dismissal then this would automatically be unlawful sex discrimination. Your employer should not count any time when you were ill with a pregnancy-related illness during your pregnancy or maternity leave in deciding whether to dismiss you, because that is also discrimination related to your pregnancy.

"I have had to extend my maternity leave with 4 weeks' certificated sickness absence. My employer has now written to say that if I do not return at the end of this he will sack me. I had a lot of sick leave during my pregnancy because of complications. Also, before my pregnancy I did have time off with sickness, which my employer was cross about, though nothing formal was done about this. Would it be legal to dismiss me in these circumstances?"

No. It is unlawful under the SDA to dismiss a woman for pregnancy-related illness after her return from maternity leave if a man would not have been dismissed for the same amount of sickness absence. Your employer cannot take into account any pregnancy-related illness which occurred during your pregnancy or maternity leave, so your employer will be discriminating against you unless it would also have dismissed a man who was ill for the same length of time as you, not counting the time you were ill while pregnant or on maternity leave.

"I am entitled to additional maternity leave, but I elected to go back to work at the end of my 26 weeks of ordinary maternity leave. I had complications and have been signed off sick. My employer says that I must take additional maternity leave, which is unpaid, rather than paid sick leave. Is this sex discrimination?"

If you have notified your employer of your intention to return at the end of ordinary maternity leave, it is almost certainly unlawful sex discrimination to refuse to allow you to return on the sick scheme, either as regards the statutory scheme, or your contractual scheme if you have one.

Health and safety

"I am a haulage driver and I cannot do the loading and unloading now that I am pregnant. I have been told that I can either do clerical work while the job lasts, on clerical pay, go off sick with statutory sick pay or leave until after the baby is born. Is this sex discrimination? One of the men injured his back and was off sick on full pay for a few months."

You have rights under the ERA and under health and safety regulations. Your employer should carry out a risk assessment of your job once they have been informed of your pregnancy and then should take temporary action to remove those risks to you and your unborn baby's health while they last. Your employer must offer you any alternative work that is available, but only if it is of a suitable kind and isn't on substantially less favourable terms than your current job. Ultimately, if this cannot be done your employer must suspend you on full pay. If they do not do these things, you would also have a sex discrimination claim. The fact that a man has been given preferential treatment helps you to show that it was your pregnancy/sex, which caused your treatment. However, even without this comparison you would still have an SDA claim.

IVF

"I have been undergoing IVF treatment and have been dismissed for the time I have had to take off for this and out of concern for my future absences if I have to repeat the treatment. Is this sex discrimination?"

Your dismissal for IVF treatment is not necessarily sex discrimination, since men undergo fertility treatment as well. You need to show that a man would not be treated so harshly. If you can show that your employer discriminated against you because of assumptions about future absence should your IVF treatment be successful, this would be direct sex discrimination.

Women require more treatment for IVF than men undergoing fertility treatment, and are therefore more likely to be disciplined as a result for absences. This could be indirect sex discrimination if you could prove that the employer's rule was unjustifiable.

Rights on return to work

"During my maternity leave my department was reorganised and my duties have been assimilated into other people's jobs. I was not consulted about the reorganisation though others were. I have been told that I must compete for jobs and that my return to work will be delayed until I am successful. Is this sex discrimination?"

It could be. There are a number of issues: not being consulted because you were on maternity leave when colleagues at work were consulted is direct sex discrimination. Reorganising your job is not necessarily sex discrimination as jobs can evolve and change to correspond with business demands. However, if you can show that your job would have remained had you not been absent on maternity leave, then you would be able to claim sex discrimination. You may need to look at how other jobs were reorganised in your department and the treatment of your colleagues in this regard. You need to establish whether you are under threat of redundancy and to look at your employer's redundancy procedure and how it is being applied to deleted posts.

You can also challenge an unfair redundancy under the ERA. Under ERA a woman who is made redundant while on maternity leave is entitled to be offered any suitable vacancy in priority to any other redundant employee. That right applies to any vacancies up to when her employment ends. The right applies whether the redundancy happens during ordinary or additional maternity leave.

"I have been given project work on my return from maternity absence but the project is of limited duration and I have lost my previous management responsibilities. The employer says that it was not practicable to return me to my substantive post because clients needed continuity of approach. Is this sex discrimination?"

It could be, and the SDA may improve on your rights under the ERA.

Under the ERA your employer can refuse to take you back to your original job after additional maternity leave if it is not reasonably practicable to take you back. You are entitled to be offered suitable alternative work if it is available. However, if there is no sound reason for not returning you to your post, this could be a 'deemed' dismissal.

Your rights under the SDA are independent of the ERA and you can succeed under the SDA where you might fail under the ERA. For a claim under the SDA you have to show that your job still exists and that 'but for' your maternity-related absence you would not have been redeployed. A tribunal may consider that moving you in these circumstances is a detriment under the SDA in its own right because you have lost a valued job. However, it may not. Compare the job you lost with the one you are doing now. It could be that you are still receiving the same pay. However, if you can show that there are substantial differences between the two jobs, for example as regards duties and responsibilities and career prospects, you should be able to prove that your treatment was sex discrimination.

"I returned to work after maternity leave but my baby will not take the bottle. I have been working from my office at home so that I can continue to breast-feed but have attended meetings at the office as required. My employer has now given me an ultimatum that I must either return to work full-time in the office, or revert to unpaid maternity absence. Is this sex discrimination?"

This may well be sex discrimination. The tribunal may accept that treating you less favourably because you are breast-feeding is automatically direct sex discrimination because only women can breast-feed and breast-feeding is closely linked to pregnancy and maternity. However, if the tribunal do not accept that argument, you may have to argue that your treatment is unlawful indirect sex discrimination. Indirect sex discrimination occurs when a provision, criterion or practice is applied equally to men and women but which affects more women than men and is not genuinely necessary. In your case, the provision would be having to work full-time in the office.

You would argue that you could not comply with that provision because you were breast-feeding and because of the particular difficulties your baby had in taking to the bottle. You would also need to show that significantly fewer women than men can comply with a requirement to work full-time. If you can do that, your employer has the opportunity to justify an indirectly discriminatory provision.

You would therefore need to counter the employer's attempts to justify requiring full-time work in the office. You can do this by bringing evidence that, for example: you had combined breast-feeding and work successfully in the past; the quality of your work had not deteriorated in any way; clients had not been inconvenienced; and management or business administration did not suffer as a result. You can also argue that your employer has breached health and safety regulations for breast-feeding mothers and that this is in itself direct sex discrimination.

Access to partnerships

"I am a doctor. Before my pregnancy the partners in the practice had agreed informally that I would become a partner. This has now been delayed and I am being cold-shouldered. What are my rights?"

The SDA covers discrimination by partners. You would have a claim of sex discrimination if you could show that your pregnancy was at the root of your treatment and that there were no other factors which were a major cause of the treatment, for example, a personality clash with the other partners. If you do not have a written offer, you will need to be precise about what was offered, when and by whom. If there is no written offer, the tribunal would have to decide whose evidence they preferred about what offer was made and on what terms.

Contract workers

"I have been employed by the same employer on a series of fixed term contracts. The company will not renew my contract now that I am pregnant, as I would be starting maternity leave at the beginning of the new contract."

Your employer cannot refuse to renew your contract for reasons connected with your pregnancy and your need for maternity leave as this would be sex discrimination. They would not be able to defend a claim with the argument that they would have made the same decision regardless of the reason for any absence and because of the job/project requirements for continuous availability. Nor would your employer be able to do so on the ground that you would be on maternity leave, either at the time the contract would have been renewed, or for part of the period covered by the contract. You may well have an unfair dismissal claim under the ERA and other rights under the Fixed Term Workers Regulations.

You need to establish the precise reasons for the refusal to renew your contract, particularly if it has been renewed before without problems and the work is ongoing. If you can pin the treatment down to your pregnancy and no other substantial cause, then you will have a claim of sex discrimination. Find out what happens to other contract workers on becoming pregnant. The information may be helpful in illustrating general practice. However, your case will stand or fall on its own facts.

"I am a contract worker and have worked for this company for 2 years, but they say that I am not their employee but the agency's, and that they do not have to give me maternity leave or statutory maternity pay. The agency says that I am not their employee either."

You should contact the Inland Revenue Officer at the local National Insurance Contributions Office who will decide whose responsibility it is to pay you SMP, if you are eligible for it. If your employer refuses to pay you SMP, you can challenge this at a tribunal as a refusal to pay your wages.

The SDA covers contract workers where the ERA may not. If you are dismissed, or denied sick leave to cover your baby's birth and your recovery, you could have a sex discrimination claim. You would need to show that there were no other major factors that were at the root of your treatment.

You should get together as much information as possible, including a copy of your contract, copies of pay slips, tax details and information about who is responsible for paying you your wages, including sick pay and annual leave.

If you have a tribunal claim, you should name both the employer and the agency as respondents; the tribunal will decide who is the responsible party for the discrimination.

Conclusion

We hope this book has given you the confidence to follow your entrepreneurial vision, and, at the very least, give some serious thought to starting the business you always wanted to, rather than leaving it as a pipe dream. We also hope that you have been inspired by the real-life case studies, and that you might aspire to follow in these formidable women's footsteps.

In the course of writing this book, we've learnt that whilst men may well be from Mars and women from Venus, it is this very difference that gives women a key role in today's fast moving business world. Women bring different skills, attitudes and opions to the workplace and their value should never be underestimated or underused.

These days women are under huge pressure to have it all – a successful career, husband and 2.4 children – and it takes a special person to cope with that balancing act.

As Faith Whittlesey said, "Remember, Ginger Rogers did everything Fred Astaire did, but she did it backwards and in high heels!"

It's our turn!

Appendices

Contents

1 – VC deal components

Major deal elements stock terms

- Dividends
- Liquidation preference
- Conversion
- Redemption
- Protective provisions
- Voting provisions

Other elements

- Registration rights
- Rights over management shares
- Pre-emptive rights
- Voting and board
- Option pool
- Operating covenants

Liquidation preference

- Preferred is paid original investment amount plus accrued dividends (if any) before common receives anything.
- 'Participating preferred' shares any remaining proceeds with common. Usually subject to a cap of 3X or 4X (including preference).
- Relative seniority of different classes of preferred
    - usually all equal if 'monotonically increasing' fortune
    - trouble – down round – new money will be senior to old money

Conversion

- Conversion events
    - Voluntary – often some % can force all of the preferred to convert
    - Automatic – upon 'Qualified IPO'
        - minimum total offering
        - minimum share price
        - Conversion Ratio – initially 1:1
            - Adjustments – stock splits, etc – price anti-dilution
- Exceptions – option pool, conversion of preferred, outstanding warrants, other existing conditions, other special exceptions

Anti-dilution

- Issuance or 'deemed issuance' of common at less than preferred issuance price
- 'Deemed issuance' – adjust upon issuance of derivative security; if common never issued, readjust later
    - options, warrants
    - convertible securities
- Conversion Ratio= Conversion Value/Conversion Price
    - Initially CV=CP so CR =1
- 'Full ratchet': Conversion Price reset to equal price at which diluting security is sold
- 'Weighted average': $CP = CP*R$
    - $R = (N + M/CP)/(N+S)$

        where   N = old shares outstanding (fully diluted)

                         S = new shares to be issued

                         M = new money (£)

Redemption

- When – typically after five years
    - often phased over three years
- Trigger
    - automatic
    - upon vote of preferred

- Price
    - price paid plus accrued dividends
    - sometimes additional return
- Different classes of preferred – later classes won't let earlier investors out first

Contractual v 'charter' rights

- Charter:
    - public document.
    - amendment requires shareholder vote.
- Contract:
    - can be kept private (until IPO).
    - amendment by a % of the parties.

Selected 'contractual' rights

- Pre-emptive rights (and rights of first refusal).
- Registration rights.
- Voting agreements.

Pre-emptive rights

- Permits investors to participate pro rata in future financings, to preserve their percentage ownership
- Subject to exclusions:
    - option pool issuances.
    - strategic alliances and licences.

Rights of first refusal

- Granted by founders/other investors.
- Gives investors the right to acquire shares offered by the grantor, pro rata.
- May be partial or 'all or nothing'.
- Exclude: VC partnership distributions, estate planning.

Registration rights

- Enables investors to sell shares publicly by means of a registered offering:
    - Sales prior to end of 1-year holding period.
    - Avoid compliance with volume limitations.
- Registration paid for by the company.
- Are founders included?

Demand registration rights

- After the IPO or within 3-7 years.
- Can be exercised 1-3 times.
- Can be exercised by holders of 20-50% of the registrable shares, with value of [£].

Incidental ('piggyback') registration rights

- Investors 'piggyback' on another registration.
- Can they participate in other shareholders' demand rights?
- Subject to underwriter 'cutback'.
- S-3 Registrations generally unlimited, too.

Voting agreements

- Board seats
    - Set size of board
    - Investor designees (1-2)
    - Founder designees
    - Independents

Source: c2ventures.com

2 – Accounting definitions

Profit and loss

Turnover
Total invoiced sales for the period, net of VAT. UK sales. Exports & overseas sales and inter-company sales will be included.

Cost of sales
Cost components directly related to turnover.

Gross profit
This indicates the profit before deducting depreciation, distribution, selling and administration costs. It is an indicator of the underlying profitability of a company's core operations.

Operating profit
Indicates the profit and loss arising from core business activities. The figure is pre-tax profit plus interest paid minus non-trading income.

Non-trading income
Comprises investment income, such as income from quoted & unquoted investments, rents received, share of profit from associated companies; as well as reserves adjustments, such as transfers from capital grant reserve. Interest relief grants. Write-offs of investments and intangibles will also be included.

Interest payable
Interest paid by the company. This will be the net charge for interest after any capitalised element. It should be noted that many private companies do not disclose this figure in full, or aggregate short and long-term, and hire purchase interest together.

Pre-tax profit
The net trading profit figure after deduction of all operating expenses including depreciation & finance charges, but before deduction of tax, dividends, subventions or group relief, and other appropriations. Where applicable it will include the share of profits and losses of associated companies. Items described by the company as exceptional are included. Extraordinary items are excluded.

Taxation
Tax charges paid against profits. This can be negative, representing a tax credit.

Profit after tax
This figure represents the profit or loss after deduction of corporation taxation but before the deduction of dividends, minority interests and any extraordinary items.

Dividends payable   This item includes both proposed and paid items and provisions/appropriations determined by FRS4.

Retained profits   This figure is after the deduction of extraordinary items, taxation, dividends and any other appropriations (e.g. minority interests). Essentially, this is the amount carried from the Profit and Loss Account balance on the Balance Sheet.

Value added   Trading profit plus salaries & wages. It should be noted that for the value added calculation, staff costs are grossed up to reflect national insurance costs. Value added represents the difference between the sales income received and bought in materials and services expended in the period.

Balance sheet

Tangible fixed assets   The sum of fixed assets and intermediate assets.

Intangible assets   Assets which do not possess any material value. Will include goodwill, trademarks, patents and copyrights, at their amortised book value. These are assets with no 'physical' existence, but are deemed to confer benefits to the company in future periods.

Total fixed assets   The total of tangible and intangible fixed assets.

Stocks   Trading stocks, sundry stocks and work in progress net of progress payments.

Trade debtors   Trade debtors, bills receivable and amounts recoverable on contracts due within one year. For smaller companies, when the figure is not disclosed the figure will represent total debtors.

Cash   Cash includes the following: cash in hand; cash at bank; cash at bank and in hand; cash balances.

Miscellaneous current assets   Short-term assets other than stocks, trade debtors or cash. Includes items such as: bank balances; bank account (where not negative); bank deposit account; building society deposit; short-term deposits; bank current account, sundry debtors; amounts due from group and related companies; called up share capital not paid; prepayments and accrued income; and current asset investments (where these are not short-term deposits).

Total current assets   The sum of stocks, trade debtors, cash and miscellaneous current assets.

Total assets   The total of current and total fixed assets.

Creditors: Amounts falling due within one year   Also referred to as total current liabilities, being the sum of trade creditors, bank overdraft and miscellaneous current liabilities.

Total assets less current liabilities   Total assets minus total current liabilities.

Total long term liabilities   The sum of long-term bank loans. Other long-term finance and other long term liabilities.

Total liabilities   The sum of current and long term liabilities.

Share capital and reserves   The sum of called up share capital and sundry reserves.

P&L account reserve   The accumulation of profits/losses from previous trading periods including the retained profit/loss from the profit and loss account.

Revaluation reserve   Also known as investment revaluation reserve, property revaluation reserve, and unrealised capital gains on valuation.

Shareholders' funds   The sum of called up share capital, sundry reserves, P&L account reserve and revaluation reserve.

Capital employed   The sum of shareholders' funds and total long-term liabilities.

Net worth   Shareholders' funds minus intangibles. Often referred to as the book value of the company. The long-term realisable value after all liabilities are cleared.

Working capital   Obtained by subtracting total current liabilities from the total current assets. This represents the surplus deficiency of funds from normal trading activities.

Contingent liabilities   These items are extracted from the notes to the accounts and includes all 'potential' liabilities such as: guarantees, indemnities, cross guarantees, HM customs and excise, letters of credit and VAT registration.

Cash flow statements

Net cash flow from operating activities   Cash receipts and payments from normal operations.

Net cash flow from rtn on inv. and servicing of finance   Cash derived from holding investments matched against the cash utilised in paying the interest on finance capital and the dividends on equity capital. This is a useful indicator of the business's performance. A negative figure would indicate poor profitability or poor management of working capital efficiency.

Net cash flow before financing   This is the total cash generated or used by the company before any funding activity and movements in the cash balances. If positive, the company has generated a cash surplus, which can be used as liquid funds or to repay debt.

Net cash flow from financing   Cash derived from the issue of equity capital or the use of loan facilities matched against the cash utilised in repaying borrowings.

Increase in net cash   A reconciliation of cash movements in terms of cash and cash equivalent balances.

Business ratios

Profit/Sales (%)   This represents the percentage of sales left as profits or losses before tax. In general, if profitability is the main driving force the higher the result the better. It should not however, be taken in isolation. Also known as the profit margin.

Profit/Capital employed (%)   Often used as a primary measure of company performance. This ratio is taken as an indication of how much profit a business yields relative to the money invested. Also referred to ass return on capital.

Profit/Total assets (%)   Shows as a percentage the value of the pre-tax profits in proportion to the value of total assets.

Profit/Shareholders funds (%)   Expresses the proportion of pre-tax profit made in relation to the value of the shareholders funds.

Sales/Total assets (%)   Shows as a percentage the value of sales in proportion to the value of total assets. Also referred to as asset utilisation.

Sales/Fixed assets	Shows as a ratio the value of sales in proportion to the value of fixed assets.
Sales/Total fixed assets (%)	Measures the level of sales generated in relation to total fixed assets. This result will be affected by the accuracy of the net book value of the assets.
Working capital/ Sales (%)	Surplus or deficiency of funds from normal trading activities in relation to its size measured by sales.
Stock turnover	Turnover divided by stocks held. Generally speaking, the number of times stock is renewed each year.
Credit period (days)	The number of days, on average, for the company to collect trade debt. Calculated by dividing trade debtors by sales and multiplying by 365 days.
Creditor days (days)	The number of days it takes the company to pay trade creditors. This ratio provides an indication of the amount of credit given to the business by its suppliers. The formulae is trade creditors divided by sales multiplied by 365 days.
Current ratio	This represents the number of times the business' short-term assets cover its current liabilities. It measures the ability to meet its day to day commitments.
Liquidity ratio	This represents the number of times a customer's quick assets can cover its current liabilities. Quick assets being defined as current assets less stock. This is taking into account the fact that it takes a reasonable amount of time for stock to be converted into cash.
Total debt/Net worth (%)	A way of measuring the 'gearing' or 'leverage' of a company, by comparing total loans (short and long-term) to net worth.
Bank overdraft & long term liabilities/Net worth	This ratio represents the relationship between the bank overdraft & long term borrowings and other amounts due over 12 months, against the net worth.
Shareholders funds/ Total liabilities	This represents the business' liabilities as a ratio of shareholders' funds. This ratio provides a measure of protection given by shareholders to other parties who contribute funds, e.g. banks, creditors etc. A falling ratio indicates increasing financial risk.
Long-Term debt/ Net worth (%)	This represents the debt outstanding beyond 12 months in relation to net worth.

Long-term liabilities/ Net worth (%)	Ratio of liabilities due over a year in relation to the net worth.
Interest/Pre-interest profit (%)	Sometimes referred to as income gearing – this measures the proportion of pre-interest profit which is required to service debt.
Total debt/Working capital	A gearing measurement which compares total borrowings with the surplus or deficit of funds from normal trading activities.
Bank overdraft & Long-term liabilities/Working capital	Ratio of bank overdraft and liabilities due over 12 month period in relation to the working capital of the company
Bank o/dft & long-term liabilities/ Total assets	This indicates the relationship between debt and asset value of the company.
Average employee remuneration (GBP)	Employee remuneration divided by the average number of employees.
Wages/Sales (%) (GBP)	Indicates the amount of sales revenue expended on employees' pay, showing the marginal cost of employment.
Profit /Employee (GBP)	Amount of profit before tax made per employee.
Sales/Employee	This is often used as a measurement of productivity. It indicates the amount of sales revenue generated by each employee.
Capital employed/ Employee (GBP)	Capital employed per employee.
Fixed assets/ Employee (GBP)	Fixed asset investment per employee.
Total assets/ Employee (GBP)	Total assets in comparison to the number of employees.
Profit/Value added (%)	Pre-tax profit as a percentage of value added.
Value added/Sales (%)	Sales figure as a percentage of value added measurement.
Value added/ Employee (GBP)	Employees in relation to the value added.

Value added/ Employee remuneration (GBP) — Employee's remuneration in relation to the value added.

Creditors/Debtors — The ratio of trade creditors to trade debtors.

Debtors/Total assets (%) — Trade debtors in relation to the total assets of the company. This measures the value of moneys owed in relation to company's asset base.

Current liabilities/ Stock — Liabilities to be paid within 12 months expressed as a ratio in relation to value of stocks.

Export/Sales (%) — Amount of sales revenue attributable to export business as a percentage of total sales.

Sales/Audit fees — Comparison of sales revenue to cost of audit.

Total assets to audit fees — Comparison of total assets to audit fees.

Shareholders' funds/ Total assets (%) — The relationship of the business' assets to shareholders' funds.

Sales/Capital employed — This measures the amount of revenue generated by a business in relation to the level of investment made. Referred to as capital utilisation and when combined with profit margin gives the principal measure of profitability, return on capital.

Stocks/Working capital (%) — The value of stocks represented as a percentage to the working capital of the company.

Current assets/ Total assets (%) — Percentage of current assets against long-term assets indicates where the asset base rests.

Profit/Current liabilities (%) — Pre-tax profit in relation to liabilities due within the next 12 months.

Sales/Current liabilities — Sales expressed as ratio to those liabilities due within next 12 months.

Net Cash/Current liabilities — Net cash (defined as cash less bank overdraft) expressed as a ratio to those liabilities due within the next 12 months.

Liquid assets/Total assets (%) — Percentage measurement of liquid assets against total asset base – good indicator of which assets could be quickly realised.

Net worth/Total assets - intangibles (%)	This measures the accounting value of the company against total assets. Intangibles are discounted as they cover perceived value such as goodwill, R&D development, patents, trademarks etc.
Net worth/Total fixed assets (%)	This measures the net worth of the company against those assets whose value may be great, but are not necessarily quick to liquidise. Fixed assets normally make up a far proportion of total assets.
Net worth/Current liabilities (%)	This measures the short-term percentage risk against the value of the company.
P&L Acct reserve/ Net Worth (%)	Accumulated profits/losses as a percentage of shareholders' funds less intangible assets.
Revaluation reserve/ Shareholders funds (%)	This takes into account revaluation of investments or properties and measures it against the shareholders' funds.
Bank overdraft/ Current assets (%)	The current bank overdraft as a percentage of short-term assets. A good measurement for using whether these assets cover the bank overdraft.

Notes to the accounts

Exports	This figure represents direct exports from the UK.
Employees' remuneration	'Wages and salaries' figure – excluding social security, pension costs etc., where possible.
Director's remuneration	All payments made to directors including pension fund contributions, benefits in kind and ex-gratia payments to their families.
Audit fees	The auditor's charge for the statutory audit, which excludes accountancy charges and other non-audit related fees.
Non audit fees	This refers to amounts charged by the auditors for services other than the audit.
Depreciation	This indicates the amount written off tangible assets (including leased assets) during the period.
Average number of employees	Average number of employees employed during the period.

Fixed assets	This represents a number of items, including the following: property, plant, fixtures, fittings, office equipment and motor vehicles, all at written down value. This will include leased and capitalised assets, and for some industries assets held on a long-term basis and constantly replaced for renting or hiring out.
Intermediate assets	This represents investments in subsidiary and associated companies, trade and other unquoted investments, long-term amounts due from other group and associated companies and any other long-term debtors.
Due from group, non current	Part of intermediate assets, amounts due from other group companies, associated companies that are received over one year, and with no stated fixed repayment terms.
Due from group, current	Amounts due from other group companies or associated companies that appear to be receivable within one year.
Trade creditors	This figure includes short-term, i.e. within one year, portion of trade creditors and trade bills payable. For smaller companies, where trade creditors have not been separated out, the figure will represent total current liabilities.
Bank overdraft	This includes overdrawn bank account, negative cash items and bank indebtedness.
Bank loans, current portion	Installment of bank loan due for repayment within 12 months.
Other short-term finance	This includes any undefined 'Loans' or 'Loans' from non-banking sources. Typically hire purchase obligations, leases, factoring advances, stocking loans, debentures, mortgages, capital creditors, amounts due to group and directors within one year.
Due to group, current	Loans due to group companies due in one year.
Due to directors	Directors loans due in one year.
Other current liabilities	This includes all other sundry creditors, accrued expenses and pre-paid income, including dividends, corporation tax, social security or other sundry amounts payable within one year.
Short-term loans	The sum of bank overdraft, bank loans (current portion) and other short-term finance.
Long-term loans	The sum of long-term bank loans and other long-term finance.

Long-term bank loans	Installments of bank loans repayable in more than one year.
Other long-term finance	This includes long-term portions of hire purchases and leasing obligations; amounts due to other group, associated or affiliated companies; portions of trade and sundry creditors payable in more than one year.
Due to group, non-current	Loans due to group/related companies over more than 12 months.
Due to directors, non-current	Directors' loans due in more than 12 months.
Other long term liabilities	This includes deferred tax, future tax, minority interests, pension fund liabilities, provisions for liabilities and pre-paid income.
Called up share capital	The total value of shares issued. This represents the share capital currently invested in the company.
Sundry reserves	This includes capital reserve, share premium, related companies' reserves, merger reserve, consolidation reserve and capital based grants.

3 – Sample press release

FOR IMMEDIATE RELEASE

Contact: Doug Morris
Phone: 212-515-1964

ENTREPRENEURS IN INDIA TARGETED TO CREATE HIGH TECH START UPS IN U.K.

Financial entrepreneur and investment expert to help Indian entrepreneurs go global

London, U.K. – May 11, 2005 – UK Trade & Investment's Global Entrepreneurs Programme (GEP) today announced the appointment of Alpesh Patel as a 'Dealmaker'. In his new role, Patel will provide guidance to a growing number of Indian life sciences and technology entrepreneurs interested in setting up their companies or pursuing opportunities in the United Kingdom. Patel is the fifth Dealmaker appointed by the GEP and the first to operate in India.

"I am very pleased to welcome Alpesh Patel to the team," said William Pedder, Chief Executive of Inward Investment for UK Trade & Investment. "Alpesh's experience as an entrepreneur and vast knowledge of British and Indian business communities will make him invaluable to the programme and to the entrepreneurs he will assist."

As a Dealmaker, Patel will assist Indian entrepreneurs by connecting them to a range of resources in the U.K. – notably business, technology and financial networks. He can also help entrepreneurs access U.K. based venture capitalists and other sources of financing, as well as connect clients with strategic partners such as suppliers and distributors, and identify and recruit senior management. Assistance in accessing these resources enables entrepreneurs to more quickly and easily develop a platform from which they can enter the European market.

"I am honoured to have the opportunity to work with the Global Entrepreneurs Programme," said Patel. "Entrepreneurs today must think about their company in terms of starting global, not becoming global. The Programme is a wonderful facilitator for entrepreneurs who possess intellectual property with truly world-wide potential."

Patel has a long record as both an entrepreneur and supporter of entrepreneurship. He has started and built five companies since 1997, including Agile Partners Asset Management, one of the best performing hedge funds in the world in 2004.

He is also a founding Board member of TiE-UK, part of a 10,000 member global network of entrepreneurs operating in nine countries, and is on the Board of Advisors for the Center for Entrepreneurship at the University of Reading. Additionally, Patel was a Visiting Fellow in Business & Industry, Corpus Christi College, Oxford University

An expert on Anglo-Indo relations, Patel has advised the U.K. government on strategies for bilateral and multilateral trade growth, and is a board member of the UK-India Roundtable and the Indo-British Partnership. Additionally, he is the U.K. representative to Beijing to chair sessions on IT and improving EU-Asian trade. Patel has also been a leader in fostering entrepreneurship in both the U.K. and India.

Patel is a regular contributing writer on investing for the *Financial Times*, is a regular stock markets commentator on BBC World, CNN and CNBC, and formerly hosted a weekly show on Bloomberg TV. In addition to his work as a commentator, Patel has authored 10 books on investing.

The Global Entrepreneurs Programme, operated by U.K. Trade & Investment, champions new business ideas by bringing together entrepreneurs and those who can best guide them towards success in the U.K. A unique and valuable aspect of the program is the Dealmaker model for mentoring life science- and technology-oriented start-ups. The Dealmakers are experienced, serial entrepreneurs who assist other entrepreneurs from the U.S. and India.

The Global Entrepreneurs Programme was launched in the U.S. and, due to that success, is expanding to India. The four Dealmakers previously appointed to the program have venture capital and entrepreneurial experience in technology and life sciences sectors in both the U.S. and U.K. These four Dealmakers have focused on assisting U.S.-based entrepreneurs in starting companies in the U.K. The GEP is already working with 85 entrepreneurs, 15 of which have successfully developed businesses or opportunities in the U.K. GEP clients include entrepreneurs in the areas of nanotechnology, information and communication technology, pharmaceutical development and diagnostic testing.

About UK Trade & Investment and The Global Entrepreneurs Programme

UK Trade & Investment is the government organisation that provides integrated support services for UK companies engaged in overseas trade and foreign businesses focused on the UK as an inward investment location. For more information visit the web site at www.uktradeinvest.gov.uk

UK Trade & Investment launched the Global Entrepreneurs Programme (GEP) in 2003 as a novel approach to economic development. Rather than focus on attracting foreign direct investments from large corporations, the GEP champions new business ideas by bringing together entrepreneurs and those who can best guide them towards success in the U.K. The Dealmakers act as a liaison between the government and entrepreneurs. For more information visit the GEP website at:

www.entrepreneurs.gov.uk

4 – Collection policy

30 days

- Give a quick call to ensure the client has the invoice.
- Re-send copy if necessary and politely ask to remit.
- Confirm payment date.

45 days

- Make a follow up call.
- Re-confirm payment date and method.
- Ask for account to be cleared up within 15 days.

60 days

- Send formal letter to demand payment.
- If dealing with payables person – follow up with their boss.
- Stop all deliveries to client.
- Demand payment immediately.

75 days

- Send formal letter – state if account is not paid within 10 days, you will turn it over to collection agency.

90 days

- Turn over to collection agency.
- Start small claims proceedings.

5 – Alphabetical list of UK networks

All are National Business Angels Network (NBAN) Associates unless otherwise stated.

Business Link for London Central
6 New Bridge Street
London
EC4V 6AB

Contact: Alastair Keir
Tel: 020 7010 1321
akeir@bl4london.com
www.businesslink4london.com

Business Link for London North
Link House
Southbury Road
Enfield
Middlesex
EN1 1TS

Contact: Kantilal Patel
Tel: 020 7010 1371
kpatel@bl4london.com
www.businesslink4london.com

Business Link for London South
1 Wandle Road
Croydon
Surrey
CR0 1DA

Contact: Nigel Dear
Tel: 020 7010 1265
ndear@bl4london.com
www.businesslink4london.com

Business Link London East
Solar House
Romford Road
London
E15 4LJ

Contact: Roger Morris
Tel: 020 7010 1355
rmorris@bl4london.com
www.businesslink4london.com

Business Link for London West
The Perfume Factory
Wales Farm Road
London
W3 6UG

Contact: Paul Coleman
Tel: 020 7010 1453
pcoleman@bl4london.com
www.businesslink4london.com

Business Link Northamptonshire
Royal Pavilion
Summerhouse Road
Northampton
NN3 6BJ

Contact: Barrie Egan
Tel: 01604 643777
Fax: 01604 670362
barrie.egan@businesslinknorthants.org
www.businesslinknorthants.org

Business Link Solutions Limited
Eastern Bypass
Thame
Oxon
OX9 3FF

Tel: 0845 606 4466
Fax: 0870 161 5852
cst@businesslinksolutions.co.uk
www.businesslinksolutions.co.uk

Business Link Staffordshire (not NBAN)
Commerce House, Festival Park
Stoke on Trent
Staffordshire
ST1 5BE

Contact: Mike Bird
Tel: 01889 508332
Fax: 01889 508089
mikebird@btinternet.com

Business Link Surrey

5th Floor, Hollywood House
Church Street East
Woking,
Surrey
GU21 1HJ

Contact: Richard Holmes
Tel: 01483 713329
Fax: 01483 771507
richard.holmes@businesslinksurrey.co.uk
www.businesslinksurrey.co.uk

Business Link Wessex

Merck House
Seldown Lane, Poole
Dorset
BH15 1TD

Contact: Lorraine Exley
Tel: 01202 785415
Fax: 01202 785401
lorraine.exley@businesslinkwessex.co.uk
www.businesslinkwessex.co.uk

Business Link West

16 Clifton Park
Bristol
BS8 9BY

Contact: Peter Hepburn
Tel: 0117 973 7373
Fax: 0117 923 8024
Mobile: 07980 165634
peter.hepburn@businesswest.co.uk
www.businesswest.co.uk

c2Ventures - Berkhamsted

Ashridge House
121 High Street
Berkhamsted
Hertfordshire
HP4 2DJ

Contact: Paul Gardner
Tel: 07050 263 500
Fax: 0870 7062199
info@c2ventures.com
www.c2ventures.com

c2Ventures - London

1 St Andrews Hill
London
EC4V 5BY

Contact: Stephen Hay
Tel: 020 7329 7070
Fax: 020 7329 2911
info@c2ventures.com
www.c2ventures.com

Cambridge Business Link

Centenary House, St. Mary's Street
Huntingdon
Cambridgeshire
PE29 3PE

Contact: John Cresswell
Tel: 01480 846414
Fax: 01480 846478
john.cresswell@c-b-s.org.uk
www.c-b-s.org.uk

Capital Connections (not NBAN)

King Business Centre
Reeds Lane
Sayers Common
Hassocks
West Sussex
BN6 9LS

Contact: Howard Matthews
Tel: 01273 835455
Fax: 01273 835466
Email: cadmus@globalnet.co.uk

Capital Partners Group

33 St SJames's Square
London
SW1Y 4YS

Contact: Claudio Rojas
Tel: 07050 804262
Fax: 08701 313502
info@CapitalPartners-PrivateEquity.com
www.CapitalPartners-PrivateEquity.com

Cavendish Management Resources
(Head Office)
31 Harley Street
London
W1G 9QS

Contact: Mike Downey
Tel: 020 7636 1744
Fax: 020 7636 5639
cmr@cmruk.com
www.cmruk.com

Chamber of Commerce Herefordshire & Worcestershire (not NBAN)
Enterprise House
Castle Street, Worcester
Worcestershire
WR1 3EN

Contact: Randesh Kalar
Tel: 01905 723200
Fax: 01905 613338
randeshk@hwchamber.co.uk
www.hwchamber.co.uk

Corbett Keeling (not NBAN)
13 St Swithins Lane
London
EC4N 8AL

Contact: Jim Keeling
Tel: 020 7626 6266

Critchleys
Boswell House
1-5 Broad Street
Oxford
OX1 3AW

Contact: Keith White
Tel: 01865 243155
Fax: 01865 200923
kwhite@critchleys.co.uk
www.critchleys.co.uk

Dunstable Management Group (not NBAN)
PO Box 18, Dereham
Norfolk
NR20 4UL

Contact: Oliver Diggle
Tel: 01362 637948
Fax: 01362 637581
odiggle@dunstablemanagement.co.uk
www.dunstablemanagement.co.uk

East Midlands Business Angels (not NBAN)
PO Box 333, Newark
Nottinghamshire
NG23 6FQ

Contact: Tom Yardley
Tel: 01636 708717
Fax: 01636 708717
emba.co.uk@virgin.net

Enbusiness
17 Erpingham Road
Putney
London
SW15 1BE

Contact: Oliver Woolley, Richard Anderson
Tel: 08707 58 59 58
Fax: 070 9216 3155
funding@enbusiness.co.uk
www.enbusiness.co.uk

The Enterprise Consortium
253 High Street
Henley in Arden
Warwickshire
B95 5BG

Contact: Bill Leech
Tel: 01564 794898
Fax: 01564 793092
Mob: 07899 792792
bill.leech@enterpriseconsortium.co.uk
www.enterpriseconsortium.co.uk

Entrust

Portman House
Portland Road
Newcastle-upon-Tyne
NE2 1AQ

Contact: Bob Marris
Tel: 0191 244 4000
Fax: 0191 244 4001
enquire@entrust.co.uk
www.investorsforum.org.uk
www.regionalfinancialservices.org.uk

Envestors

17 Erpingham Road
London
SW15 1BE

Contacts: Richard Anderson, Oliver
Woolley
Tel: 0870 758 5958
Fax: 070 9207 5437
funding@enbusiness.co.uk
www.enbusiness.co.uk

EquityLink Hertfordshire (Head office)

Business Link Hertfordshire
45 Grosvenor Road
St Albans
Hertfordshire
AL1 3AW

Contacts: Martin Carr, Stuart
McRoberts, Sara Fecamp
Tel: 01727-813495
Fax: 01727-813757
stuartm@exemplas.com
www.equitylink.co.uk

EquityLink Essex

12 Colneford Hill
White Colne
Colchester
CO6 2PJ

Contact: Bob Westrip
Tel: 01787 222427
Fax: 01787 222427
bob.westrip@virgin.net
www.equitylink.co.uk

EquityLink Kent

Business Link Kent
26 Kings Hill Avenue
Kings Hill
West Malling
Kent
ME19 4AE

Contact: Ian Netherton
Tel: 01732 878051
Fax: 01732 874818
ian.netherton@businesslinkkent.com
www.equitylink.co.uk

EquityLink Milton Keynes, Oxfordshire and Buckinghamshire

Eastern Bypass
Thame
Oxon
OX9 3FF

Contact: Customer service team
Tel: 0845 606 4466
Fax: 0870 161 5852
cst@businesslinksolutions.co.uk
www.businesslinksolutions.co.uk

EquityLink Surrey

Hollywood House
Church Street East
Woking
Surrey
GU21 1HJ

Contacts: Andrea Card, Richard
Holmes
Tel: 01483 713329
Fax: 01483 771501
andrea.card@businesslinksurrey.co.uk
richard.holmes@businesslinksurrey.co.uk
www.equitylink.co.uk

E-Synergy

Bride House
18-20 Bride Lane
London
EC4Y 8BT

Contact Andrew Stevenson
Tel: 020 7583 3503
Fax: 020 7583 3474
enquiries@e-synergy.com
www.e-synergy.com

First Stage Capital (not NBAN)

Elsinore House
77 Fulham Palace Road
London, England
W6 8JA

Contact: Paul Fisher
Tel: 020 8563 1563
Direct dial: 020 8563 1685
Fax: 020 8563 2767
Paul.Fisher@firststagecapital.com

www.firststagecapital.com

Fleming Lincoln (not NBAN)

Rewitt House, Culworth
Banbury
Oxfordshire
OX17 2HJ

Contact: Angus Fleming
Tel: 01295 768808
Fax: 0870 4601019
agf@fleminglincoln.co.uk
www.fleminglincoln.co.uk

Gorilla Park

1-2 Domingo Street
London
EC1Y 0TA

Contact: Russ Campey
Tel: 020 7014 8906
Fax: 020 70148901
Mob: 07971 988609
russ@gorillapark.com
www.gorillapark.com

Great Eastern Investment Forum

Richmond House
16-20 Regent Street
Cambridge
Cambridgeshire
CB2 1DB

Contacts: Andrea Blakesley, Hugh
Parnell
Tel: 01223 467296
Fax: 01223 720258
andrea.blakesley@geif.co.uk
hugh.parnell@nwbrown.co.uk
www.geif.co.uk

Hanley & Co
Spring Court
Spring Road, Hale
Cheshire
WA14 2UQ

Contact: John Sheehan
Tel: 0161 928 7100
Fax: 0161 928 7419
johnshee@hanleyandco.com
www.hanleyandco.com

Harben Barker
Drayton Court, Drayton Road
Shirley, Solihull
West Midlands
B90 4NG

Contact: Chris Barker
Tel: 0121 704 4004
Fax: 0121 711 3520
hb@harbenbarker.co.uk
www.harbenbarker.co.uk

Haslam Tunstall
14 Bold Street
Warrington
Cheshire
WA1 1DL

Contact: Neil Duncan
Tel: 01925 633214
Fax: 01925 418987
neilduncan@haslamtunstall.co.uk
www.haslamtunstall.co.uk

Helm Financial Management (not NBAN)
Vigilant House
120 Wilton Road
London
SW1V 1JZ

Contact: Russell Wynn Jones
Tel: 020 7808 7117
Fax: 020 7808 7118
Mob: 07774 757900
russell@helm-group.com
www.helm-group.com

Henley Business Partnership
31 Valley Road
Henley-on-Thames
Oxon
RG9 1RL

Contact: John Quinton
Tel: 01491 576616
Fax: 01491 411076
jbquinton@compuserve.com

Hotbed
Ibex House
Keller Close
Milton Keynes
MK11 3LL

Contact: Claire Madden
Tel: 01908 571500
Fax: 01908 571599
enquiries@hotbed.uk.com
www.hotbed.uk.com

Humphrey & Co Chartered Accountants

8-9 The Avenue
Eastbourne
East Sussex
BN21 3YA

Contact: Eric Hylton
Tel: 01323 730 631
Fax: 01323 738 355
info@humph.co.uk
www.humph.co.uk

IDJ (not NBAN)

81 Piccadilly
London
W1J 8HY

Contact: Charles Sebag-Montefiore
Tel: 020-7355 1200
Fax: 020-7495 1149
csmontefiore@idj.co.uk
www.idj.co.uk

Intellect

20 Red Lion Street
London
WC1R 4QN

Contact: John Parkinson
Tel: 07887 520146
Fax: 020 7404 4119
john.parkinson@intellectuk.org
www.intellectuk.org

Inter - Alliance Group

1st Floor, 26 Southampton Buildings
London
WC2A 1AN

Contact: Darren Levene
Tel: 020 7074 3000
Fax: 020 7074 3001/2
darren.levene@inter-alliance.com
www.inter-alliance.com

Ivo Associates

Chestnut House
1c Sheepfold
St Ives
Cambridge
PE27 5FY

Contact: Dennis Camilleri
Tel: 01480 390648
Fax: 01480 390648
dennis.camilleri@ntlworld.com

James & Cowper Chartered Accountants

Buxton Court
3 West Way
Botley
Oxford
OX2 0JB

Contact: Steve Clarke
Tel: 01865 200 500
Fax: 01865 200 501
sclarke@jamescowper.co.uk
www.jamescowper.co.uk

K@talyst

24 High Street
Whittlesford
Cambridgeshire
CB2 4LT

Contact: Anthony Collinson
Tel: 01223 492180
Fax: 01223 492189
anthony@katalystventures.com
www.katalystventures.com

Kingston Business Angels

Kingston Innovation Centre
Unit 3, Kingsmill Business Park
Chapel Mill Road
Kingston-upon-Thames
Surrey
KT1 3GZ

Contact: Barry Akid
Tel: 020 8781 1142
Fax: 020 8781 1142
info@akid.co.uk
www.akid.co.uk

Kingston Smith

Devonshire House
60 Goswell Road
London
EC1M 7AD

Contact: David Masterson
Tel: 020 7566 4000
Fax: 020 7566 4010
dmasterson@kingstonsmith.co.uk
www.kingstonsmith.co.uk

Latitude LLP (not NBAN)

68 Charlotte Street
London
W1T 4QF

Contact: Steve Hacking
Tel: 020 7637 3330
Fax: 020 7636 3104
steve@latitude.co.uk
www.latitude.co.uk

LINC Scotland (not NBAN)

Queens House
19 St Vincent Place
Glasgow
G1 2DT

ContactsDavid Grahame,Allison
Owens
Tel: 0141-221 3321
Fax: 0141-221 2909
info@lincscot.co.uk
www.lincscot.co.uk

London Partnership

4 Creed Court
5 Ludgate Hill
London
EC4M 7AA

Contact: Krishna Visuvanat
Tel: 020 7248 0656
Fax: 020 7213 0591
Mob: 07940 510051
info@londonpartnership.co.uk
www.londonpartnership.co.uk

Maclay, Murray & Spens

151 St Vincent Street
Glasgow
G2 5NJ

Contact: Andrew Buchan
Tel: 020 7606 6130
Fax: 020 7600 0992/3
jm@mms.co.uk
www.mms.co.uk

MBAngels

16 The Crescent
Burton Latimer
Northants
NN15 5NQ

Contact: Bill Nelson
Tel: 01536 724486
Mob: 07950 038065
MBAngels@talk21.com

MBI/MBO

20 Garrick Street
London
WC2E 9AX

Contact: Brian Duffy
Tel: 020 7664 7801
Fax: 020 7664 6396
kingsley@the-generator.co.uk

McCabes

56 Palmerston Place
Edinburgh
EH12 5AY

Contact: Jeff Meek
Tel: 0131 225 6366
Fax: 0131 220 1041
Mob: 07957 860929
jeff@mccp.co.uk
www.mccp.co.uk

Menzies Chartered Accountants

Victoria House, Victoria Road
Farnborough
Hampshire
GU14 7PG

Contact: John Biffen
Tel: 01252 541244
Fax: 01252 524000
jbiffen@menzies.co.uk
www.menzies.co.uk

Mercantile 100 (not NBAN)

Baker Till Chartered Accountants
Breckenridge House
274 Sauchiehall Street
Glasgow
G2 3EH

Contact: Simon Sweeney
Tel: 0141 307 5000

Morpheus Consulting (not NBAN)

1 Hadham, Mill Cottages
Hertford
Hertfordshire
SG10 6EY

Contact Andrew Lloyd-Skinner
Tel: 01279 843302
Fax: 01279 843302
alloydskinner@dial.pipex.com

New Sarum Enterprises

8 Centre One
Lysander Way
Salisbury
Wiltshire
SP4 6B

Contact: Dr J McArdell
Tel: 01722 415 026
Fax: 01722 415 028
nse@dial.pipex.com

Numerica Group (not NBAN)

66 Wigmore Street
London
W1U 2HQ

Contact: Shirin Gandhi
Tel: 020 7467 4159
Fax: 020 7467 4040
shirin.gandhi@numerica.biz

www.numerica.biz

One London Business Angels

28 Park Street
London
SE1 9EQ

Contact: Aisha Ejaz
Tel: 020 7940 1562
Fax: 020 7403 1742
aisha.e@one-london.com
www.one-london.com

Oury Clark

PO Box 150, Herschel House
58 Herschel Street, Slough
Berkshire
SL1 1HD

Contact: Russell James
Tel: 01753 551111
Fax: 01753 550544
russell.james@ouryclark.com
www.ouryclark.com

Oxford Investment Opportunity Network

Oxford Centre for Innovation
Mill Street, Oxford
Oxfordshire
OX2 0JX

Contact: Alistair Cavanagh
Tel: 01865 811143
Fax: 01865 209044
a.cavanagh@oxin.co.uk
www.oxin.co.uk

Pacific Continental

111 Cannon Street
London
EC4N 5AR

Contact: Janine Daines
Tel: 020 7769 7778
Fax: 020 7769 7789
jdaines@pacconsec.com
www.pacconsec.com

Pi Capital Limited

7 Old Park Lane
London
W1K 1QR

Contact: David Giampaolo
Tel: 020 7629 9949
Fax: 020 7491 1015
pi@picapital.co.uk
www.picapital.co.uk

J.G. Pflaumer & Associates (not NBAN)

Berkshire House
12 Sandown Road
Slough
SL2 1TU

Contact: Geoff Pflaumer
Tel: 0870 710 6778
Fax: 0870 710 6778
Mob: 07817 959722
jgcp@jgpflaumer.com
www.jgpflaumer.com

Price Bailey

93 Regent Street
Cambridge
Cambridgeshire
CB2 1AW

Contact: Lawrence Bailey
Tel: 01223 507617
Fax: 01223 565035
lawrenceb@pricebailey.co.uk
www.pricebailey.co.uk

Pridie Brewster

Carolyn House,
29-31 Greville Street
London
EC1N 8RB

Contact: Peter Petyt
Tel: 020 7831 8821
Fax: 020 7474 3069
ppetyt@london.pridie-brewster.com
www.london.pridie-brewster.com

Propeller Capital

Milford Suite 1, Millpool House
Mill Lane
Godalming
GU7 1EY

Contact: John White
Tel: 01483 869898
Fax: 01483 869898
enquiries@propellercapital.com
www.propellercapital.com

Prosper Group
Tamar Science Park
Derriford
Plymouth
PL6 8BT

Contact: Ralph Stratton
Tel: 01752 785785
Fax: 01752 770925
ralph.stratton@prosper-group.co.uk
www.prosper-group.co.uk

Reeves & Neylan Chartered Accountants
37 St. Margarets Street
Canterbury
Kent
CT1 2TU

Contact: Paul Wood
Tel: 01227 768 231
Fax: 01227 458 383
paul.wood@reeves-neylan.com
www.reeves-neylan.com

Reynolds Porter Chamberlain Solicitors
Chichester House
278/282 High Holborn
London
WC1V 7HA

Contact: Ron Norman
Tel: 020 7242 2877
Fax: 020 7242 1431
rbn@rpc.co.uk
www.rpc.co.uk

Saffery Champness
(Head Office)
72-75 Red Lion Street
London
WC1R 4GB

Contact: Lorenzo Mosca
Tel: 020 7841 4000
Fax: 020 7841 4100
lorenzo.mosca@saffery.com
www.saffery.com

SE Private Equity
Greenacre Court, Station Road
Burgess Hill
West Sussex
RH15 9DS

Contact: Terry Rainback
Tel: 01444 259259
Fax: 01444 259190
sepe@sussexenterprise.co.uk
www.sussexenterprise.co.uk

The Share Centre
PO Box 2000
Aylesbury
Bucks
HP21 8ZB

Contact: Lindsey Wilkins
Tel: 01296 414144
Fax: 01296 414440
sharemark@share.co.uk
www.share.co.uk

Shaw & Company (Corporate Finance)
195 Banbury Road
Oxford
Oxfordshire
OX2 7AR

Contact: Peter O'Connell
Tel: 01865 310031
Fax: 01865 310025
basf@shaw-and-co.com
www.shaw-and-co.com

SL Corporate Finance
37 Warren Street
London
W1T 6AD

Contact: Mason Bloom
Tel: 0207 380 3406
Fax: 0207 383 3260
mason.bloom@slcf.co.uk
www.slcf.co.uk

South Yorkshire Investment Fund Capital Network
Reresby House, Bow Bridge Close
Bradmarsh Business Park
Templeborough
Rotherham
S60 1BY

Contact: Lynne Martin
Tel: 01709 386387
Fax: 01709 386383
Mob: 07990 976110
lynnem@syif.com
www.syif.com

Spofforths Chartered Accountants
30 Worthing Road
Horsham
West Sussex
RH12 1SL

Contact: Kevin Johnson
Tel: 01403 253282
Fax: 01403 250926
kevinjohnson@spofforths.co.uk
www.spofforths.co.uk

Square Root Solutions (not NBAN)
Laurel Rise
Dorchester Hill
Blandford St Mary
DT11 9AB

Contact: Ian Botwright
Tel: 01258 454031

TechInvest
North West Development Agency
Renaissance House
PO Box 37, Centre Park
Warrington
WA1 1XB

Contact: Vivienne Upcott-Gill
Tel: 01925 400301/2/3
Fax: 01925 400400
techinvest@nwda.co.uk
www.nwda.co.uk

Tetheringstones
16 The Crescent
Burton Latimer
Northants
NN15 5NQ

Contact: Bill Nelson
Tel: 01536 724486
Mob: 07950 038065
bill-nelson@lineone.net

UMS Finance
Wyddial Croft
Wyddial
Buntingford
Herts
SG9 0UH

Contact: Harry Ignatian
Tel: 0845 120 6274
Fax: 0845 120 6275
harryi@ums-group.co.uk
www.ums-group.co.uk

The University of Warwick Science Park (NBAN)
Minerva Business Angels Network
Barclays Venture Centre
Sir William Lyons Road
Coventry
CV4 7EZ

Contacts: Harry Stott, Clare Wood
Tel: 024 7632 3114
Fax: 024 7632 3001
capital@uwsp.co.uk
www.warwicksciencepark.co.uk

The Venture Site
5 The Maltings, Walkern
Stevenage
Hertfordshire
SG2 7NB

Contact: Paul Verschuur
Tel: 07092 161866
Fax: 01438 860447
paul@venturesite.org
www.venturesite.org

Waste and Resources Action Programme (WRAP)
The Old Academy
21 Horse Fair
Banbury
OX16 0AH

Contact: Erry Parker
Tel: 01295 819900
Fax: 01295 819911
erry.parker@wrap.org.uk
www.wrap.org.uk

Wilson Sandford & Co.
85 Church Road
Hove
East Sussex
BN3 2BB

Contact: Robin Wilson
Tel: 01273 821441
Fax: 01273 326724
wilsonsandford@hove.sagehost.co.uk

Winsec Corporate Exchange
1 The Centre
Church Road
Colchester
Essex
CO5 0HF

Contact: Christopher Meynell
Tel: 01621 810263
Fax: 01621 817965
corpex@winsec.co.uk
www.winsec.co.uk

Xénos - The Wales Business Angel Network
3rd Floor, Oakleigh House
Park Place
Cardiff
CF10 3DQ

Contact: Anne Vincent
Tel: 029 2033 8144
Fax: 029 2033 8145
Email: info@xenos.co.uk
www.xenos.co.uk

Yorkshire Association of Business Angels
Unit 1, Hornbeam House
Hornbeam Park
Hookstone Road
Harrogate
HG2 8QT

Contacts: Barbara Greaves, Andrew Burton
Tel: 01423 810149
Fax: 01423 810086
admin@yaba.org.uk
www.yaba.org.uk

6 – Positions held by women in companies in the FTSE Indices

FTSE Index	Sector	Director's Name	D.O.B.	Company	Position	Salary	Cash Bonus	Fees	Other Rem
FTSE 100	Investment Companies	Hogg, Baroness Sarah Elizabeth Mary	14-May-46	3i Group plc	Chairman			220000	
FTSE 100	Investment Companies	Morin-Postel, Ms Christine	06-Oct-46	3i Group plc	Non-executive Director			34000	
FTSE 100	Banks	Cairncross, Miss Frances Anne	20-Aug-44	Alliance & Leicester plc	Non-executive Director			50000	
FTSE 100	Pharmaceuticals & Biotechnology	Barra, Ms Ornella	01-Jan-54	Alliance UniChem plc	Director	270000	108000		5000
FTSE 100	Mining	Marques, Dr Maria Silvia	01-Jan-57	Anglo American Bastos plc	Non-executive Director			3000	
FTSE 100	Pharmaceuticals & Biotechnology	Henney, Dr Jane	26-Mar-47	AstraZeneca plc	Non-executive Director			49000	
FTSE 100	Pharmaceuticals & Biotechnology	Hooper, Ms Michele	01-Jan-52	AstraZeneca plc	Non-executive Director			19000	
FTSE 100	Pharmaceuticals & Biotechnology	Moller, Ms Erna	01-Jan-41	AstraZeneca plc	Non-executive Director			49000	
FTSE 100	Pharmaceuticals & Biotechnology	Ogilvie, Dame Bridget M	01-Jan-39	AstraZeneca plc	Non-executive Director			49000	
FTSE 100	Life Assurance	Piwnica, Ms Carole	01-Jan-58	AVIVA plc	Non-executive Director			27000	
FTSE 100	Life Assurance	Vallance, Dr Elizabeth Mary	01-Apr-45	AVIVA plc	Non-executive Director			40000	
FTSE 100	Transport	Ewing, Ms Margaret	01-Jan-55	BAA plc	Finance Director	370000	110000		20000
FTSE 100	Transport	Kong, Ms Janis	01-Jan-51	BAA plc	Director	219000	68000		
FTSE 100	Aerospace & Defence	Birley, Prof Sue	01-Jan-44	BAE SYSTEMS plc	Non-executive Director			44000	18000
FTSE 100	Banks	Cropper, Dame Hilary Mary	09-Jan-41	Barclays plc	Non-executive Director			57000	

FTSE Index	Sector	Director's Name	D.O.B.	Company	Position	Salary	Cash Bonus	Fees	Other Rem
FTSE 100	Banks	Dawson, Prof Sandra	01-Jan-47	Barclays plc	Non-executive Director			44000	
FTSE 100	Oil & Gas	Rimington, Dame Stella	01-Jan-36	BG Group plc	Non-executive Director			47500	
FTSE 100	Chemicals	Baddeley, Ms Julie M	21-Mar-51	BOC Group plc	Non-executive Director			43000	
FTSE 100	General Retailers	Bennink, Ms Jan	01-Jan-57	Boots Group plc	Non-executive Director			35000	
FTSE 100	General Retailers	Ploix, Ms Hélène	01-Jan-45	Boots Group plc	Non-executive Director			37000	
FTSE 100	Oil & Gas	Julius, Dr DeAnne Shirley	01-Jan-49	BP plc	Non-executive Director			80000	
FTSE 100	Transport	O'Cathain, Baroness Detta	03-Feb-38	British Airways plc	Non-executive Director			34000	1000
FTSE 100	Transport	Reed, Mrs Alison	01-Jan-57	British Airways plc	Non-executive Director			10000	
FTSE 100	Tobacco	Llopis, Ms Ana Maria	01-Jan-51	British American Tobacco plc	Non-executive Director			42628	
FTSE 100	Media & Entertainment	Rebuck, Ms Gail	01-Jan-52	British Sky Broadcasting Group plc	Non-executive Director			43600	
FTSE 100	Telecommunication Services	Jay of Paddington, Baroness	18-Nov-39	BT Group plc	Non-executive Director			39000	
FTSE 100	Food Producers & Processors	Wilcox, Baroness Judith	31-Oct-40	Cadbury Schweppes plc	Non-executive Director			42000	
FTSE 100	Leisure & Hotels	Hogg, Baroness Sarah Elizabeth Mary	14-May-46	Carnival plc	Non-executive Director	38674.03			3069.38
FTSE 100	Utilities - Other	Alexander, Ms Helen	01-Jan-57	Centrica plc	Non-executive Director			35000	

FTSE 100	Utilities - Other	Mann, Miss Patricia Kathleen Randall	01-Jan-38	Centrica plc	Senior Non-executive Director	35000	
FTSE 100	Support Services	Gooding, Miss Valerie Frances	01-Jan-50	Compass Group plc	Non-executive Director	43000	
FTSE 100	Beverages	Lilja, Ms Maria	01-Jan-44	Diageo plc	Non-executive Director	62000	1000
FTSE 100	General Retailers	Clifton, Ms Rita	01-Jan-58	Dixons Group plc	Non-executive Director	20000	
FTSE 100	Media & Entertainment	Jones, Mrs Karen Elisabeth Dind	29-Jul-56	Emap plc	Non-executive Director	35000	
FTSE 100	Life Assurance	Carnwath, Mrs Alison J	01-Jan-53	Friends Provident plc	Non-executive Director	85000	
FTSE 100	Life Assurance	Thomas, Lady Barbara	28-Dec-46	Friends Provident plc	Deputy Chairman & SNED	67000	
FTSE 100	Tobacco	Carnwath, Mrs Alison J	01-Jan-53	Gallaher Group plc	Non-executive Director	38000	
FTSE 100	Pharmaceuticals & Biotechnology	Shapiro, Dr Lucy	01-Jan-41	GlaxoSmithKline plc	Non-executive Director	57000	
FTSE 100	General Retailers	Patten of Wincanton, Lady Louise Alexandra Virginia	02-Feb-54	GUS plc	Non-executive Director	37779	
FTSE 100	Construction & Building Materials	Noakes, Baroness Sheila	01-Jan-50	Hanson plc	Non-executive Director	51000	
FTSE 100	Support Services	Knox, Mrs Lesley Mary S	19-Sep-53	Hays plc	Non-executive Director	45000	
FTSE 100	Banks	McConville, Ms Coline	01-Jan-65	HBOS plc	Non-executive Director	57000	
FTSE 100	Banks	Dunn, The Rt Hon Baroness Lydia	29-Feb-40	HSBC Holdings plc	Joint Deputy Chair & SNED	35000	

FTSE Index	Sector	Director's Name	D.O.B.	Company	Position	Salary	Cash Bonus	Fees	Other Rem
FTSE 100	Banks	Hintze, Miss Sharon	23-Sep-44	HSBC Holdings plc	Non-executive Director			35000	
FTSE 100	Banks	Taylor, Ms Carole	16-Nov-45	HSBC Holdings plc	Non-executive Director			64000	
FTSE 100	Food & Drug Retailers	de Moller, Mrs June Frances	25-Jun-47	J Sainsbury plc	Non-executive Director			35000	
FTSE 100	Food & Drug Retailers	Macaskill, Mrs Bridget A	05-Aug-48	J Sainsbury plc	Non-executive Director			35000	
FTSE 100	General Retailers	Salmon, Mrs Margaret	01-Jan-48	Kingfisher plc	Non-executive Director			41000	
FTSE 100	Life Assurance	Avery, Ms Kate	01-Jan-60	Legal & General Group plc	Director	267000	100000		18000
FTSE 100	Life Assurance	Heaton, Mrs Frances Anne	11-Aug-44	Legal & General Group plc	Non-executive Director			57000	1000
FTSE 100	Life Assurance	Hodson, Ms Beverley C	01-Jan-51	Legal & General Group plc	Non-executive Director			57000	
FTSE 100	Banks	Julius, Dr DeAnne Shirley	01-Jan-49	Lloyds TSB Group plc	Non-executive Director			45000	
FTSE 100	Speciality & Other Finance	Carnwath, Mrs Alison J	01-Jan-53	Man Group plc	Non-executive Director			50000	
FTSE 100	General Retailers	Reed, Mrs Alison	01-Jan-57	Marks & Spencer Group plc	Finance Director	352000			36000
FTSE 100	Utilities - Other	Richter, Ms Maria C	19-Oct-54	National Grid Transco plc	Non-executive Director			29000	
FTSE 100	Banks	Pease, Ms Nichola	01-Jan-62	Northern Rock plc	Non-executive Director			36000	
FTSE 100	Media & Entertainment	Fairhead, Ms Rona	01-Jan-62	Pearson plc	Finance Director	363000	116000		14000
FTSE 100	Media & Entertainment	Scardino, Ms Marjorie	25-Jan-47	Pearson plc	Chief Executive	625000	200000		54000

Index	Sector	Name	DOB	Company	Role				
FTSE 100	Life Assurance	Macaskill, Mrs Bridget A	05-Aug-48	Prudential plc	Non-executive Director			17000	
FTSE 100	Life Assurance	O'Donovan, Ms Kathleen A	01-Jan-57	Prudential plc	Non-executive Director			35000	
FTSE 100	Personal Care & Household Products	Llopis, Ms Ana Maria	01-Jan-51	Reckitt Benckiser plc	Non-executive Director			48000	
FTSE 100	Personal Care & Household Products	Sprieser, Ms Judith	08-Mar-53	Reckitt Benckiser plc	Non-executive Director			14000	
FTSE 100	Aerospace & Defence	Bondurant, The Hon Amy	01-Jan-51	Rolls-Royce Group plc	Non-executive Director			9000	
FTSE 100	Banks	Mackay, Miss Eileen Alison	07-Jul-43	Royal Bank of Scotland Group plc	Non-executive Director			64000	
FTSE 100	Beverages	De Lisi, Ms Nancy Jane	01-Jan-51	SAB Miller plc	Non-executive Director				
FTSE 100	Electricity	Rice, Ms Susan	01-Jan-46	Scottish & Southern Energy plc	Non-executive Director			24000	
FTSE 100	Electricity	Johansen, Ms Judi	01-Jan-59	Scottish Power plc	Director	206600	258300		3200
FTSE 100	Utilities - Other	Cassoni, Ms Marisa	01-Jan-52	Severn Trent plc	Non-executive Director			40700	1600
FTSE 100	Oil & Gas	Buttle, Dr Eileen	19-Oct-37	Shell Transport & Trading Company plc	Non-executive Director			50000	
FTSE 100	Oil & Gas	Henderson, Ms Mary R (Nina)	06-Jul-50	Shell Transport & Trading Company plc	Non-executive Director			63500	
FTSE 100	Health	Kirby, Dr Pamela Josephine	23-Sep-53	Smith & Nephew plc	Non-executive Director			35000	
FTSE 100	Banks	Markland, Ms Ruth	01-Jan-53	Standard Chartered plc	Non-executive Director			6747.26	
FTSE 100	Food & Drug Retailers	Morali, Ms Veronique	01-Jan-59	Tesco plc	Non-executive Director			44000	

FTSE Index	Sector	Director's Name	D.O.B.	Company	Position	Salary	Cash Bonus	Fees	Other Rem
FTSE 100	Food Producers & Processors	Chalker of Wallasey, The Rt Hon Baroness Lynda	01-Jan-43	Unilever plc	Non-executive Director			35000	26400
FTSE 100	Utilities - Other	Newell, Ms Jane	01-Jan-44	United Utilities plc	Non-executive Director			55000	
FTSE 100	Telecommunication Services	Hughes, Ms Penny Lesley	31-May-59	Vodafone Group plc	Non-executive Director			90000	
FTSE 100	Leisure & Hotels	Leith, Miss Prudence (Prue) M	01-Jan-40	Whitbread plc	Non-executive Director			29500	
FTSE 100	Food & Drug Retailers	Melnyk, Miss Marie Margaret	10-Jun-58	WM Morrison Supermarkets plc	Joint Managing Director	456000	22000		27000
FTSE 100	Media & Entertainment	Axelrod, Ms Beth	01-Jan-63	WPP Group plc	Director	336000	252000		12000
FTSE 100	Media & Entertainment	Dyson, Ms Esther	01-Jan-52	WPP Group plc	Non-executive Director			25000	
FTSE 250	Engineering & Machinery	George, Miss Judy	01-Jan-40	Aga Foodservice Group plc	Director	94000	9000		2000
FTSE 250	Engineering & Machinery	Mahy, Ms Helen	01-Jan-61	Aga Foodservice Group plc	Non-executive Director			20000	
FTSE 250	Insurance	Atkins, Ms Amanda J	01-Jan-58	Alea Group Holdings (Bermuda) Ltd	Finance Director	32076			4501
FTSE 250	Investment Companies	Ruckley, Mrs Sheila M	01-Jan-49	Alliance Trust plc, The	Director	85875			1679
FTSE 250	Construction & Building Materials	Hesse, Ms Martha Ossian	01-Jan-43	AMEC plc	Non-executive Director			78000	
FTSE 250	Transport	Palmer, Mrs A Veronica M	01-Jan-41	ARRIVA plc	Non-executive Director			28500	
FTSE 250	Transport	Colyer, Ms Lesley	01-Jan-53	Avis Europe plc	Director	186000	98697		20004
FTSE 250	Utilities - Other	Heaton, Mrs Frances Anne	11-Aug-44	AWG plc	Non-executive Director			36000	

FTSE 250	Utilities - Other	Lyons, Mrs Sue	01-Jan-53	AWG plc	Non-executive Director		30000	
FTSE 250	General Retailers	Miller, Ms Irene	01-Jan-52	Body Shop International plc	Non-executive Director		36000	
FTSE 250	General Retailers	Roddick, Mrs Anita Lucia	23-Oct-42	Body Shop International plc	Non-executive Director		30000	195000
FTSE 250	Construction & Building Materials	MacDonagh, Mrs Lesley A	01-Apr-52	Bovis Homes Group plc	Non-executive Director		13000	
FTSE 250	Construction & Building Materials	Morgan (Lady Balfour), Dr Janet P	05-Dec-45	BPB plc	Non-executive Director		39000	
FTSE 250	Banks	Patten of Wincanton, Lady Louise Alexandra Virginia C	02-Feb-54	Bradford & Bingley plc	Non-executive Director		1798	
FTSE 250	Banks	Thorne, Ms Rosemary Prudence	12-Feb-52	Bradford & Bingley plc	Finance Director	309375	128000	24891
FTSE 250	Investment Companies	Blomfield-Smith, Mrs Rosamund	01-Jan-49	British Empire Securities & General Trust plc	Non-executive Director		15500	
FTSE 250	Real Estate	Patten of Wincanton, Lady Louise Alexandra Virginia C	02-Feb-54	Brixton plc	Chairman		70000	
FTSE 250	General Retailers	Bravo, Ms Rose Marie	01-Jan-51	Burberry Group plc	Chief Executive	922352.9	922352.94	253329.41
FTSE 250	General Retailers	Cartwright, Ms Stacey	18-Nov-63	Burberry Group plc	Finance Director	29000	29000	6000
FTSE 250	General Retailers	Marland, Mrs Caroline Ann	14-Apr-46	Burberry Group plc	Non-executive Director		40000	
FTSE 250	Media & Entertainment	Schwarz, Ms Nathalie	01-Jan-70	Capital Radio plc	Director	192000	62000	
FTSE 250	Media & Entertainment	Smith, Ms Linda	01-Jan-63	Capital Radio plc	Director		62000	13000

FTSE Index	Sector	Director's Name	D.O.B.	Company	Position	Salary	Cash Bonus	Fees	Other Rem
FTSE 250	Media & Entertainment	Thomas, Lady Barbara	28-Dec-46	Capital Radio plc	Non-executive Director			30000	
FTSE 250	General Retailers	Wilcox, Baroness Judith	31-Oct-40	Carpetright plc	Non-executive Director			31000	
FTSE 250	Investment Companies	Weir, Ms Helen A	01-Jan-63	City of London Investment Trust plc, The	Non-executive Director			16500	
FTSE 250	Speciality & Other Finance	Smith, Mrs Helen Louise	01-Jan-72	Collins Stewart Tullett plc	Finance Director	100000	800000		1000
FTSE 250	Engineering & Machinery	de Moller, Mrs June Frances	25-Jun-47	Cookson Group plc	Non-executive Director			39500	
FTSE 250	Chemicals	Richmond, Mrs Barbara Mary	28-Jul-60	Croda International plc	Finance Director	244008			25801
FTSE 250	Leisure & Hotels	Hewitt, Ms Deborah (Debbie)	31-Aug-63	De Vere Group plc	Non-executive Director			30000	
FTSE 250	Investment Companies	Mackay, Ms Eileen	01-Jan-44	Edinburgh Investment Trust plc, The	Senior Non-executive Director			24351	
FTSE 250	Investment Companies	Ralston, Ms Nicola	01-Jan-56	Edinburgh Investment Trust plc, The	Non-executive Director			11112	
FTSE 250	Media & Entertainment	O'Donovan, Ms Kathleen A	01-Jan-57	EMI Group plc	Non-executive Director			46500	
FTSE 250	Media & Entertainment	Alfano, Ms Diane	01-Jan-56	Euromoney Institutional Investor plc	Director	100868	188619		4124
FTSE 250	Leisure & Hotels	Chapman, Ms Clare	01-Jan-61	First Choice Holidays plc	Non-executive Director			19000	
FTSE 250	Investment Companies	Fukuda, Miss Haruko	21-Jul-46	Foreign & Colonial Investment Trust plc	Non-executive Director			24000	

Index	Sector	Name	Date	Company	Role				
FTSE 250	Food Producers & Processors	Scriven, Mrs Jane Katherine	05-Oct-59	Geest plc	Director	187000			18000
FTSE 250	Construction & Building Materials	Cross, Ms Christine	01-Jan-51	George Wimpey plc	Non-executive Director			31191	
FTSE 250	Construction & Building Materials	Dean of Thornton-le-Fylde, Baroness Brenda	01-Jan-44	George Wimpey plc	Non-executive Director			7016	
FTSE 250	Real Estate	Pease, Ms Nichola	01-Jan-62	Grainger Trust plc	Non-executive Director			30000	
FTSE 250	Food & Drug Retailers	Johnson, Ms Susan	01-Jan-58	Greggs plc	Non-executive Director			22250	
FTSE 250	Media & Entertainment	Barnes, Ms Mair	24-Dec-44	GWR Group plc	Non-executive Director			23000	
FTSE 250	Media & Entertainment	Hodgson, Ms Patricia	01-Jan-57	GWR Group plc	Non-executive Director			5000	
FTSE 250	Media & Entertainment	Pallot, Ms Wendy	01-Jan-65	GWR Group plc	Finance Director	150000	57000		10000
FTSE 250	Media & Entertainment	Pirie, Mrs Stella Jane	01-Jan-51	GWR Group plc	Non-executive Director			37000	
FTSE 250	Insurance	Engler, Dr Carol Franklin	31-Mar-51	Hiscox plc	Non-executive Director			35000	
FTSE 250	General Retailers	Knox, Mrs Lesley Mary S	19-Sep-53	HMV Group plc	Non-executive Director			31000	
FTSE 250	Speciality & Other Finance	Fukuda, Miss Haruko	21-Jul-46	Investec plc	Non-executive Director			26250	
FTSE 250	Leisure & Hotels	Baker, Ms Suzanne	01-Jan-63	J D Wetherspoon plc	Commercial Director	133000	36000		14000
FTSE 250	Insurance	Wade, Ms Vyvienne Y A C	01-Jan-62	Jardine Lloyd Thompson Group plc	Director	200000	200000		39000
FTSE 250	Media & Entertainment	King, Ms Martina	01-Jan-61	Johnston Press plc	Non-executive Director			20000	

FTSE Index	Sector	Director's Name	D.O.B.	Company	Position	Salary	Cash Bonus	Fees	Other Rem
FTSE 250	General Retailers	Touraine, Ms Agnes	01-Jan-55	lastminute.com plc	Non-executive Director			6667	
FTSE 250	Software & Computer Services	Knight, Mrs Angela A	01-Jan-51	LogicaCMG plc	Non-executive Director			36000	
FTSE 250	Real Estate	de Moller, Mrs June Frances	25-Jun-47	London Merchant Securities plc	Non-executive Director			30000	
FTSE 250	Speciality & Other Finance	Cohen of Pimlico, Rt Hon Baroness	01-Jan-41	London Stock Exchange plc	Non-executive Director			33000	
FTSE 250	Speciality & Other Finance	Furse, Ms Clara	01-Jan-58	London Stock Exchange plc	Chief Executive	351000	186000		3000
FTSE 250	Leisure & Hotels	Wilding, Ms Linda	01-Jan-59	Luminar plc	Non-executive Director			30000	
FTSE 250	Information Technology Hardware	Flaherty, Ms Kathleen R	01-Jan-51	Marconi Corporation plc	Non-executive Director			26000	29000
FTSE 250	General Retailers	Knox, Mrs Lesley Mary S	19-Sep-53	MFI Furniture Group plc	Non-executive Director			32000	
FTSE 250	Leisure & Hotels	Weller, Ms Sara	01-Jan-62	Mitchells & Butlers plc	Senior Non-executive Director			23000	
FTSE 250	Support Services	McGregor-Smith, Mrs Ruby	01-Jan-63	MITIE Group plc	Finance Director	150000	127000		16000
FTSE 250	Investment Companies	Ferguson, Ms Carol	16-Nov-46	Monks Investment Trust plc, The	Non-executive Director			10007	
FTSE 250	Investment Companies	Glen, Ms Marian	27-Feb-60	Murray Income Trust plc	Non-executive Director			13000	
FTSE 250	Investment Companies	Morgan (Lady Balfour), Dr Janet P	05-Dec-45	Murray International Trust plc	Non-executive Director			3500	
FTSE 250	Transport	Lyons, Mrs Sue	01-Jan-53	National Express Group plc	Non-executive Director			35000	

Index	Sector	Name	DOB	Company	Position				
FTSE 250	Real Estate	Hollendoner, Ms Nancy Jane	01-Jan-55	NHP plc	Non-executive Director			16874	
FTSE 250	Food Producers & Processors	Ni-Chionna, Mrs Orna	21-Feb-56	Northern Foods plc	Non-executive Director			30500	
FTSE 250	Food Producers & Processors	O'Driscoll, Ms Pat	01-Jan-59	Northern Foods plc	Chief Executive	5423			7493
FTSE 250	Utilities - Other	Williams, Ms Jenny	01-Jan-49	Northumbrian Water Group plc	Non-executive Director				
FTSE 250	Automobiles & Parts	Sykes, Ms Hilary C	01-Jan-61	Pendragon plc	Director & Company Secretary	98000	48000		12000
FTSE 250	Utilities - Other	Mortimer, Ms Katharine Mary Hope	01-Jan-46	Pennon Group plc	Non-executive Director			31000	
FTSE 250	Utilities - Other	Nichols, Ms Dinah A	01-Jan-44	Pennon Group plc	Non-executive Director			24000	
FTSE 250	Construction & Building Materials	Morin-Postel, Ms Christine	06-Oct-46	Pilkington plc	Non-executive Director			25000	
FTSE 250	Real Estate	MacNaughton, Ms Joan	01-Jan-51	Quintain Estates & Development plc	Non-executive Director				
FTSE 250	Real Estate	Thomas, Lady Barbara	28-Dec-46	Quintain Estates & Development plc Director	Senior Non-executive			35000	5000
FTSE 250	Real Estate	Worthington, Ms Rebecca	01-Jan-72	Quintain Estates & Development plc	Finance Director	125000	55000		19000
FTSE 250	Support Services	Hewitt, Ms Deborah (Debbie)	31-Aug-63	RAC plc	Director	187775	76049		16990
FTSE 250	Support Services	Thompson, Ms Dianne	01-Jan-51	RAC plc	Non-executive Director			28000	10
FTSE 250	Media & Entertainment	Crouch, Mrs Sunny	01-Jan-43	Scottish Radio Holdings plc	Non-executive Director			20000	
FTSE 250	Investment Companies	Knox, Mrs Lesley Mary S	19-Sep-53	Second Alliance Trust plc	Chairman			11250	

FTSE Index	Sector	Director's Name	D.O.B.	Company	Position	Salary	Cash Bonus	Fees	Other Rem
FTSE 250	Investment Companies	Ruckley, Mrs Sheila M	01-Jan-49	Second Alliance Trust plc	Director	29168			
FTSE 250	Support Services	Ford, Mrs Margaret	16-Dec-57	Serco Group plc	Non-executive Director			7785	
FTSE 250	Speciality & Other Finance	Rutherford, Dr Sarah	01-Jan-59	Singer & Friedlander Group plc	Non-executive Director			19882	
FTSE 250	Food & Drug Retailers	Patten of Wincanton, Lady Louise Alexandra Virginia C	02-Feb-54	Somerfield plc	Senior Non-executive Director			45000	200
FTSE 250	Media & Entertainment	Baldry, Mrs Lorraine	01-Jan-49	St Ives plc	Non-executive Director			20000	
FTSE 250	Media & Entertainment	Tinson, Dame Susan (Sue) Myfanwy	01-Jan-43	St Ives plc	Non-executive Director			11700	
FTSE 250	Transport	Gloag, Ms Ann Heron	01-Jan-43	Stagecoach Group plc	Non-executive Director			30000	
FTSE 250	Transport	Morgan (Lady Balfour), Dr Janet P	05-Dec-45	Stagecoach Group plc	Non-executive Director			30000	
FTSE 250	Food Producers & Processors	Piwnica, Ms Carole	01-Jan-58	Tate & Lyle plc	Non-executive Director			233000	
FTSE 250	Media & Entertainment	Studer, Ms Sharon	01-Jan-51	Taylor Nelson Sofres plc	Non-executive Director			5000	
FTSE 250	Construction & Building Materials	Innes Ker, Lady Katherine (Robin)	01-Jan-60	Taylor Woodrow plc	Non-executive Director			38000	
FTSE 250	Transport	Price, Mrs Caroline Fiona	01-Jan-65	TBI plc	Finance Director	300000	175000		17000
FTSE 250	Telecommunication Services	Connell, Mrs Josephine (Jo) Lilian	26-Jan-48	Thus Group plc Director	Non-executive			30000	
FTSE 250	Telecommunication Services	Ford, Mrs Margaret	16-Dec-57	Thus Group plc	Non-executive Director			30000	

Index	Sector	Name	Date	Company	Role			
FTSE 250	Investment Companies	Burton, Ms Caroline Mary	01-Jan-50	TR Property Investment Trust plc	Non-executive Director			15000
FTSE 250	Media & Entertainment	Bailey, Sly	01-Jan-63	Trinity Mirror plc	Chief Executive	458000	458000	10000
FTSE 250	Media & Entertainment	Hughes, Ms Penny Lesley	31-May-59	Trinity Mirror plc	Non-executive Director		40000	
FTSE 250	Oil & Gas	Spottiswoode, Ms Claire	20-Mar-53	Tullow Oil plc	Non-executive Director		25000	
FTSE 250	Aerospace & Defence	Blackstone, Baroness Tessa	27-Sep-42	VT Group plc	Non-executive Director		5000	
FTSE 250	Insurance	Letsinger, Ms Katherine L	01-Jan-63	Wellington Underwriting plc	Finance Director	232000	313000	
FTSE 250	General Retailers	Hodson, Ms Beverley C	01-Jan-51	WH Smith plc	Director	330000		107000
FTSE 250	General Retailers	Rainey, Ms Mary Teresa	01-Jan-55	WH Smith plc	Non-executive Director		31000	
FTSE 250	General Retailers	Leith, Miss Prudence (Prue) M	01-Jan-40	Woolworths Group plc	Non-executive Director		32000	
FTSE 250	Real Estate	Carragher, Miss Madeleine	15-Feb-55	Workspace Group plc	Operations Director	175000	139100	11400
SmallCap	Investment Companies	Tozer, Ms Jane	01-Jan-47	3i European Technology Trust plc	Non-executive Director		18000	
SmallCap	Electronic & Electrical Equipment	Rice-Jones, Ms Margaret	01-Jan-61	Abacus Group plc	Non-executive Director		19000	
SmallCap	Transport	James, Mrs Lesley	01-Jan-50	Alpha Airports Group plc	Non-executive Director		30000	
SmallCap	Transport	McRae, Ms Heather	01-Jan-62	Alpha Airports Group plc	Finance Director & Company Sec	155000	29000	15000
SmallCap	Household Goods & Textiles	Mountford, Ms Margaret	01-Jan-52	Amstrad plc	Non-executive Director		28000	

FTSE Index	Sector	Director's Name	D.O.B.	Company	Position	Salary	Cash Bonus	Fees	Other Rem
SmallCap	Pharmaceuticals & Biotechnology	Hacker, Mrs Ann	01-Jan-51	Antisoma plc	Non-executive Director			27000	
SmallCap	Pharmaceuticals & Biotechnology	Ney, Dr Ursula	01-Jan-52	Antisoma plc	Chief Operating Officer	79000			5000
SmallCap	Pharmaceuticals & Biotechnology	Norinder, Mrs Birgit	01-Jan-48	Antisoma plc	Non-executive Director			15000	
SmallCap	Mining	Markus, Mrs Catherine E	01-Jan-58	Aquarius Platinum Ltd	Non-executive Director			21516.1	
SmallCap	Insurance	Dandridge, Ms Christine	01-Jan-57	Atrium Underwriting plc	Director	180000	481000		1000
SmallCap	Software & Computer Services	Thomas, Lady Barbara	28-Dec-46	Axon Group plc	Senior Non-executive Director			35000	
SmallCap	General Retailers	Aston, Miss Susan (Sue) Mary	24-Jan-55	Beattie (James) plc	Director	97000	8000		5000
SmallCap	Media & Entertainment	Calder, Ms Elisabeth Nicole (Liz)	10-Jan-38	Bloomsbury Publishing plc	Director	92000	65000		10000
SmallCap	Support Services	Chandler, Mrs Lynn Angharad	05-Apr-61	BPP Holdings plc	Finance Director	155000	17000		12000
SmallCap	Support Services	Cohen of Pimlico, Rt Hon Baroness	01-Jan-41	BPP Holdings plc	Chairman & SNED			60000	
SmallCap	Support Services	Thorburn, Mrs Anne	01-Jan-61	British Polythene Industries plc	Finance Director	99000	49000		11000
SmallCap	Support Services	Brooke, Mrs Consuelo C	01-Jan-47	BTG plc	Senior Non-executive Director			35508	
SmallCap	Leisure & Hotels	D'Arcy, Ms Lynne	01-Jan-58	Burtonwood Brewery plc	Managing Director	133000	39000		8000
SmallCap	Health	James, Mrs Lesley	01-Jan-50	Care UK plc	Non-executive Director			20000	

									Other
SmallCap	Speciality & Finance	Hanratty, Miss Judith Christine	01-Jan-44	Charles Taylor Consulting plc	Non-executive Director			14000	
SmallCap	Investment Companies	Vallance, Dr Elizabeth Mary	01-Apr-45	Charter Pan-European Trust plc	Non-executive Director			11000	
SmallCap	General Retailers	Darlington, Mrs Debbie	01-Jan-69	Clinton Cards plc	Director	141000			32000
SmallCap	Construction & Building Materials	Colgrave, Ms Wendy	13-Jan-65	Countryside Properties plc	Finance Director	100000	101000		24000
SmallCap	Construction & Building Materials	Gupta, Ms Trisha	30-May-47	Countryside Properties plc	Director	85000	101000		19000
SmallCap	Software & Computer Services	Gradden, Ms Mandy	01-Jan-68	Detica Group plc	Finance Director & Company Sec	99000	27000		9000
SmallCap	Real Estate	Mitchell, Ms Victoria	09-Sep-50	Development Securities plc	Non-executive Director			20000	
SmallCap	Real Estate	Lesniak, Ms Alicja	04-Dec-51	DTZ Holdings plc	Non-executive Director				4000
SmallCap	Investment Companies	Matterson, Ms Jean	01-Jan-57	Dunedin Income Growth Investment Trust plc	Senior Non-executive Director			11000	
SmallCap	Software & Computer Services	Breger, Ms Ruth	01-Jan-52	Emblaze Ltd Director	Non-executive			20000	
SmallCap	Automobiles & Parts	Wilson, Ms Ann Chrisette	09-Jan-56	European Motor Holdings plc	Finance Director	344000	250000		32000
SmallCap	Investment Companies	Bates, Mrs Sarah	01-Jan-59	F&C Pacific Investment Trust plc	Non-executive Director			1500	
SmallCap	Investment Companies	Nott, Mrs Gillian	01-Jan-46	F&C Pacific Investment Trust plc	Non-executive Director			18000	
SmallCap	Investment Companies	Renwick, Ms Vanessa	01-Jan-61	Finsbury Growth & Income Trust plc	Non-executive Director			12000	

FTSE Index	Sector	Director's Name	D.O.B.	Company	Position	Salary	Cash Bonus	Fees	Other Rem
SmallCap	Investment Companies	Dixon, Ms Josephine	01-Jan-59	Finsbury Worldwide Pharmaceutical Trust plc	Non-executive Director			2613	
SmallCap	Media & Entertainment	Gordon, Ms Lisa J	01-Jan-66	Future Network plc, The	Non-executive Director			24000	
SmallCap	Insurance	Merry, Ms Barbara J	01-Jan-58	Hardy Underwriting Group plc	Chief Executive	175000	150117		3641
SmallCap	Investment Companies	Davis, Ms Sally	01-Jan-54	Henderson Smaller Companies Investment Trust plc	Non-executive Director			15000	
SmallCap	Investment Companies	Unwin, Ms Judith	01-Jan-55	Henderson TR Pacific Investment Trust plc	Non-executive Director			14500	
SmallCap	Insurance	Kellie, Ms Judy	01-Jan-48	Highway Insurance Holdings plc	Non-executive Director			29000	
SmallCap	Speciality & Other Finance	Iversen, Ms Barbara Anne	01-Jan-55	Hitachi Capital (UK) plc	Finance Director	120000	44000		12000
SmallCap	General Retailers	Grunewald, Ms Sarah	01-Jan-62	Homestyle Group plc	Non-executive Director			8000	
SmallCap	General Retailers	Quant, Miss Mary	01-Jan-34	House of Fraser plc	Non-executive Director			25000	
SmallCap	Investment Companies	Bates, Mrs Sarah	01-Jan-59	INVESCO English & International Trust plc	Non-executive Director			13000	
SmallCap	Media & Entertainment	Erem, Ms Ceyda	01-Jan-52	ITE Group plc	Director	137000			
SmallCap	Software & Computer Services	Blow, Ms Bridget Penelope	01-Jan-50	ITNET plc	Chief Executive	278000	142000		24000

SmallCap	Support Services	Wilcox, Baroness Judith	31-Oct-40	Johnson Service Group plc	Non-executive Director			6000	
SmallCap	Investment Companies	Airey, Ms Elisabeth Patricia (Liz)	28-Jan-59	JPMorgan Fleming European Fledgling Investment Trust plc	Non-executive			16500	19000
SmallCap	Investment Companies	Walter, Mrs Davina J	01-Jan-55	JPMorgan Fleming US Discovery	Non-executive Director			11000	
SmallCap	Investment Companies	Hollond, Mrs Beatrice Hannah Millicent	01-Jan-60	Keystone Investment Trust plc	Non-executive			10000	38000
SmallCap	Construction & Building Materials	Mattar, Miss Deena E	01-Jan-65	Kier Group plc	Finance Director & Company Sec	207000	42000		
SmallCap	General Retailers	Mohd-Saaid, Ms Ainum	01-Jan-46	Laura Ashley Holdings plc	Joint Chief Executive	83000			
SmallCap	General Retailers	Mooi, Ms Sally Cheong Siew	01-Jan-53	Laura Ashley Holdings plc	Non-executive Director			10000	7000
SmallCap	General Retailers	Navarednam, Ms Rebecca Annapillai	01-Jan-47	Laura Ashley Holdings plc	Joint Chief Executive	83000			
SmallCap	Investment Companies	Banszky, Ms Caroline J	24-Jul-53	Law Debenture Corporation plc, The	Managing Director	253990	55000		449
SmallCap	Leisure & Hotels	Lillis, Ms Linda	15-May-57	London Clubs International plc	Finance Director	170000			13000
SmallCap	Investment Companies	Long, Ms Tracy	04-Jun-62	Lowland Investment Company plc	Non-executive Director			2750	
SmallCap	Investment Companies	Leates, Ms Gillian	01-Jan-57	Majedie Investments plc	Director	122000	25000		11000
SmallCap	Support Services	Cohen of Pimlico, Rt Hon Baroness	01-Jan-41	Management Consulting Group plc	Senior Non-executive Director			10186	
SmallCap	Investment Companies	Nott, Mrs Gillian	01-Jan-46	Martin Currie Portfolio Investment Trust plc	Non-executive Director			16000	

FTSE Index	Sector	Director's Name	D.O.B.	Company	Position	Salary	Cash Bonus	Fees	Other Rem
SmallCap	Personal Care & Household Products	Bogdanowicz-Bindert, Ms Christine A	01-Jan-51	McBride plc	Non-executive Director			20000	
SmallCap	General Retailers	Wadeley, Mrs Melanie	01-Jan-69	Merchant Retail Group plc	Director	92000	25000		13000
SmallCap	Media & Entertainment	Reed, Ms Leslie-Ann	01-Jan-60	Metal Bulletin plc & Company Sec	Finance Director	124500	12500		18200
SmallCap	Construction & Building Materials	Gallacher, Ms Geraldine	01-Jan-60	Morgan Sindall plc	Non-executive Director			25000	
SmallCap	General Retailers	Brady, Ms Karren	01-Jan-69	Mothercare plc	Non-executive Director			22000	
SmallCap	Health	Alexander, Ms Ingrid C	01-Jan-52	Nestor Healthcare Group plc	Non-executive Director			29000	
SmallCap	Support Services	Goodey, Ms Felicity	01-Jan-49	Nord Anglia Education plc	Non-executive Director			16000	
SmallCap	Support Services	Simpson, Ms Lorene	01-Jan-62	Nord Anglia Education plc	Finance Director & Company Sec	124000	37000		4000
SmallCap	Software & Computer Services	Beckett, Ms Nikaila (Nikki) Susan	01-Jan-61	NSB Retail Systems plc	Chief Executive	265000	132500		17004
SmallCap	Pharmaceuticals & Biotechnology	Kingsman, Prof Susan Mary	25-Jun-52	Oxford BioMedica plc	Director	134445	23108		7682
SmallCap	Telecommunication Services	Barnes, Ms Mair	24-Dec-44	Patientline plc	Senior Non-executive Director			20000	
SmallCap	General Retailers	Alexander, Mrs Paula	01-Jan-56	Peacock Group plc	Senior Non-executive Director			27000	
SmallCap	Support Services	Oakes, Ms Gillian Philippa	01-Jan-54	PSD Group plc	Senior Non-executive Director			22000	

SmallCap	Support Services	Robinson, Ms Francesca Mary	01-Jan-60	PSD Group plc	Chief Executive	350000	2000	19000
SmallCap	Speciality & Other Finance	Burton, Ms Caroline Mary	01-Jan-50	Rathbone Brothers plc	Non-executive Director			4000
SmallCap	Speciality & Other Finance	Michel, Ms Katrina	01-Jan-56	Rensburg plc	Non-executive Director			23000
SmallCap	Leisure & Hotels	Corzine, Ms Patricia A	01-Jan-58	Restaurant Group plc, The	Director	29000	14000	3000
SmallCap	Software & Computer Services	Coutu, Ms Sherry L	01-Jan-64	RM plc	Senior Non-executive Director			23000
SmallCap	Construction & Building Materials	Camm, Ms Gillian	01-Jan-60	Rok Property Solutions plc	Non-executive Director			28000
SmallCap	Media & Entertainment	Sharp, Ms Tina M	01-Jan-62	Sanctuary Group plc, The	Non-executive Director			58000
SmallCap	Real Estate	Wicker-Miurin, Ms Fields	01-Jan-59	Savills plc	Non-executive Director			26042
SmallCap	Investment Companies	Pirie, Mrs Stella Jane	01-Jan-51	Schroder UK Growth Fund plc	Non-executive Director			11500
SmallCap	Investment Companies	Morgan (Lady Balfour), Dr Janet P	05-Dec-45	Scottish American Investment Company plc, The	Non-executive Director			12000
SmallCap	Investment Companies	Frew, Ms Anita M	24-Jun-57	Securities Trust of Scotland plc	Non-executive Director			11500
SmallCap	Investment Companies	Davidson, The Hon Joanna R	01-Jan-58	Shires Income plc	Non-executive Director			11000
SmallCap	Support Services	Lancaster, Ms Emma	01-Jan-70	SHL Group plc	Finance Director	159000	18000	2000
SmallCap	Leisure & Hotels	Revitt, Ms Kathryn	01-Jan-65	Sportech plc	Non-executive Director			
SmallCap	Software & Computer Services	Tozer, Ms Jane	01-Jan-47	SurfControl plc	Non-executive Director			19337

FTSE Index	Sector	Director's Name	D.O.B.	Company	Position	Salary	Cash Bonus	Fees	Other Rem
SmallCap	Automobiles & Parts	Joyce, Ms Rebecca	01-Jan-61	Torotrak plc	Finance Director & Company Sec	130000			
SmallCap	Media & Entertainment	Morrow, Mrs M (Helen)	23-Jan-56	Ulster Television plc	Non-executive Director			20600	
SmallCap	Food Producers & Processors	Young, Ms Margaret Anne	01-Jan-55	Uniq plc	Non-executive Director			33000	
SmallCap	Investment Companies	Lascelles, Mrs Angela Marion	25-Aug-47	Value and Income Trust plc	Non-executive Director				
SmallCap	Pharmaceuticals & Biotechnology	Ferguson, Ms Carol	16-Nov-46	Vernalis plc	Non-executive Director			11000	
SmallCap	Chemicals	Frew, Ms Anita M	24-Jun-57	Victrex plc	Senior Non-executive Director			22050	
SmallCap	Automobiles & Parts	Lyons, Mrs Sue	01-Jan-53	Wagon plc	Non-executive Director			26667	
SmallCap	Health	Jovan, Dr Morana		Whatman plc	Non-executive Director			30000	
SmallCap	Support Services	Brown, Ms Caroline	01-Jan-63	WSP Group plc	Non-executive Director			12000	
SmallCap	Software & Computer Services	Barrat, Mrs Lyndley (Lyn) Kay	18-Sep-47	Xansa plc	Commercial Director	200000			18197
SmallCap	Software & Computer Services	Brooke, Mrs Consuelo C	01-Jan-47	Xansa plc	Non-executive Director			30000	
SmallCap	Information Technology Hardware	Airey, Ms Elisabeth Patricia (Liz)	28-Jan-59	Zetex plc	Chairman			44000	

Total numbers of women in business by post type in FTSE All-Share

Chairman & SNED	1
Chief Operating Officer	1
Deputy Chairman & SNED	1
Director & Company Sec	1
Joint Deputy Chair & SNED	1
Joint Managing Director	1
Operations Director	1
Commercial Director	2
Joint Chief Executive	2
Managing Director	2
Chairman	4
Finance Director & Company Sec	6
Chief Executive	9
Senior Non-executive Director	14
Finance Director	20
Director	27
Non-executive Director	189

Posts held by women in the FTSE 100

Chairman		**1**
Hogg, Baroness Sarah Elizabeth Mary 3i Group plc		
CEO		**1**
Scardino, Ms Marjorie	Pearson plc	
FD		**3**
Fairhead, Ms Rona	Pearson plc	
Reed, Mrs Alison	Marks & Spencer Group plc	
Ewing, Ms Margaret	BAA plc	

Busy ladies

2 Posts	**29**
3 Posts	**5**
Carnwath, Mrs Alison J	
Cohen of Pimlico, Rt Hon Baroness	
de Moller, Mrs June Frances	
Lyons, Mrs Sue Count	
Wilcox, Baroness Judith	
4 Posts	**4**
Thomas, Lady Barbara	
Patten of Wincanton, Lady Louise Alexandra Virginia C	
Morgan (Lady Balfour), Dr Janet P	
Knox, Mrs Lesley Mary S	

Most women-friendly sectors

Investment Companies	36
Media & Entertainment	28
General Retailers	28
Support Services	18
Banks	13
Construction & Building Materials	13
Transport	12
Leisure & Hotels	11
Pharmaceuticals & Biotechnology	11
Real Estate	11
Software & Computer Services	10
Speciality & Other Finance	10
Utilities - Other	10

Least women-friendly sectors

Electronic & Electrical Equipment	1
Household Goods & Textiles	1
Beverages	2
Electricity	2
Information Technology Hardware	2
Mining	2
Tobacco	2

Age distribution

70+	1
66-70	6
61-65	30
56-60	60
51-55	67
46-50	60
41-45	42
35-40	13
<35	2

Above 60 age group

Executive	2
Non-executive	35

Source: Manifest (www.manifest.co.uk)

Index